UNDERDEVELOPMENT IS A STATE OF MIND

The Latin American Case

Lawrence E. Harrison

Published by

The Center for International Affairs,
Harvard University *and*

★BOOKS★

Copyright © 1985 by

The President and Fellows of Harvard College

Madison Books

4720 Boston Way
Lanham, MD 20706

3 Henrietta Street
London WC2E 8LU England

All rights reserved

Printed in the United States of America

British Cataloging in Publication Information Available

The Center for International Affairs provides a
forum for the expression of responsible views.
It does not necessarily agree with those views.

Co-published by arrangement with
The Center for International Affairs,
Harvard University

Library of Congress Cataloging-in-Publication Data

Harrison, Lawrence E.
Underdevelopment is a state of mind.

Reprint. Originally published: Lanham, MD : Center
for International Affairs, Harvard University and
University Press of America, c1985.
Bibliography: p.
Includes index.
1. Latin America—Economic conditions—1945-
2. Economic development—Social aspects.   3. Culture.
4. Economic development—Psychological aspects.
I. Harvard University. Center for International
Affairs.   II. Title.
[HC125.H384   1988]   330.98'0038   87-24678
ISBN 0-8191-6490-9 (pbk. : alk. paper)

All Madison Books are produced on acid-free
paper which exceeds the minimum standards set by the National
Historical Publications and Records Commission.

The Center For International Affairs Executive Committee, 1984–85

Samuel P. Huntington, *Eaton Professor of the Science of Government; Director, Center for International Affairs*

Lisa Anderson, *Director of Student Programs; Assistant Professor of Government*

Leslie H. Brown, *Director of the Fellows Program*

Seyom Brown, *Acting Director, University Consortium for Research on North America*

Richard N. Cooper, *Maurits C. Boas Professor of International Economics*

Paul M. Doty, *Mallinckrodt Professor of Biochemistry; Director, Center for Science and International Affairs*

Stephan Haggard, *Acting Director of Student Programs; Assistant Professor of Government*

Chester D. Haskell, *Executive Officer*

Douglas A. Hibbs, *Professor of Government*

Stanley Hoffmann, *C. Douglas Dillon Professor of the Civilization of France; Chairman, Center for European Studies*

Herbert Kelman, *Richard Clarke Cabot Professor of Social Ethics*

Joseph S. Nye, *Clarence Dillon Professor of International Affairs*

Dwight H. Perkins, *Harold Hitchings Burbank Professor of Political Economy; Director, Harvard Institute for International Development*

Robert D. Putnam, *Chairman, Department of Government; Professor of Government*

Louise Richardson, *Ph.D. Candidate in Government*

Sidney Verba, *Director of the University Library; Carl H. Pforzheimer University Professor*

Ezra Vogel, *Director, Program on U.S. – Japan Relations; Professor of Sociology*

The Center for International Affairs is a multidisciplinary research institution within Harvard University. Founded in 1958, the Center seeks to provide a stimulating environment for a diverse group of scholars and practitioners studying various aspects of international affairs. Its purpose is the development and dissemination of knowledge concerning the basic subjects and problems of international relations. Major Center research programs include national security affairs, U.S. relations with Europe, Japan, Africa, and other areas of the world, nonviolent sanctions in conflict and defense, international economic policy, and other critical issues. At any given time, over 160 individuals are working at the Center, including faculty members from Harvard and neighboring institutions, practitioners of international affairs, visiting scholars, research associates, post-doctoral fellows, and graduate and undergraduate student associates.

Acknowledgment

I am indebted to a large number of people who have contributed to the realization of this book, principally by criticism but often with their encouragement.

Several have focused on individual chapters: Robert Angyal, Arturo Cruz, Jack Harris, Eduardo Lizano, Tomás Pastoriza, León Tenembaum, and Bernardo Vega. Several others have read the entire book and provided me with helpful comments: Shirley Christian, Luigi Einaudi, Amy Firfer, Georgie Anne Geyer, James Goodsell, Neil Isaacs, Annik LaFarge, Michael Novak, Lawrence Pezzullo, Carlos Rangel, Reese Schonfeld, Michael Scully, Francis X. Sutton, and Sidney Weintraub.

I am particularly indebted to the Center for International Affairs at Harvard University, which provided me with an ideal setting for writing the book for the better part of two years. The comments and encouragement of Samuel Huntington and Dwight Perkins were of particular importance. Evelyn Brew did a magnificent job in typing the manuscript. Chet Haskell played a key role in the Center's decision to publish the book, and Virginia Livingston skillfully shepherded the manuscript through the publishing process. And it was the Center that located Nancy Macmillan to do her superb job of editing.

I am above all indebted to Jorge Domínguez, who studied the entire manuscript and whose scholarly insights, criticisms, challenges, and encouragement were invaluable.

Finally, I owe a special debt to my wife, Polly Fortier Harrison, whose decision in 1971 to pursue graduate work in anthropology, whose subsequent professional career in development anthropology, and whose insightful comments on the manuscript have all played an important part in the evolution of my thinking on the relationship between culture and development.

Not all of the people mentioned above agree with everything the book says. I alone bear the full responsibility for that.

Lawrence E. Harrison

To Polly, Julia, Beth, and Amy

Underdevelopment is not just a collection of statistical indices which enable a socio-economic picture to be drawn. It is also a state of mind, a way of expression, a form of outlook and a collective personality marked by chronic infirmities and forms of maladjustment.

Augusto Salazar Bondy
A Peruvian Intellectual

Contents

Introduction

From May 1962 to March 1982, I worked in the U.S. Agency for International Development (AID), specializing in Latin America. During thirteen of those almost twenty years, I lived in five Latin American countries. I was director of the AID missions in Costa Rica (1969 – 71, and also served there in 1964 – 65), Haiti (1977 – 79), and Nicaragua (1979 – 81); director of the Regional Mission for Central America, in Guatemala (1975 – 77); and deputy director of the mission in the Dominican Republic (1965 – 68).

Like many young people who worked for AID in the early years of the Alliance for Progress (inaugurated on August 17, 1961, at Punta del Este, Uruguay), I was convinced that Latin America was in trouble principally because of U.S. neglect, and that a combination of money, Yankee ingenuity, and good intentions would transform the region to one of rapidly developing, vigorous democracies in a decade or two. After all, we in the U.S. shared the hope and the wealth of the New World with Latin America, we gained our independence at roughly the same time, and their constitutions and rhetoric sounded pretty much like ours. They hadn't done as well as we, but that could be remedied. The spectacular success of the Marshall Plan was much on our minds.

Less than seven years after Punta del Este, Teodoro Moscoso, the first U.S. coordinator of the Alliance for Progress and one of its most ardent and optimistic early promoters, had this to say:

> The Latin-American case is so complex, so difficult to solve, and so fraught with human and global danger and distress that the use of the word "anguish" is not an exaggeration.
> The longer I live, the more I believe that, just as no human being can save another who does not have the will to save himself, no country can save others no matter how good its intentions or how hard it tries.[1]

A few years later, in an article in *Foreign Policy* in which I quoted Moscoso, I made the following observation:

> The differences between North America and Latin America are enormous, covering virtually all aspects of human life. The North American and the Latin American have differing concepts of the individual, society, and the relationship between the two; of justice and law; of life and death;

of government; of the family; of relations between the sexes; of organization; of time; of enterprise; of religion; of morality. These differences have
contributed to the evolution of societies which are more unlike one another
than our past policymakers appear to have appreciated. In fact, it can be
argued that there are some Asian societies (Japan is an obvious candidate)
which have more in common with the societies of North America than do
most of the societies of Latin America.[2]

In the thirteen years since I wrote those words, I have been increasingly
persuaded that, more than any other of the numerous factors that influence
the development of countries, it is culture that principally explains, in most
cases, why some countries develop more rapidly and equitably than others.
By "culture" I mean the values and attitudes a society inculcates in its people
through various socializing mechanisms, e.g., the home, the school, the
church.

In this book I try to support that thesis. In the first chapter I explain
what I understand by the word "development" and what I think makes
development happen, and then suggest how culture can either facilitate or
get in the way of development. In the second chapter, I summarize the
views of a number of social scientists who have considered the relationship
between development and culture.

The next six chapters examine the experience of pairs of countries or
regions, most of which started with the same basic resource endowment but
have developed very differently. The exception is the chapter that treats
Spain and Latin America. There, it is the similarities rather than the differences that are of most interest.

The book concludes with a chapter that asks the question: If the thesis
is valid, what does it mean in terms of the choices countries face in their
efforts to improve well-being? What can be done to reinforce the cultural
characteristics that impel or facilitate development and diminish those that
impede or undermine it?

I want to assure the reader of my appreciation of the many factors
other than culture that affect development. Resource endowment obviously
plays an important role: that Venezuela's per-capita income is twice the
Latin American average is clearly a result of its rich oil deposits. A country's
size — in both space and population and the proportion between the two —
has much to do with how it develops: Brazil, Argentina, and Mexico can
be more optimistic about their futures than Haiti, El Salvador, or Panama,
in part because their national markets are large enough to support a varied
industrial and agricultural base.

Soil quality and other factors affecting agriculture are important, both
because of their influence on overall prosperity and because the kinds of
crops for which they are suitable will influence economic and social structure.

Geography plays a role in other ways, as well. Proximity to large and
vigorous markets (e.g., Mexico's proximity to the United States) is clearly

advantageous. In contrast, geographic barriers to communication (e.g., Bolivia's inaccessibility) impede development. Climatic factors also can be important: rainfall, amount of sunlight, and temperature place limits on agriculture, and temperature may affect human motivation. That most poor countries are found in tropical climates cannot be ignored.

Clearly, government policies and the effectiveness with which they are pursued can be crucial, particularly when development is viewed in the short run — in terms of years or a decade or two. I would argue, however, that the cultural environment importantly influences the process through which leaders gain their positions, the priorities they apply in shaping policies, and the people, institutions, and practices they use to execute those policies. Leadership, on the other hand, can in extraordinary cases have such a profound influence on the course of a country that it introduces important modifications in national values and attitudes, e.g., Kemal Ataturk in Turkey, Mao in China, Lincoln and Franklin Roosevelt in the United States.

Nor can we ignore, in this listing of noncultural factors that affect development, the vagaries of history, international economic forces often beyond the control of a country, and sometimes sheer luck. And we have still far from exhausted the list.

I have taken the time to carry the list this far to satisfy the reader of my appreciation of the enormous complexity of the development process. This complexity notwithstanding, I want to repeat my belief that culture, more than any other factor, explains why some countries grow faster and more equitably than others.

This thesis will collide with the deeply felt reluctance of most anthropologists to make value judgments in comparing cultures.[3] I hope the book will demonstrate how one culture may make progress easier for its people than another. According to my values, which are, I believe, generally shared by most people in both the developed and underdeveloped worlds, progress-prone cultures are better places for human beings to live than traditional, static cultures. And the most progressive cultures that humankind has thus far evolved follow the democratic model of the West.

The thesis may appear to some to be racist. They misunderstand. I start with the strong belief that there are no culturally significant genetic differences between races or ethnic groups, and that culture, particularly as it affects progress, is transmitted socially. People are socialized by their parents, peers, churches, schools, media, governments, etc., to see the world in ways that determine how they develop as individuals and as a society. That culture is transmitted socially is underscored in several chapters of this book. For example, the blacks of Haiti and the blacks of Barbados both have their roots in West Africa. Both came to this hemisphere as slaves. But whereas Haiti is today still basically an African country, contemporary Barbadians are much closer to being Englishmen than Africans. Similarly, Hispanic culture is the dominant culture for some full-blooded Indians and blacks as well as for most mestizos and whites in Hispanic-American societies.

Culture, then, is transmitted and received, and it changes. Racist theories imply that culture is inborn and static. Those theories are totally inconsistent with the thesis of this book.

Finally, I appreciate that the book does not present conclusive evidence for the validity of the thesis. I have written it because the significance of culture is by far the most important insight to come out of my twenty years in development assistance. One of my principal hopes is that others will be stimulated by the book to undertake the research that will either verify, expand, or modify the thesis. Above all, I hope the book will encourage political and intellectual leaders to give greater consideration to cultural factors as they grapple with the anguish, to use Moscoso's word, of modernization.

NOTES

1. Lawrence E. Harrison, "Waking from the Pan American Dream," pp. 170 – 71.
2. *Ibid.*, p. 164.
3. For the dissenting views of an atypical anthropologist, see the comment of Arthur Hippler on page 18.

1

What makes development happen?

Development, most simply, is improvement in human well-being.[1] Most people today aspire to higher standards of living, longer lives, and fewer health problems; education for themselves and their children that will increase their earning capacity and leave them more in control of their lives; a measure of stability and tranquillity; and the opportunity to do the things that give them pleasure and satisfaction. A small minority will take exception to one or more of these aspirations. Some others may wish to add one or more. For the purposes of this book, however, I think the list is adequate.

The enormous gap in well-being between the low-income and the industrialized countries is apparent from the following summary table, the source of which is the World Bank's *World Development Report 1982*. A similar but expanded table, broken down by country, appears later in this chapter.

Table 1.

	Low-income countries	Industrialized countries
Total population (mid-1980)	2.2 billion	671 million
Annual average population growth rate (1970 – 80)	2.1%	.8%
Average per-capita gross national product (1980)	$260	$10,320
Average life expectancy at birth (1980)	57 years	74 years
Average adult literacy (1977)	50%	99%

What explains the gap? What have the industrialized countries done that the low-income countries have not? Why was the Marshall Plan a monumental success, the Alliance for Progress much less successful? What makes development happen or not happen?

There are those who will say that what the industrialized countries have done that the low-income countries have not is to exploit the low-income countries; that development is a zero-sum game; that the rich countries are rich because the poor countries are poor. This is doctrine for Marxist-Leninists, and it has wide currency throughout the Third World.

To be sure, colonial powers often did derive great economic advantage from their colonies, and u.s. companies have made a lot of money in Latin America and elsewhere in the Third World, particularly during the first half of this century. But the almost exclusive focus on "imperialism" and "dependency" to explain underdevelopment has encouraged the evolution of a paralyzing and self-defeating mythology. The thesis of this book is in diametrical contrast. It looks inward rather than outward to explain a society's condition.

I believe that the creative capacity of human beings is at the heart of the development process. What makes development happen is our ability to imagine, theorize, conceptualize, experiment, invent, articulate, organize, manage, solve problems, and do a hundred other things with our minds and hands that contribute to the progress of the individual and of humankind. Natural resources, climate, geography, history, market size, governmental policies, and many other factors influence the direction and pace of progress. But the engine is human creative capacity.

The economist Joseph Schumpeter (1883 – 1950) singled out the entrepreneurial geniuses — the Henry Fords of the world — as the real creators of wealth and progress, as indeed they must have appeared in the early years of Schumpeter's life. Economist and political scientist Everett Hagen was less elitist: "The discussion of creativity refers . . . not merely to the limiting case of genius but to the quality of creativity in general, in whatever degree it may be found in a given individual."[2]

My own belief is that the society that is most successful at helping its people — *all* its people — realize their creative potential is the society that will progress the fastest.

It is not just the entrepreneur who creates progress, even if we are talking narrowly about material — economic — progress. The inventor of the machine employed by the entrepreneur; the scientist who conceived the theory that the inventor turned to practical use; the engineer who designed the system to mass-produce the machine; the farmer who uses special care in producing a uniform raw material to be processed by the machine; the machine operator who suggests some helpful modifications to the machine on the basis of long experience in operating it — all are contributing to growth. So is the salesman who expands demand for the product by conceiving a new use for it. So, too, are the teachers who got the scientist, the inventor, and the engineer interested in their professions and who taught the farmer agronomy.[3]

Production takes place within a broader society, and the way that society functions affects the productive process. Good government can assure stability and continuity, without which investment and production will falter. Good government can provide a variety of services that facilitate production. And the policies government pursues, e.g., with respect to taxation, interest rates, support prices for agricultural products, will importantly affect producer decisions. Thus, the creativity and skill of government officials play a key role in economic development. It can be argued, in fact, that an effective government policymaker — e.g., a Treasury Secretary — is worth many Henry Fords.[4] W. Arthur Lewis observes, "The behaviour of government plays as important a role in stimulating or discouraging economic activity as does the behaviour of entrepreneurs, or parents, or scientists, or priests."[5]

But our definition of development is far broader than just the productive dimension of human existence. It also embraces the social dimension, particularly health, education, and welfare. It is government that bears the principal responsibility for progress in these sectors, and, as with economic progress, innovation and creativity are at the root of social progress. The people who conceive the policies that expand and improve social services are thus comparable in their developmental impact to industrial entrepreneurs, as are public-sector planners, administrators, technicians, and blue-collar workers to their private-sector counterparts.

It is not difficult to see how this view of what makes development happen can be extended to virtually all forms of work, intellectual and physical, performed within a society. While it is obvious that the contribution of some will be greater than that of others, and while the role of gifted people can be enormously important, all can contribute. It is thus probably more accurate, at least in the contemporary world, to think of development as a process of millions of small breakthroughs than as a few monumental innovations, the work of geniuses. A society that smooths the way for these breakthroughs is a society that will progress.

How does a society encourage the expression of human creative capacity? Basically, in seven ways:

1. Through creation of an environment in which people expect and receive fair treatment.
2. Through an effective and accessible education system: one that provides basic intellectual and vocational tools; nurtures inquisitiveness, critical faculties, dissent, and creativity; and equips people to solve problems.
3. Through a health system that protects people from diseases that debilitate and kill.
4. Through creation of an environment that encourages experimentation and criticism (which is often at the root of experimentation).
5. Through creation of an environment that helps people both discover their talents and interests and mesh them with the right jobs.
6. Through a system of incentives that rewards merit and achievement (and, conversely, discourages nepotism and "pull").
7. Through creation of the stability and continuity that make it possible to plan ahead with confidence. Progress is made enormously more difficult by instability and discontinuity.

Two examples in Nicaragua

My recent experience in Nicaragua provides two examples that symbolize what societies can do to nurture or frustrate human creative capacity.

The United States ambassador to Nicaragua during my two years there was Lawrence A. Pezzullo. Larry Pezzullo grew up in the Bronx, the son of an immigrant Italian butcher. His mother, also an immigrant, was illiterate. He attended public schools in New York City, served in the u.s. Army in Europe during World War ii, and returned to New York to attend Columbia University under the GI bill. Following graduation, he taught in a public high school on Long Island for six years, then joined the Foreign Service. He rose steadily through the ranks, served as deputy assistant secretary of state for congressional affairs from 1975 to 1977, and was named ambassador to Uruguay in 1977. He became ambassador to Nicaragua in July 1979, simultaneous with the installation of the revolutionary Government of National Reconstruction.

Larry Pezzullo is a person of extraordinary talent. He has great capacity for understanding complicated political processes. But he also has a flair for conceiving and orchestrating responses to the circumstances he faces, and an unerring sense of timing. He is a diplomatic entrepreneur who, in Nicaragua, was the right man in the right place at the right time. (He has since become executive director of Catholic Relief Services.)

Rosa Carballo was born into similar humble circumstances, but in Nicaragua. She is a woman in her sixties, highly intelligent, dignified, and self-disciplined. She has a profound understanding of human nature and sees well below the surface of the political process in her country. With those qualities, she might well have been a successful professional in another society. In Nicaragua she is a domestic servant. She is effectively illiterate.

I want to note in passing that, today, there are few countries that could not virtually eradicate illiteracy within a generation if the will to do so existed.

Values and attitudes that foster progress

We now have to ask what values and attitudes foster the conditions that facilitate the expression of human creative capacity — and development. In this discussion, I will be referring to Figure 1. Diagrams often both oversimplify and confuse. Figure 1, however, has helped me think through the complicated relationships between culture and development, and the reader may find it helpful, too. I want to stress that it is a simplification of an enormously complicated system, and that cause and effect probably move both up and down, both left and right.

The society's world view is the source of its value and attitude systems. The world view is formed by a complex of influences, including geography, economic organization, and the vagaries of history. The world view and its

Figure 1

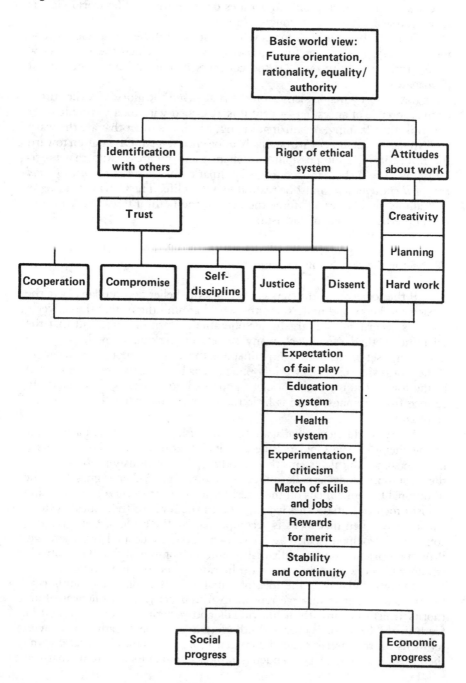

related value and attitude systems are constantly changing, but usually at a very slow pace, measurable in decades or generations. The world view is expressed at least in part through religion.

Of crucial importance for development are: (1) the world view's time focus — past, present, or future; (2) the extent to which the world view encourages rationality; and (3) the concepts of equality and authority it propagates.

If a society's major focus is on the past — on the glory of earlier times or in reverence of ancestors — or if it is absorbed with today's problems of survival, the planning, organizing, saving, and investment that are the warp and woof of development are not likely to be encouraged. Orientation toward the future implies the possibility of change and progress. And that possibility, as Max Weber stressed in his landmark work *The Protestant Ethic and the Spirit of Capitalism*, must be realizable in this life. The Calvinist concepts of "calling" and "election" force the eyes of the faithful toward the future. So do the basic tenets of Judaism:

> Judaism clings to the idea of Progress. The Golden Age of Humanity is not in the past, but in the future.[6]

If the society's world view encourages the belief that humans have the capacity to know and understand the world around them, that the universe operates according to a largely decipherable pattern of laws, and that the scientific method can unlock many secrets of the unknown, it is clearly imparting a set of attitudes tightly linked to the ideas of progress and change. If the world view explains worldly phenomena by supernatural forces, often in the form of numerous capricious gods and goddesses who demand obeisance from humans, there is little room for reason, education, planning, or progress.

Many world views propagate the idea of human equality, particularly in the theme of the Golden Rule and its variations. The idea is stressed more in some ethical systems than in others. It is obviously present in both the Protestant and Catholic ethical systems. But Weber argues that the traditional Catholic focus on the afterlife, in contrast to the Protestant (and Jewish) focus on life in this world, vitiates the force of the ethical system, particularly when that focus is accompanied by the cycle of transgression/confession/absolution.[7] One possible consequence may be a relatively stronger Protestant orientation toward equality and the community, and a relatively stronger Catholic orientation toward hierarchy and the individual.

Directly related to the idea of equality is the concept of authority. Subsequent chapters observe repeatedly the negative consequences of authoritarianism for growth of individuals and societies. There may well be truth in the belief of Weber and others that traditional Catholicism, with its focus on the afterlife and the crucial role of the church hierarchy and the priest, encouraged a dependency mindset among its adherents that was an obstacle to entrepreneurial activity. Martin Luther, by contrast, preached "the priesthood of all believers;"[8] "every Christian had to be a monk all his life."[9]

But there are also some religions — including, to be sure, some Protestant denominations — whose basic tenets embrace the idea of inequality. Traditional Hinduism comes immediately to mind, as do Gunnar Myrdal's comments on South Asia:

> . . . Social and economic stratification is accorded the sanction of religion. . . . the inherited stratification implies low social and spatial mobility, little free competition in its wider sense, and great inequalities.[10]

> It should be an hypothesis for further study that people in this region are not inherently different from people elsewhere, but that they live and have lived for a long time under conditions very different from those in the Western world, and that this has left its mark upon their bodies and minds. Religion has, then, become the emotional container of this whole way of life and work and by its sanction has rendered it rigid and resistant to change.[11]

The fundamental questions of future versus past and present orientation, encouragement or discouragement of rationality, and emphasis on equality versus emphasis on authority strongly influence three other cultural factors that play an important role in the way a society develops: (1) the extent of identification with others, (2) the rigor of the ethical system, and (3) attitudes about work.

Several of the people whose works are discussed in the following chapter (e.g., Weber, Myrdal, David McClelland) have emphasized the importance for progress of a radius of identification and trust that embraces an entire society. There is evidence that the extended family is an effective institution for survival but an obstacle to development.[12] Weber observes, "The great achievement of ethical religions, above all of the ethical and ascetistic sects of Protestantism, was to shatter the fetters of the sib [i.e., the extended family]."[13]

The social consequences of widespread mistrust can be grave. Samuel Huntington makes the point:

> . . . the absence of trust in the culture of the society provides formidable obstacles to the creation of public institutions. Those societies deficient in stable and effective government are also deficient in mutual trust among their citizens, in national and public loyalties, and in organization skills and capacity. Their political cultures are often said to be marked by suspicion, jealousy, and latent or actual hostility toward everyone who is not a member of the family, the village, or, perhaps, the tribe. These characteristics are found in many cultures, their most extensive manifestation perhaps being in the Arab world and in Latin America . . . In Latin America . . . traditions of self-centered individualism and of distrust and hatred for other groups in society have prevailed.[14]

A whole set of possibilities opens up when trust is extended beyond the family, possibilities that are likely to be reflected in both economic and social development. Myrdal observes, ". . . a more inclusive nationalism then becomes a force for progress . . . a vehicle for rationalism and for the ideals of planning, equality, social welfare, and perhaps democracy."[15] In such an environment, the idea of cooperation will be strengthened, with all that implies for modern production techniques, community problem-solving, and political stability. The idea of compromise, which is central to the working of a pluralistic system, is also reinforced.[16] When the idea of compromise — i.e., that a relationship is important enough to warrant seeking to avoid confrontation, even if some concession is necessary — is weak, the likelihood of confrontation is increased. Constant confrontation undermines stability and continuity, which, as noted earlier, are crucial to development.

There is a gap in all societies between the stated ethical system and the extent to which that system is honored in practice. Religions' treatment of ethical issues obviously has something to do with the size of the gap. Broad identification among the members of a society will strengthen the impact of the ethical system. Where the radius of identification and trust is small, there may effectively be no operative ethical system.

The rigor of the effective ethical system will shape attitudes about justice, which are central to several major development issues. If the members of a society expect injustice, the ideas of cooperation, compromise, stability, and continuity will be undermined. Corruption and nepotism will be encouraged. And the self-discipline necessary to keep a society working well (e.g., payment of taxes, resistance to the temptation to steal) will be weakened. The system of criminal and civil jurisprudence will be politicized and corrupted and will not be taken seriously by the citizenry. The idea of justice is also central to crucial social issues: the fairness of income distribution, availability of educational opportunities and health services, and promotion by merit.

Another link to these questions of radius of identification, rigor of the effective ethical system, and justice is the idea of dissent.[17] Its acceptance is fundamental to a functioning pluralistic political system, and it is clearly related to the idea of compromise. But it is also an important idea for creativity: what the inventor and the entrepreneur do is a kind of creative dissent.

Attitudes about work link back to several of these ideas, but particularly to future orientation. If the idea of progress is well established in the culture, there is a presumption that planning and hard work will be rewarded by increased income and improved living conditions. When the focus is on the present, on day-to-day survival, the ceiling on work may be the amount necessary to survive.

This brings us back to the seven conditions that encourage the expression of human creative capacity:

1. The expectation of fair play
2. Availability of educational opportunities
3. Availability of health services
4. Encouragement of experimentation and criticism
5. Matching of skills and jobs
6. Rewards for merit and achievement
7. Stability and continuity

Taken together, the seven conditions describe a functional modern democratic capitalist society. The extent to which countries realize their potential is determined, I believe, by the extent to which these conditions exist. This assertion is supported by Table 2: the seven conditions substantially exist in the fifteen countries whose per-capita gross national product (GNP) is the highest in the world (excluding four oil-rich Arab countries). These same fifteen countries accounted for 83 percent of the Nobel Prize winners from 1945 to 1981.

A breakdown of progress by country

I conclude this chapter with the country-by-country Table 2, which is drawn from the World Bank's *World Development Report 1982.* The table will be useful in the following chapters to give at least a sense of the different development levels achieved by the pairs of countries considered.

I am aware of the shortcomings of per-capita GNP as an indicator. For example, it is distorted by exchange-rate conversions and it tells nothing about income distribution. But it continues to be the single most widely used indicator of development, and at least some of its shortcomings are mitigated by the inclusion of adult literacy and life expectancy data.

Table 2. Basic indicators

	Population (millions) mid-1980	Area (thousands of square kilometers)	GNP per capita Dollars 1980	Adult literacy (percent) 1977[a]	Life expectancy at birth (years) 1980	Average annual growth of population 1970–80 (percent)
Low-income economies	2,160.9 t	30,714 t	260 w	50 w	57 w	2.1 w
China and India	1,649.9 t	12,819 t	270 w	54 w	59 w	1.9 w
Other low-income	511.0 t	17,895 t	230 w	34 w	48 w	2.6 w
1 Kampuchea, Dem.	6.9	181	—		—	−0.2
2 Lao PDR	3.4	237	—	41	43	1.8
3 Bhutan	1.3	47	80	—	44	2.0
4 Chad	4.5	1,284	120	15	41	2.0
5 Bangladesh	88.5	144	130	26	46	2.6
6 Ethiopia	31.1	1,222	140	15	40	2.0
7 Nepal	14.6	141	140	19	44	2.5
8 Somalia	3.9	638	—	60	44	2.3
9 Burma	34.8	677	170	70	54	2.4
10 Afghanistan	15.9	648	—	12	37	2.5
11 Viet Nam	54.2	330	—	87	63	2.8
12 Mali	7.0	1,240	190	9	43	2.7
13 Burundi	4.1	28	200	23	42	2.0
14 Rwanda	5.2	26	200	50	45	3.4
15 Upper Volta	6.1	274	210	5	39	1.8

16 Zaire	28.3	2,345	220	58	47	2.7
17 Malawi	6.1	118	220	25	44	2.9
18 Mozambique	12.1	802	230	28	47	4.0
19 India	673.2	3,288	240	36	52	2.1
20 Haiti	5.0	28	270	23	53	1.7
21 Sri Lanka	14.7	66	270	85	66	1.6
22 Sierra Leone	3.5	72	280	—	47	2.6
23 Tanzania	18.7	945	280	66	52	3.4
24 China	976.7	9,561	290	66	64	1.8
25 Guinea	5.4	246	290	20	45	2.9
26 Central African Rep.	2.3	623	300	39	44	2.1
27 Pakistan	82.2	804	300	24	50	3.1
28 Uganda	12.6	236	300	48	54	2.6
29 Benin	3.4	113	310	25	47	2.6
30 Niger	5.3	1,267	330	5	43	2.8
31 Madagascar	8.7	587	350	50	47	2.5
32 Sudan	18.7	2,506	410	20	46	3.0
33 Togo	2.5	56	410	18	47	2.5
Middle-income economies	1,138.8 t	41,614 t	1,400 w	65 w	60 w	2.4 w
Oil exporters	496.8 t	16,135 t	1,160 w	57 w	56 w	2.6 w
Oil importers	642.0 t	25,479 t	1,580 w	73 w	63 w	2.3 w
34 Ghana	11.7	239	420	—	49	3.0
35 Kenya	15.9	583	420	50	55	3.4
36 Lesotho	1.3	30	420	52	51	2.3
37 Yemen, PDR	1.9	333	420	40	45	2.4
38 Indonesia	146.6	1,919	430	62	53	2.3

Table 2. continued

	Population (millions) mid-1980	Area (thousands of square kilometers)	GNP per capita Dollars 1980	Adult literacy (percent) 1977[a]	Life expectancy at birth (years) 1980	Average annual growth of population 1970–80 (percent)
39 Yemen Arab Rep.	7.0	195	430	21	42	2.9
40 Mauritania	1.5	1,031	440	17	43	2.5
41 Senegal	5.7	196	450	10	43	2.8
42 Angola	7.1	1,247	470	—	42	2.4
43 Liberia	1.9	111	530	25	54	3.4
44 Honduras	3.7	112	560	60	58	3.4
45 Zambia	5.8	753	560	44	49	3.1
46 Bolivia	5.6	1,099	570	63	50	2.5
47 Egypt	39.8	1,001	580	44	57	2.1
48 Zimbabwe	7.4	391	630	74	55	3.3
49 El Salvador	4.5	21	660	62	63	2.9
50 Cameroon	8.4	475	670	—	47	2.2
51 Thailand	47.0	514	670	84	63	2.5
52 Philippines	49.0	300	690	75	64	2.7
53 Nicaragua	2.6	130	740	90	56	3.4
54 Papua New Guinea	3.0	462	780	32	51	2.3
55 Congo, People's Rep.	1.6	342	900	—	59	2.8
56 Morocco	20.2	447	900	28	56	3.0
57 Mongolia	1.7	1,565	—	—	64	2.9
58 Albania	2.7	29	—	—	70	2.5

59 Peru	17.4	1,285	930	80	58	2.6
60 Nigeria	84.7	924	1,030	30	49	2.5
61 Jamaica	2.2	11	1,040	90	71	1.5
62 Guatemala	7.3	109	1,080	—	59	3.0
63 Ivory Coast	8.3	322	1,150	41	47	5.0
64 Dominican Rep.	5.4	49	1,160	67	61	3.0
65 Colombia	26.7	1,139	1,180	—	63	2.3
66 Ecuador	8.0	284	1,270	81	61	3.0
67 Paraguay	3.2	407	1,300	84	65	3.2
68 Tunisia	6.4	164	1,310	62	60	2.1
69 Korea, Dem. Rep.	18.3	121	—	—	65	2.6
70 Syrian Arab Rep.	9.0	185	1,340	58	65	3.6
71 Jordan	3.2	98	1,420	70	61	3.4
72 Lebanon	2.7	10	—	—	66	0.7
73 Turkey	44.9	781	1,470	60	62	2.4
74 Cuba	9.7	115	—	96	73	1.3
75 Korea, Rep. of	38.2	98	1,520	93	65	1.7
76 Malaysia	13.9	330	1,620	—	64	2.4
77 Costa Rica	2.2	51	1,730	90	70	2.5
78 Panama	1.8	77	1,730	—	70	2.3
79 Algeria	18.9	2,382	1,870	35	56	3.2
80 Brazil	118.7	8,512	2,050	76	63	2.2
81 Mexico	69.8	1,973	2,090	81	65	3.1
82 Chile	11.1	757	2,150	—	67	1.7
83 South Africa	29.3	1,221	2,300	—	61	2.7

Table 2. continued

	Population (millions) mid-1980	Area (thousands of square kilometers)	GNP per capita Dollars 1980	Adult literacy (percent) 1977ᵃ	Life expectancy at birth (years) 1980	Average annual growth of population 1970–80 (percent)
84 Romania	22.2	238	2,340	98	71	0.9
85 Portugal	9.8	92	2,370	—	71	1.3
86 Argentina	27.7	2,767	2,390	93	70	1.6
87 Yugoslavia	22.3	256	2,620	85	70	0.9
88 Uruguay	2.9	176	2,810	94	71	0.3
89 Iran	38.8	1,648	—	50	59	3.1
90 Iraq	13.1	435	3,020	—	56	3.3
91 Venezuela	14.9	912	3,630	82	67	3.3
92 Hong Kong	5.1	1	4,240	90	74	2.5
93 Trinidad and Tobago	1.2	5	4,370	95	72	1.3
94 Greece	9.6	132	4,380	—	74	0.9
95 Singapore	2.4	1	4,430	—	72	1.5
96 Israel	3.9	21	4,500	—	72	2.6
High-income oil exporters	14.4 t	4,012 t	12,630 w	25 w	57 w	5.0 w
97 Libya	3.0	1,760	8,640	—	56	4.1
98 Saudi Arabia	9.0	2,150	11,260	16	54	4.4
99 Kuwait	1.4	18	19,830	60	70	6.0
100 United Arab Emirates	1.0	84	26,850	56	63	13.2

Industrial market economies

	714.4 t	30,935 t	10,320 w	99 w	74 w	0.8 w
101 Ireland	3.3	70	4,880	98	73	1.1
102 Spain	37.4	505	5,400	—	73	1.0
103 Italy	56.9	301	6,480	98	73	0.6
104 New Zealand	3.3	269	7,090	99	73	1.5
105 United Kingdom	55.9	245	7,920	99	73	0.1
106 Finland	4.9	337	9,720	100	73	0.5
107 Australia	14.5	7,687	9,820	100	74	1.4
108 Japan	116.5	372	9,890	99	76	1.1
109 Canada	23.9	9,976	10,130	99	74	1.1
110 Austria	7.5	84	10,230	99	72	0.0
111 United States	227.7	9,363	11,360	99	74	1.0
112 Netherlands	14.1	41	11,470	99	75	0.8
113 France	53.5	547	11,730	99	74	0.5
114 Belgium	9.8	31	12,180	99	73	0.2
115 Norway	4.1	324	12,650	99	75	0.5
116 Denmark	5.1	43	12,950	99	75	0.4
117 Sweden	8.3	450	13,520	99	75	0.3
118 Germany, Fed. Rep.	60.9	249	13,590	99	73	(.)
119 Switzerland	6.5	41	16,440	99	75	0.3

Table 2. continued

	Population (millions) mid-1980	Area (thousands of square kilometers)	GNP per capita Dollars 1980	Adult literacy (percent) 1977[a]	Life expectancy at birth (years) 1980	Average annual growth of population 1970–80 (percent)
Nonmarket industrial economies	353.3 t	23,155 t	4,640 w	100 w	71 w	0.8 w
120 Poland	35.8	313	3,900	98	72	0.9
121 Bulgaria	9.0	111	4,150	—	73	0.6
122 Hungary	10.8	93	4,180	99	71	0.4
123 USSR	265.5	22,402	4,550	100	71	0.9
124 Czechoslovakia	15.3	128	5,820	—	71	0.7
125 German Dem. Rep.	16.9	108	7,180	—	72	−0.1

a. Figures in italics are for years other than that specified.

16

NOTES

1. "Development" and "progress" are used synonymously in this book.
2. Everett E. Hagen, *On the Theory of Social Change: How Economic Growth Begins*, p. 88.
3. Hagen makes similar points on p. 11 of *On the Theory of Social Change*.
4. This point is elaborated in Lawrence E. Harrison, "Some Hidden Costs of the Public Investment Fixation," pp. 20 – 23.
5. W. Arthur Lewis, *The Theory of Economic Growth*, p. 376.
6. The words of a former Chief Rabbi of Great Britain in J. H. Hertz (ed.), *The Pentateuch and Haftorahs*, p. 196.
7. Clearly, contemporary Catholicism is moving toward the Protestant and Jewish focus on this life, particularly since Pope John XXIII.
8. Quoted in David C. McClelland, *The Achieving Society*, p. 48.
9. Max Weber, *The Protestant Ethic and the Spirit of Capitalism*, p. 121.
10. Gunnar Myrdal, *Asian Drama: An Inquiry into the Poverty of Nations*, p. 104.
11. *Ibid.*, p. 112.
12. The conditions for human progress and happiness are still worse where trust extends no further than the nuclear family, as in Banfield's "Montegrano" (see the next chapter). In that case, both development and survival are threatened.
13. Max Weber, *The Religion of China*, p. 237.
14. Samuel P. Huntington, *Political Order in Changing Societies*, p. 28.
15. Myrdal, *Asian Drama*, p. 122.
16. It is, I believe, significant that there is no truly apt Spanish word for "compromise" (see Chapter 7).
17. It also seems significant that there is no truly apt Spanish word for "dissent" (see Chapter 7).

2

What others have said

A number of scholars have addressed the relationship between culture and development. Some have examined the extent to which conditions similar to the seven listed in the preceding chapter exist in reality, not just in rhetoric, and have analyzed the cultural factors they believe lie behind the question of how well a society works for all its people. Some have focused more narrowly on the question of entrepreneurship, particularly why it is more in evidence in some societies than others.

Most of the analytical work has been done by economists, political scientists, and sociologists. Interestingly, the contribution of anthropologists has been quite limited, particularly when it comes to comparing the performance of two or more countries. Most anthropologists subscribe to the theory of cultural relativism, which insists that each culture must be viewed on its own terms — that comparative value judgments cannot be made. One anthropologist who rejects this view is Arthur Hippler, who had this to say in the 1981 *American Anthropologist*: "I propose a basic criterion for looking at culture as a human tool: Cultures are better or worse depending on the degree to which they support innate human capacities as those emerge."[1]

Gunnar Myrdal (1898 –)

Foremost among those who have studied the cultural roots of how well a society works is Swedish economist Gunnar Myrdal. Myrdal's three-volume work, *Asian Drama: An Inquiry into the Poverty of Nations*, is a milestone in our efforts to understand poverty and development. Myrdal dedicated ten years to an attempt to describe, explain, and prescribe for the tragic poverty of South Asia. He concluded that cultural factors are the principal obstacles to modernization: not just that they get in the way of entrepreneurial activity, but that they permeate, rigidify, and dominate the entire national system in all its political, economic, and social dimensions; "that even in their economic choices people are conditioned by their total mental make-up and, in particular, by the community in which they live . . ."[2]

In expressing disappointment that social anthropologists and sociologists have failed "to provide the more broadly based system of theories and concepts needed for the scientific study of the problem of development," Myrdal observes, "For this there may seem to be an obvious explanation,

18

that the factors abstracted from in the economic analysis — attitudes, institutions, modes and levels of living, and, broadly, culture — are so much more difficult to grasp in systematic analysis than are the so-called economic factors."[3]

Myrdal starts by describing South Asia's "modernization ideals" — the consensus of *articulated* (principally by the elite) values and attitudes during the 1960s. He points out that "the modernization ideals [e.g., rationality, social and economic equality, political democracy] are all, in a sense, alien to the region, since they stem from foreign influences."[4] He then examines the traditional, often unarticulated values and attitudes that largely govern the actions of the masses and, indeed, the entire society (including the elite). The contrast between the two is often dramatic, and imparts a strong sense of the enormity of the cultural obstacles to development.

In describing traditional South Asian culture,[5] Myrdal first looks at an idealized and largely mythological stereotype:

> A central claim is that people in Asia are more spiritual and less materialistic than Westerners. They are other-worldly, selfless, and disposed to disregard wealth and material comfort. They sustain poverty with equanimity and even see positive virtues in it. They have a special respect for learning and a capacity for contemplation and meditation. Their intellectual strength lies in intuition more than in reason and hard calculation. In current affairs their main criterion is the moral worth of a person or a policy, and they are apt to censure expediency and opportunism in politics. With spiritual concerns and personal salvation paramount, the external world takes on an illusory and transient aspect. The attitude toward the environment tends to be timeless, formless, and therefore carefree and even fatalistic. The ideal is alleged to be detachment, withdrawal, if not renunciation and asceticism. This bent of mind, it is said, gives Asians serenity and the capacity to endure extreme physical suffering. They are pictured as tolerant, non-aggressive, and non-militant in their social relations and their international politics. They are said to dislike definitive legal principles and to prefer to settle conflicts by mutual agreement rather than by formal procedures; to regard status as more important than contracts; to desire peace with their neighbors and the world, and peace in their souls.[6]

Myrdal analyzes each of these idealized qualities, frequently employing Jawaharlal Nehru's words as well as his own:

> Myrdal:
>   . . . the charity and tolerance often attributed to the Indians is in direct contradiction to the extreme intolerance bred by rigid social stratification and the callousness toward those in a lower social stratum that is found among the most cultivated Indians and soon adopted by Westerners who live in India for any length of time . . . Indians are generally felt to be haughty and intolerant . . . non-violence is certainly not a national trait in India, as demonstrated by the Hindu-Moslem strife at the time of parti-

tion . . . A propensity for narrow materialism in all social strata is commonly observed . . .[7]

Nehru:

    A country under foreign domination seeks escape from the present in dreams of a vanished age, and finds consolation in visions of past greatness.[8] That is a foolish and dangerous posture in which many of us indulge. An equally questionable practice for us in India is to imagine that we are still spiritually great though we have come down in the world in other respects. Spiritual or any other greatness cannot be founded on lack of freedom and opportunity, or on starvation and misery.[9]

I won't put it that way, that Indians are 'more spiritual.' I would say that a static society talks more about so-called spirituality.[10]

Nor do I appreciate in the least the idealisation of the 'simple peasant life.' I have almost a horror of it. . . . What is there in the 'Man with the Hoe' to idealize over? Crushed and exploited for innumerable generations he is only little removed from the animals who keep him company.[11]

    Myrdal concludes this examination of myth and reality by observing that the idealized and largely mythological stereotype is getting in the way of achievement of the modernization ideal.

    Myrdal's views on South Asian religion recapitulate Marx and Weber: he believes that religion usually acts as a tremendous force for social inertia[12] and that it encourages irrationality. The caste system "tends to make the existing inequalities particularly rigid and unyielding"[13] and "fortifies the prevalent contempt and disgust for manual work."[14] It is here that Myrdal touches on an idea that is the theme of John Kenneth Galbraith's subsequent book, *The Nature of Mass Poverty*:

    . . . the survival-mindedness of the people, their unresponsiveness to opportunities for betterment, and their scorn of manual labor, especially work for an employer, may result, directly or indirectly, from long ages of hopeless poverty.[15]

    South Asia's experience under the British brought with it some important benefits, in Myrdal's view: ". . . with all its shortcomings, the colonial period provided these countries with more 'development' than they had ever had."[16] One aspect of this development was the concept of nationhood, which had not existed before, and which Myrdal sees as potentially ". . . a vehicle for rationalism and for the ideals of planning, equality, social welfare, and perhaps democracy."[17]

    Karl Marx said essentially the same thing in 1853. In that year he wrote two articles for *The New York Daily Tribune*[18] in which he expressed the opinion that, through the introduction of such innovations as a professional army, the free press, a national education system, and steam propulsion, England was "causing a social revolution in Hindustan" and undermining an "undignified, stagnatory, and vegetative life [that] evoked . . . wild, aimless, unbounded forces of destruction."[19] He also stressed the crucial importance of the British contribution to the concept of Indian nationhood.

Myrdal believes, along with several others,[20] that fragmentation of loyalties — what I referred to earlier as a limited radius of identification and trust — is a major impediment to the building of a modern nation. He believes that the lack of loyalty to the society as a whole is a major contributor to corruption and, particularly, nepotism. He speculates, "Is there . . . a general asociality that leads people to think that anybody in a position of power is likely to exploit it in the interest of himself, his family, or other social groups to which he has a feeling of loyalty?"[21]

Culture is neither immutable nor immune to change by planned intervention, in Myrdal's view. He believes such change should be a high-priority focus of government planning. He sees education, defined broadly to include child and adult education, government reform, and media attention, as a particularly promising tool. "From a development point of view, the purpose of education must be to rationalize attitudes as well as to impart knowledge and skills."[22]

W. Arthur Lewis (1915 –)

W. Arthur Lewis, who was born in St. Lucia, West Indies, was among the first economists to treat the cultural dimensions of economic development. In *The Theory of Economic Growth* (1955), Lewis relates cultural influences both to entrepreneurship and to the broader question of the sociopolitical environment for growth. Particularly in the latter, his views parallel those of Myrdal: "Economic growth depends on attitudes to work, to wealth, to thrift, to having children, to invention, to strangers, to adventure, and so on, and all these attitudes flow from deep springs in the human mind."[23]

Lewis sees religion as an important influence on development for good or bad, depending on whether it promotes honesty, saving, risk-taking, and rationality. But he also thinks that religion reflects as well as determines economic attitudes. He shares Myrdal's (and others') belief that the extended family is often an impediment to progress because it gets in the way of national cohesion. As a former British colonial subject, his views on imperialism are particularly interesting:

> The best empires have added greatly to human happiness; they have established peace over wide areas, have built roads, have improved public health, have stimulated trade, have brought improved systems of law, have introduced new technical knowledge, and so on. Whereas the worst empires have brought pillage, and slaughter and slavery in their train.[24]

Like Myrdal, Lewis considers attitudes and institutions that perpetuate social rigidity (e.g., slavery, caste, race barriers, snobbery) as highly prejudicial to growth. His views on slavery parallel those of a number of other writers, from Max Weber to Carlos Rangel (both of whom will be discussed later in the chapter):

> . . . in the slave communities of the New World, the plutocracies were much given to going on picnics and to having a good time, and there was much absentee ownership. The middle and working classes of these communities to this day show a greater propensity to consume lavishly than they do to work, and this may plausibly be explained by saying that they have inherited the idea that work is only fit for slaves.[25]

Lewis was among the first theorists to recognize the importance to development of women, whom he views as a major neglected resource. He singles out the traditional roles of women as obstacles to development and the consequence of male "snobbery." And he observes that "one of the quickest ways of increasing the national output is to open factories offering light jobs of the kind which women do most easily."[26]

Of particular interest to Lewis was why some countries produce proportionately more entrepreneurs than others. As mentioned above, he believes religion is relevant: he sees, for example, a pattern of achievement among persecuted religious groups (e.g., Jews, Huguenots, Quakers, Parsees). He also believes groups that have lost prestige may develop an extraordinary drive for achievement, as occurred in Japan's Meiji Restoration.[27] But he believes that the principal determinant of the incidence of entrepreneurship is the extent to which a society attaches prestige and other incentives to it.

Let us digress briefly to look at the views of three people who have paid special attention to this question of entrepreneurship/achievement.

Entrepreneurship: Max Weber (1864 – 1930); Joseph A. Schumpeter (1883 – 1950); David C. McClelland (1917 –)

Many social scientists have studied why some groups or societies achieve more than others. Perhaps the first to address the question in depth was Max Weber, a German who is considered one of the fathers of sociology. In *The Protestant Ethic and the Spirit of Capitalism*, which he wrote in 1904 – 05, Weber examined evidence from the records of the city of Baden suggesting that Protestants were higher achievers than Catholics (and that Jews were even higher achievers than Protestants). This led him to the study of religion as a determinant of achievement in this and subsequent books.

We have already touched on some of Weber's ideas. He believed that at the root of achievement is a set of values and attitudes we associate with the Protestant ethic: hard work, thrift, honesty, rationality, austerity — in sum, "asceticism." Particularly in the Protestant denominations influenced by Calvinism, they operate in a mutually reinforcing way. The Calvinist concept of "calling" — "the fulfillment of the obligations imposed on the individual by his position in the world"[28] — coupled with the concept of "election" — the belief that God has blessed a chosen few whose state of grace is apparent from their prosperity — "must have been the most powerful conceivable lever for the expansion of that attitude toward life which we have called the spirit of capitalism." And, "when the limitation of consumption is combined with this release of acquisitive activity, the inevitable practical result is obvious: accumulation of capital through ascetic compulsion to save."[29]

Weber believed that Roman Catholic emphasis on the afterlife and, particularly, what he perceived as a more flexible ethical system put Catholics at a disadvantage to Protestants and Jews in this life. "The God of Calvinism demanded of his believers not single good works, but a life of good works combined into a unified system. There was no place for the very human Catholic cycle of sin, repentance, atonement, release, followed by renewed sin."[30] Weber also believed that what he perceived as the less paternalistic relationship between Protestant (and Jewish) lay people and their clergy also had a salutary effect on achievement, if for no other reason than that it encouraged the literacy necessary for reading the Bible.

Weber's study of Asia, and particularly Eastern religions, led him to conclude that the values and attitudes inculcated by these religions explained why Asia's economic development was far behind Europe's. In *The Religion of China* (1915) and *The Religion of India* (1916 – 17), Weber catalogued the contrasts between the Protestant ethic and the "highly anti-rational world of universal magic"[31] of Confucianism and Hinduism.

These traditional religions, like traditional religions the world over, explained natural phenomena by supernatural events, by the actions of pantheons of greater and lesser spirits, by magic.[32] Human beings were objects acted upon by these supernatural forces, not independent actors themselves, capable of making things happen, of bringing about change.

The "irrationality"[33] of oriental religions was thus in Weber's view a major barrier to development. But these religions also propagated a "non-ethical" (particularly by contrast with Protestant asceticism) set of values and attitudes that got in the way of change. The only ethical sins "consisted of offenses against traditional authorities, parents, ancestors, and superiors in the hierarchy of office."[34] Family piety dominated thought and action, and it, coupled with the absence of a broader social ethic, led to dishonesty in dealings outside the family. This, in turn, led to widespread mistrust, a major obstacle to economic activity.

Weber focused on religion to the virtual exclusion of other cultural elements embraced in "ethnicity." Partly as a result, exceptions to his thesis keep popping up. Weber died long before overseas Chinese demonstrated very high economic achievement indeed in such places as Taiwan, Hong Kong, and Singapore, to say nothing of Hawaii and other parts of the United States. (Galbraith explains this phenomenon by the self-selection of achievers implicit in the decision to migrate from a culture of mass poverty.) Nor did Weber live to see the Chinese revolution of 1946, which some might interpret as Mao's confirmation of Weber's views. It is, in any event, interesting to note the concern of the current Chinese leadership to encourage entrepreneurship.

Although there may be a number of exceptions to Weber's thesis, religion does appear to be an important factor in several of the cases treated later in this book.

Seven years after Weber completed *The Protestant Ethic and the Spirit of Capitalism*, Joseph Schumpeter published *The Theory of Economic Development*, which identified the entrepreneurial function as the critical catalyst for development. He believed that human creative genius was at the root of economic growth. His definition of that genius was a narrow, elitist, even romantic one, excluding the inventor and the capitalist:

> . . . the function of entrepreneurs is to reform or revolutionize the pattern of production by exploiting an invention or, more generally, an untried technological possibility for producing a new commodity or producing an old one in a new way, by opening up a new source of supply of materials or a new outlet for products, by reorganizing industry and so on. . . . To act with confidence beyond the range of familiar beacons and to overcome . . . resistance requires aptitudes that are present in only a small fraction of the population. . . . This function does not essentially consist in either inventing anything or otherwise creating the conditions which the enterprise exploits. It consists in getting things done.[35]

Henry Ford is a prototype of the Schumpeterian entrepreneur. Thomas Edison is not. The true entrepreneur possesses ". . . the dream and the will to found a private kingdom . . . a dynasty . . . the will to conquer: the impulse to fight to prove oneself superior to others, to succeed for the sake, not of the fruits of success but of success itself. . . . Finally, there is the joy of creating, of getting things done, or simply of exercising one's energy and ingenuity."[36]

Schumpeter believed democratic capitalism provided the best environment for the entrepreneur and assured the greatest good for the greatest number. But he also predicted the demise of the entrepreneur with the increasing bureaucratization of life and the inevitable hostility of intellectuals, who are also nurtured by democratic capitalism.

David McClelland is a psychologist who has devoted much of his career to trying to understand what makes some countries develop more rapidly

than others. His book *The Achieving Society* (1961) makes an important contribution to the literature of development by focusing on human motivation.
He observes at the outset:

> It would certainly not surprise us to discover that [the forces that produce
> rapid economic development] lie largely in man himself — in his funda-
> mental motives and in the way he organizes his relationships to his fellow
> men.[37]

Like Lewis, Schumpeter, and Weber, McClelland believes it is the
entrepreneur who makes development happen. Societies that produce proportionally more entrepreneurs will advance faster than societies that produce proportionally fewer. The big question is the same one Weber tried
to answer: What makes some societies produce more entrepreneurs than
others?

McClelland attempts to isolate and study what he labels "the need for
achievement" among men around the world.[38] He examines the Protestant/
Catholic contrast that fascinated Weber and finds substantial — although
not total — support for Weber's thesis. Using children's stories as indicators
of value and attitude systems,[39] McClelland then seeks to correlate evidence
of high need for achievement in the stories of thirty countries with actual
economic performance. There is a very close correlation, not with growth
at the time the stories were popular, but with subsequent growth. There
is thus, he believes, a lag between periods of intense concern for achievement
and the fruition in actual progress as more highly motivated new generations
mature and start to exert their influence.

In searching for the explanation of why some societies produce proportionately more entrepreneurs than others, McClelland focuses on child-
rearing. Psychologists have traditionally identified the first few years of life
as the period when personality is largely formed. McClelland believes that,
at least when it comes to achievement motivation, the years between five
and twelve are crucial. He cites evidence that during this key growth period,
moderate parental pressures are optimal and that achievement tendencies in
children are reinforced by reasonably high parental standards at a time when
a child can handle them; by limited parental interference; and by expressed
parental pleasure in their children's achievements.

McClelland stresses two points that echo the views of others. As Weber
observed, ascetic sects *do* seem to be unusually successful economically,
e.g., the Quakers, Hassidic Jews, the Jains of India. Their values that are
relevant to achievement include anti-authoritarianism, a reverence for life,
and rejection of a priestly caste ("everyone is a priest"). Like Lewis and
Carlos Rangel, McClelland also sees the institution of slavery as totally
undermining of achievement motivation in the slave (American blacks were
significantly lower in achievement motivation than practically all the other
groups tested), but also to some extent in the master.

McClelland concludes with some advice to politicians, planners, and economists:

> Pay attention to the effects that your plans will have on the values, motives and attitudes of people because *in the long run* it is these factors that will determine whether the plans are successful in speeding economic development.[40]

He goes on to mention the following as ways in which values and attitudes can be made more progress-prone: expanded mass communication, concerted effort to reduce corruption, emancipation of women, encouragement of group play by children, reduced father dominance in parenting (because it tends to be authoritarian), religious reform, and educational reform that stresses group participation and achievement.

This concludes the entrepreneurship/achievement digression. Let us now return to consider the views of others who have studied the broader context within which progress does or does not occur.

Gabriel A. Almond (1911 –) and Sidney Verba (1932 –)

Gabriel A. Almond and Sidney Verba are political scientists who produced the pioneering work *The Civic Culture* in 1963. Roughly one thousand interviews were conducted in each of five countries — the United States, Great Britain, Germany, Italy, and Mexico — to determine variations in values and attitudes that might be correlated with the degree of political cohesiveness and progress achieved in each country. The survey tested such questions as feelings toward government and politics, patterns of partisanship, the sense of civic obligation, the political sophistication of the citizenry, attitudes about organization, and concepts of cooperation. The goal is "the civic culture," which may be thought of as the values and attitudes of the elite and the people in general that make possible democracy and its "great ideas — the freedoms and dignities of the individual [and] the principle of government by consent of the governed."[41]

The links of the foregoing to culture are well summarized in a subsequent book, *Political Culture and Political Development*, edited by Verba and Lucian Pye, also a political scientist. Pye observes that ". . . analysis which focuses on the phenomenon of culture may be peculiarly well adapted for comparing and classifying political systems . . ."[42] Verba then elaborates this point, drawing on what he had learned as coauthor of *The Civic Culture*:[43]

> In a culture in which men's orientation toward nature is essentially one of fatalism and resignation their orientation toward government is likely to be much the same. . . . The beliefs described in southern Italy and pre-revolutionary Mexico are examples of that orientation and suggest that such a combination of fatalism toward nature and government may be general in peasant societies.

In Italy and Ethiopia a deeply felt sense of distrust in people is reflected in a striking sense of distrust within the realm of politics.

Perhaps the most crucial political belief involves that of political identity. Of what political unit does the individual consider himself a member, and how deep and unambiguous is the sense of identification?

A second significant dimension of identification is the horizontal identification with one's fellow citizens . . . the sense of integration individuals have with other people who inhabit the political system.

. . . the extent to which members of a political system have trust and confidence in their fellow political actors is a crucial aspect of the horizontal integration of a political culture. It is likely to be closely related to one's general view of human nature: some cultures incorporate much more favorable views of one's fellow men than do others.

This sense of confidence in other political actors is a particularly crucial aspect of a democratic political culture. Unless individuals trust their political opponents they are going to be rather unwilling to turn over government power to those opponents.

As with the general basic value structure of a culture, basic political values are quite probably set fairly firmly early in life. . . . The most important early experiences with implications for basic political values, however, may have no explicit political content at all. In early social situations the child will learn certain basic lessons about the nature of authority, the trustworthiness and supportiveness of other people, the manipulability of the environment, and the desirability of such manipulation. . . . In Italy, children learn to distrust others.

Edward C. Banfield (1916 –)

In 1954 and 1955, political scientist Edward C. Banfield lived for nine months among the peasants of an extremely poor and backward town in the south of Italy. Banfield gives the town the fictitious name of Montegrano in his book *The Moral Basis of a Backward Society*.

Banfield's curiosity was piqued initially by the almost total absence of organizations in Montegrano. He contrasts the town in this respect with comparably sized and comparably remote St. George, Utah, which is a beehive of organized activity, and observes:

We are apt to take it for granted that economic and political associations will quickly arise wherever technical conditions and natural resources permit. . . . The assumption is wrong because it overlooks the crucial importance of culture.[44]

As he seeks to understand why there are no organizations, Banfield becomes familiar with other facets of the Montegranesi's lives that are clearly getting in the way of their development as individuals and as a community:

. . . not only is public-spiritedness lacking, but many people positively want to prevent others from getting ahead. . . . there is a tremendous envy of either money or intelligence.[45]

In the Montegrano mind, any advantage that may be given to another is necessarily at the expense of one's family.[46]

Because manual labor is degrading, a landowner who can do so without starving hires someone to do his work for him.[47]

If they could do so, the people of Montegrano would migrate to the United States *en masse*.[48]

(the comment of a Montegrano peasant) 'The peasant always keeps his place; others have the possibility of improving themselves.'[49]

In Montegrano and nearby towns an official is hardly elected before the voters turn violently against him.[50]

Many think of God as a hostile, aggressive force which must be propitiated.[51]

Banfield concludes that, while innumerable forces help to explain the misery of the peasants of Montegrano — he subsequently mentions "poverty, ignorance, and a status system which leaves the peasant almost outside the larger society"[52] — the strategic or limiting factor is what he calls amoral familism — "the inability of villagers to act together for their common good or, indeed, for any end transcending the immediate, material interest of the nuclear family."[53] In his view, the unspoken cardinal rule of the Montegranesi is, "Maximize the material short-run advantage of the nuclear family; assume that all others will do likewise."[54] He develops seventeen corollaries[55] to this rule that are worth noting here because they so commonly apply to traditional societies:

1. No one furthers the interest of the group except as his own interest is furthered.
2. Only officials will concern themselves with public affairs.
3. There will be few checks on the activities of officials.
4. Organizations will be difficult to achieve and maintain.
5. Office-holders will work only as hard as necessary to stay in office.
6. The law will be disregarded when there is no reason to fear punishment.
7. Office-holders will take bribes when they can get away with it.
8. The weak will favor a strong-handed regime.
9. Anybody who invokes public-spiritedness as a motive will be regarded as a fraud.
10. There will be no relationship between abstract political principle and concrete behavior in everyday life.
11. There will be no leaders and no followers.

1 2. People will vote only in the interest of their short-term gain.
1 3. Individuals will support community activities only if there is direct gain for themselves.
1 4. Little confidence will be placed in the promises of political parties.
1 5. People in power will be assumed to be self-serving and corrupt.
1 6. There will be no political organizations worthy of the name.
1 7. Party workers will sell their services to the highest bidder.

This list of values and attitudes may be representative of far more of Italy than just Montegrano or the Italian south. In *The Civic Culture*, Almond and Verba observe:

> The picture of Italian political culture that has emerged from our data is one of relatively unrelieved political alienation and of social isolation and distrust. The Italians are particularly low in national pride, in moderate and open partisanship, in the acknowledgment of the obligation to take an active part in local community affairs, in the sense of competence to join with others in situations of political stress . . . and in their confidence in the social environment.[56]

Banfield concludes his description of the Montegranesi in very strong terms:

> It is not too much to say that most people of Montegrano have no morality except, perhaps, that which requires service to the family. . . . To 'do wrong' usually means 'to act so as to bring punishment or misfortune upon oneself' . . . The implications of all this for political life are clear. The State exists to force men to do good. A regime is worthy of respect if it has plenty of power and uses it rigorously to enforce obedience and to maintain law and order.[57]

Like McClelland, Banfield views child-rearing practices as crucial to how societies perform. Montegranesi parents are extremely permissive and hypersensitive about the health of their children. But they often beat, threaten, and frighten them without real provocation. A premium is placed on deception by the child: "The typical parent – child relation is that of Gepetto to Pinocchio: the father long-suffering and forgiving, the child cruelly exploiting his love until finally overcome with remorse."[58]

There are two salient — and highly destructive — features of Montegranesi child-rearing in Banfield's summary:

> 1. The indulgence of parents toward children and their willingness to allow children to be selfish and irresponsible . . . until all at once at the time of marriage the grown child must assume the burden of looking after a family of his own. Perhaps it is not too much to say that the Montegranesi act like selfish children because they are brought up as selfish children.

2. The reliance upon blows to direct behavior and the capricious manner in which punishment is given. Punishment . . . is unrelated to any principle of "oughtness"; at one moment the parent kisses and at the next he cuffs. If gratification and deprivation — "good" and "bad" — depend upon the caprice of one who has power, no general principles can be internalized as conscience. . . . To receive ill will be "bad fortune" and to receive good will be "good fortune". . . . *His relation to all holders of power — the State and God, for example — will be formed on the model supplied by his parents.*[59] (italics mine)

Banfield devotes his final chapter to speculation on what might be done to help Montegrano progress. Some forces may already be in play, such as advancing health technology: the availability of antibiotics is lowering the death rate, the fear of premature death is subsiding, and peasants are raising smaller families. Others that could make a difference include the development of a sense of social responsibility by the middle and upper classes; decentralization of more power to the town; improvement of schools; public television; a newspaper (there is none); a soccer team (there is none); and the introduction of Protestant missionaries. But Banfield concludes on a pessimistic note:

If all of the measures that have been suggested here were pursued actively and effectively, there would be no dramatic improvement in the economic position of the village . . . it will be a very long time before the people of Montegrano have enough to eat. Nor would there be a dramatic change in the ethos of the Montegranesi if such measures . . . were carried out. . . . Finally, it must be said that there is little likelihood that any such measures will be tried. . . . Nations do not remake themselves in fundamental ways by deliberate intention any more than do villages.[60]

Carlos Rangel (1929 –)

Carlos Rangel is a Venezuelan journalist who has written a controversial book about Hispanic America's condition. The book was first published in 1976 in French with the title *Du Bon Sauvage au Bon Révolutionnaire* (*From the Noble Savage to the Noble Revolutionary*) and in 1977 in English with the title *The Latin Americans: Their Love-Hate Relationship with the United States.*

The French title (and the Spanish *Del Buen Salvaje al Buen Revolucionario*) refers to a kind of mythology about Latin America that is reminiscent of Myrdal's — and Nehru's — treatment of the idealized South Asian stereotype. The "noble savage" is the pre-Columbian Indian, whose allegedly idyllic existence (the reality for most was far from idyllic) was destroyed by the arrival of the Europeans. The "noble revolutionary" is the contemporary Marxist-Leninist whose role is to cleanse Latin American society from the corrupting exploitative influence of bourgeois Europe and, particularly, the United States. The sensitive, artistic, intellectual Latin American of Rodó's *Ariel*[61] is a myth, as is his counterpoise — the money-grubbing,

brutish, pragmatic North American Caliban. And perhaps the biggest myth —
and the most pernicious for Latin America, in Rangel's view — is the belief
that Latin America's condition is the result of Yankee imperialism.

Rangel believes Latin America's "failure" (his word — he has particularly in mind the contrast with the "success" of the United States and
Canada) is principally attributable to Hispanic culture:

> . . . It was Latin America's destiny to be colonized by a country that,
> though admirable in many ways, was at the time beginning to reject the
> emerging spirit of modernism, and to build walls against the rise of ration-
> alism, empiricism, and free thought — that is to say, against the very bases
> of the modern industrial and liberal revolution, and of capitalist economic
> development.[62]

Among the Spanish characteristics transmitted to the New World were
an antisocial individualism, an aversion to work, and an affinity for violence
and authoritarianism. Rangel believes the Spanish colonial experience reinforced these characteristics:

> The agricultural or, preferably, mining work was done for him by slaves
> who were organized into encomiendas and later into haciendas — institu-
> tions that displayed all of the defects and none of the good qualities of the
> socioeconomic structures of medieval Europe.[63]

Rangel, like Lewis and others, sees the experience of slavery as highly
debilitating to long-term development:

> It is not surprising to find that a number of factors inhibit the development
> of societies formerly based on slavery: the passive resistance to work that is
> the earmark of the slave; the absurd prestige of idleness that afflicts his
> master; and, finally, a rhythm of life so little concerned with punctual-
> ity . . .[64]

The Spanish mercantilist system was also a major obstacle to New
Spain's development. Spanish insistence that its colonies trade exclusively
with the mother country and Spain's discouragement of industry in the
New World imposed economic stagnation on the colonies. As Rangel observes, "Monopoly practices, privileges, restrictions placed on the free activity of individuals in the economic and other domains, are traditions
profoundly anchored in societies of Spanish origin."[65]

Rangel sees the Spanish American elite as the principal carrier of the
culture that has bred the inequities, institutional debilities, and *caudillismo*
(dictatorship) so common to the countries of Latin America. After independence,

> . . . the ruling class was an oligarchy concerned with no interests but its
> own and with the maintenance of social structures founded on the existing

land-tenure systems and peon labor. The frequent governmental changes, termed "Latin American" revolutions, in no way affected the basic situation.[66]

and,

Because they do not quite identify with the society in which they live, the members of the Spanish American ruling classes in general do not give themselves wholly to that society.[67]

Rangel reserves some of his strongest criticism for the Catholic Church, particularly its absolutism, and it is a criticism with echoes of Weber:[68]

No other institution has contributed as much as the Catholic Church to determining what Latin America has and has not become.

. . . Latin America's history bears witness to the failure of Catholicism, in contradistinction to Protestantism, or, at least, to the defeat of the Catholic ethic by the Protestant ethic, which shaped the development of the United States.

. . . The North American Protestant society appears more Christian, or perhaps less anti-Christian, than Latin American, Catholic society. It demands of its followers a pattern of social behavior that dictates reasonably good faith in daily affairs and in interpersonal relations and requires socially constructive action even of those in opposition.

Catholic, Latin American society is readily satisfied with appearances: with a show of being a good parent, of behaving well, of possessing talent, honesty, erudition, patriotism; with the outward trappings of revolutionary radicalism or proper sexual conduct; *with a show of religion*. At the same time, our societies have set very strict limits on openly permissible behavior. Only North American influence has in recent years led us to become somewhat more tolerant of nonconformist behavior patterns.

Protestant North American society, by way of comparison, demands men and women far more strictly to give proof of what they really are, as against what they claim to be. This pragmatic, commonsense requirement has given the country its dynamism, for it insures a constant number of tried citizens with dominant roles in the key sectors of national policy and development.[69]

Rangel's views will be discussed further in Chapters VII (Spain and Spanish America) and, particularly, VIII (Spanish America and the United States).

We shall now proceed to the six case studies mentioned in the introduction. They will, I believe, document many of the insights of the authors discussed in this chapter as well as my own more general thesis.

NOTES

1. Arthur E. Hippler, "The Yolngu and Cultural Relativism: A Response to Reser," pp. 393 – 97. With respect to the prominence of economists in the literature that links development with culture, I am reminded of the comment of a friend who is a noted Latin American economist, educated in the United States: "The older I get, the less I am an economist and the more I am an anthropologist."

2. Myrdal, *Asian Drama*, p. 6.

3. *Ibid.*, pp. 27 – 28.

4. *Ibid.*, p. 73.

5. Myrdal believes the generalizations that follow, while based on India, are valid for other South Asian countries.

6. *Ibid.*, p. 95.

7. *Ibid.*, pp. 97 – 98.

8. Earlier (p. 77), Myrdal had noted, "In India . . . there is a rich mythology about the ancient village as a perfect democracy with a rational cooperative organization of production and community life, where caste observance was less rigid and degrading and women enjoyed a higher status." There is an interesting parallel here with the mythology of the Noble Savage who shares the Spanish title of Carlos Rangel's book with the Noble Revolutionary (see pp. 30 – 32).

9. Quoted in Myrdal, *Asian Drama*, p. 100.

10. *Ibid.*,

11. *Ibid.*

12. *Ibid.*, p. 103.

13. *Ibid.*, p. 104.

14. *Ibid.*

15. *Ibid.*, p. 112.

16. *Ibid.*, p. 113.

17. *Ibid.*, p. 122.

18. Henry M. Christman, ed., *The American Journalism of Marx and Engels*, pp. 93 – 109.

19. *Ibid.*, p. 100. Marx states, of course, that "England . . . was actuated only by the vilest interests . . ."

20. E.g., Weber, McClelland, W. Arthur Lewis, Edward Banfield, Gabriel Almond, and Sidney Verba.

21. Myrdal, *Asian Drama*, p. 937.

22. *Ibid.*, p. 1621; Galbraith makes essentially the same plea for education in *The Nature of Mass Poverty*.

23. Lewis, *The Theory of Economic Growth*, p. 14.

24. *Ibid.*, p. 371.

25. *Ibid.*, p. 37.

26. *Ibid.*, p. 116.

27. This is the central theme of Hagen's *On the Theory of Social Change*.

28. Max Weber, *The Protestant Ethic and the Spirit of Capitalism*, p. 79.

29. *Ibid.*, p. 172.

30. *Ibid.*, p. 117.

31. Max Weber, *The Religion of India*, p. 336.

32. See, for example, the discussion of Vodun in Haiti, Chapter 4.

33. This word will be used throughout this book to contrast with Western "rationality." I appreciate that what I have labeled "irrational" may be quite rational when viewed from within the culture in question.

34. Max Weber, *The Religion of China*, p. 229.

35. Joseph A. Schumpeter, *Capitalism, Socialism, and Democracy*, p. 132.

36. Lewis, *The Theory of Economic Development*, pp. 93 – 94.

37. McClelland, *The Achieving Society*, p. 3.

38. The almost total ignoring of women in this and other works up until quite recently leaves the reader of the 1980s incredulous.

39. In justifying this methodology, McClelland (p. 71) quotes Margaret Mead: " . . . a culture has to get its values across to its children in such simple terms that even a behavioral scientist can understand them."

40. McClelland, *The Achieving Society*, p. 393.

41. Gabriel A. Almond and Sidney Verba, *The Civic Culture*, p. 3.

42. Sidney Verba and Lucian Pye, eds., *Political Culture and Political Development*, p. 6.

43. *Ibid.*, pp. 522, 529, 535, 536, 551 – 53.

44. Edward C. Banfield, *The Moral Basis of a Backward Society*, p. 8.

45. *Ibid.*, p. 18. The same attitude about the success of others has been noted in many traditional societies. It is at the essence of the common Haitian self-judgment, "*Haitien jalou*" ("The Haitian is jealous"). Maurice Cargill notes in *Jamaica Farewell* (Secaucus, N.J.: Lyle Stuart Inc., 1978) the saying in Jamaica, "Nayga [the Negro] can't bear to see Nayga prosper." Subsequently, Banfield reminds us (p. 143) that it was not long ago in Montegrano that magic was used to get back at people, as it is to this day in Haiti.

46. *Ibid.*, pp. 114.

47. *Ibid.*, p. 50.

48. *Ibid.*, p. 59. This is also reminiscent of Haiti. An American anthropologist friend took an informal poll a few years ago in the rural Haitian town in which he lived. The question was "Would you migrate to the u.s. if you could?" One hundred percent of the respondents answered, "Yes."

49. *Ibid.*, p. 65.

50. *Ibid.*, p. 28.

51. *Ibid.*, p. 130.

52. *Ibid.*, p. 163.

53. *Ibid.*, p. 10.

54. *Ibid.*, p. 85.

55. *Ibid.*, pp. 85 – 104.

56. Almond and Verba, *Civic Culture*, p. 308.

57. Banfield, *Backward Society*, p. 141.

58. *Ibid.*, p. 159.

59. *Ibid.*, pp. 160 – 161.

60. *Ibid.*, p. 175.

61. José Enrique Rodó, an Uruguayan, published *Ariel* in 1900. It has been extremely popular in Latin America, particularly with the youth.

62. Carlos Rangel, *The Latin Americans: Their Love-Hate Relationship With the United States*, p. 182.

63. *Ibid.*, p. 184. The *encomienda* was a system that assigned Indians in a given area to a Spanish colonist for the purpose of Christianizing them; the usual consequence was effective enslavement of the Indians. The *hacienda* is a plantation.

64. *Ibid.*, p. 193.

65. *Ibid.*, p. 203.

66. *Ibid.*, p. 20.

67. *Ibid.*, p. 209.

68. For a parallel view on the role of the Church in Latin America see Michael Novak, *The Spirit of Democratic Capitalism*.

69. Rangel, *The Latin Americans*, pp. 141, 144, 145, 147, 147 – 148.

3

Nicaragua and Costa Rica

Nicaragua and Costa Rica are so unlike in their development it is difficult to believe they are neighbors. Nicaragua's history is tortured, bloody, and tragic; its leaders have often been authoritarian, corrupt, and rapacious. Its people have been repressed and exploited almost continually since the Spanish arrived in 1522. Indeed, the masses were treated similarly by the Indian theocracies before the Spanish arrived.

Costa Rica, by contrast, has experienced sustained political, economic, and social progress, particularly since the mid-nineteenth century. Today, it is Latin America's most firmly-rooted democracy. It is far ahead of Nicaragua in economic and social development, as is apparent from this extract from Table 2:

	Nicaragua	Costa Rica
per-capita GNP 1980	$740[1]	$1,730
adult literacy 1977	57%[2]	90%
life expectancy 1980	56 years	70 years
average annual population growth 1970 – 80	3.4%	2.5%

Crossing the border from Nicaragua to Costa Rica is not as dramatic as crossing from Haiti to the Dominican Republic. But the differences between Nicaragua and Costa Rica are palpable: in the more substantial, often painted houses of Costa Rican peasants; in the larger number of schools; in the tidier towns; in the more extensive electricity and telephone systems.

Resource endowment favors Nicaragua, which is almost three times the size of Costa Rica. Nicaragua is slightly larger than Arkansas; Costa Rica is about the size of New Hampshire and Vermont combined. Nicaragua's population (about 2.5 million) is only slightly larger than Costa Rica's (about 2.3 million), but its arable land resources are substantially greater. Nicaragua has mineral resources, particularly gold, that are being exploited; Costa Rica's mineral resources are inconsequential.

Some may explain Nicaragua's relative poverty as the result of economic exploitation by the United States. Yet, while U.S. influence on the Somoza dynasty was substantial, the U.S. business presence in Nicaragua has never been very large. In 1978, the book value of u.s. investment in Nicaragua totaled $121 million, on the order of 2 percent of total investment. In 1982, u.s. investment in Costa Rica totaled $550 million, or about 4 percent of total investment.[3]

If resource endowment favors Nicaragua — and if the u.s. transnational corporations have "exploited" Costa Rica more (which, according to those who subscribe to "dependency theory," should have made Costa Rica poorer) — how can we explain Costa Rica's being so far ahead of Nicaragua? I believe the explanation resides principally in the differences between the ways that Nicaraguans and Costa Ricans see themselves, their compatriots, and the world. We are talking about two very different cultures.

Nicaragua's anguish

The differences between the motives of the English settlers of North America, who came to the New World to build a new life, and the Spanish conquistadors have been commented upon frequently. In his *Historia de Nicaragua*, published in 1889, José Dolores Gámez stresses that, in 1492, Spain had suffered two physically and morally destructive experiences: the expulsion of hundreds of thousands of Jews (". . . industrialists, manufacturers, and businessmen, who sustained the admirable prosperity of the Kingdom of Granada, emigrated from Spain to enrich other European countries with their industry and knowledge . . .");[4] and ten years of bloody warfare against the Moors, which, to be sure, left the Spaniards in control of their own country, but also left them bellicose, greedy, and inured to human suffering.

> Poor America, which was asleep, dreaming the dreams of the lazy and the innocent, was to be the victim [of what had happened in Spain]. Its lands, full of enchantment and blessings, its forests, its birds, in a word, its treasures, were never sufficient to appease the unleashed greed of the marauding hordes that, for the space of 300 years, converted America into perpetual war booty . . .[5]

Gámez points out that, while Spain in general had been corrupted by the events of the decade before Columbus's first voyage, the tragic consequences for Spanish America were magnified because the conquistadors were "the scum of Spanish society,"[6] interested only in getting rich quick and returning to Spain. And Central America got the worst of the worst:

> The remote provinces of Central America, which scarcely received attention from the greedy Castilians, had the bad luck to receive the worst part of the Spanish emigration . . . a brutal and superstitious soldiery, collected from gambling houses, taverns, and, often, penitentiaries . . .[7]

The greed of the conquistadors was matched by the greed of the Spanish aristocracy, "which took account solely of its own interests and almost never of the unhappy American people."[8] Thus, in the race for gold and silver, agriculture was neglected, systems of heavy taxation were established, and the colonies were made totally dependent on Spain for trade.

Control of the Indians, their exploitation as a resource, and the flow of riches to Spain were all furthered by the *encomienda* system, which Gámez describes as follows:

> . . . with the pretext of religious instruction, each soldier was the owner of a considerable number of Indians, who worked the mines, the gold processing plants, and the fields, and who were treated with such cruelty that the *encomienda* was worse than slavery.[9]

With the notable exception of Padre Bartólome de Las Casas,[10] who spent a number of years in Central America, and a few others, the representatives of the Roman Catholic Church were powerful accomplices of the conquistadors. Las Casas forced the Spanish monarchy and church hierarchy to face the moral implications of the treatment of the Indians. But of the two "strong and resolute" faces of the coin of Spanish character described by historian Lewis Hanke — "One face is that of an imperialistic conquistador and the other is a friar devoted to God"[11] — it is clear that the conquistador was dominant:

> Another example of the strength of religious formalism has been well described by Alonso de Ercilla in his great epic poem *La Araucana* (1569) on the conquest of Chile. The Araucanian chief Caupolicán had been captured and was about to be put to death when he expressed a desire to be baptized and become a Christian. "This caused pity and great comment among the Castilians who stood around," according to Ercilla, and Caupolicán was baptized "with great solemnity, and instructed in the true faith as well as possible in the short time available." After this, the Spaniards made him sit on a sharp stake and shot him through and through with arrows.[12]

Salvador Mendieta, a Nicaraguan who early in this century probed deeply and objectively the anguish of Central America, observed:

> Everything in Spain was dominated by religious feeling, a most vigorous, aggressive, intolerant, and implacable feeling. While the germ of religious reform began to ferment in other parts of Europe preparing the way for the protest of Luther, Spain was in the process of reestablishing the Inquisition and expelling the Jews.[13]

Gámez adds:

> The Catholic clergy, which . . . could have served to moderate the colonial yoke, was with very few exceptions another terrible scourge for the colonies. Wanting to break the chains of their priestly vows, especially that of poverty, a large number of priests came to the colonies hoping to enjoy a

new existence, carefree and comfortable, and especially to satisfy their earthly ambitions.[14]

The priests undertook a campaign to convert the Indians, but conversion gave them little protection against the exploitation and cruelty of the Spaniards.[15] The cruelties visited on them have been widely commented upon. What is not generally appreciated is the extent to which the Indians were enslaved and exported to other countries. According to Murdo J. MacLeod,[16] approximately 200,000 Indians — about one-third of the total Indian population — were exported from Nicaragua to Panama and Peru as slaves between 1528 and the late 1540s. Nicaragua was the center of the Central American slave trade.

The slave trade and the search for gold dominated Nicaragua's economic history during the sixteenth century. Its political history was dominated by a line of despotic Spanish governors that continued into the early nineteenth century and by the bloody rivalries of those vying for power. The *encomienda* evolved into the *hacienda*, and the slave trade ceased, but the lives of the Indians — and the blacks who began to be imported to meet labor shortages — were scarcely more bearable.

In the second half of the sixteenth century, European pirates, principally English, appeared on the Atlantic coast of Nicaragua, initiating a British interest in that coast that endured through much of the nineteenth century. Francis Drake also attacked the Pacific coast. Pirate attacks, in which booty and slaves were taken, intensified during the seventeenth century; the cities of Granada and León were repeatedly plundered; and, in 1685, both were occupied by pirate forces.

Gámez summarizes the seventeenth century as one "of depredations, slavery, and extermination" for Nicaragua.[17] Spain, far from the power it was a century earlier and absorbed in its domestic problems, left Nicaragua unprotected against the repeated pirate attacks. Industry, agriculture, and commerce were at a standstill. And the Spanish governors sustained the tradition of corruption, brutality, and ineptitude. The Church continued as a negative force: "Each bishop was effectively a petty king, as despotic and unbearable as the Spanish governors . . ."[18]

By early in the eighteenth century, the British had established settlements on the Atlantic coast, had developed close relations with the largely Indian and black population there, and were engaged in profitable timber operations. The first half of the century was relatively peaceful, by Nicaraguan standards, as the country benefited from the enlightened policies of the Spanish Bourbon kings Felipe V and Fernando VI. Agriculture began to thrive, particularly cacao, sugar, cattle, indigo, and tobacco. British-inspired incursions from the Atlantic coast continued, however, and in 1762, a fleet of fifty British ships inaugurated a twenty-five-year period of British attacks. The British finally withdrew, more victims of tropical diseases than of Spanish arms.

Its growing agricultural production notwithstanding, Nicaragua was, at the end of the eighteenth century, a political, intellectual, and moral wasteland. Spanish rule was little more enlightened than in the sixteenth century, and there was now an intensifying tension between the *peninsulares* (those born in Spain), who were in charge, and the *criollos* (those born in the New World). Education, which was dominated by irrelevant Roman classicism, was accessible only to the elite. (Gámez reports that the teaching of chemistry, physics, mathematics, and natural sciences did not begin in Central America until 1795.)[19] The Church was rich and powerful. The stultifying economic system was based on monopoly, restrictions, and burdensome taxes. The penal system was, as described by Gámez, horribly cruel.

Independence: the anguish continues

The movement for Central American independence began in earnest in 1811, triggered by the abortive declaration of independence by Padre Miguel Hidalgo in Mexico in 1810. Central America achieved independence without violence and with the greatest tranquillity"[20] on September 15, 1821. It was an independence without significant change for anyone, however, except the former Spanish administrators. The rhetoric of the revolution echoed the rhetoric of the American and French revolutions, but the similarities stopped there.

After a brief flirtation with Mexico, the five Central American states (Guatemala, El Salvador, Honduras, Nicaragua, and Costa Rica) formed a new country in 1824: the United Provinces of Central America. What followed was fourteen years of continual bickering, plotting, secession, alliances, and warfare as the new nation tore itself apart. Nicaragua's chronic instability and chaos contributed to the tragic process of disintegration.

It was at this moment that Guanacaste, Nicaragua's southernmost province, proclaimed its affiliation with Costa Rica, because, as Gámez observed, the Guanacastecos saw "that Nicaragua could not get itself together and that on the Costa Rican side [they] would enjoy the peace and tranquillity that the constant anarchy [of Nicaragua] denied them . . ."[21]

The first responsible and effective chief of state in Nicaragua's history, Dionisio Herrera, was elected in 1829 and served until 1833. "The administration of . . . Herrera [was] a veritable convalescence for Nicaragua. [He was] conciliatory . . . dignified . . . wise . . . [his was] a model of good government."[22] However, ". . . the wise administration of Herrera, even though a reorganizing and moderate government like no other in those times, suffered a defect then common to all Latin America. To survive in an incipient society, anarchic and lacking in political morality, it had to seek the support of the military, the dismal plague which has weighed so harshly on our young republic."[23]

Nicaraguan militarism was fed by the no-holds-barred rivalry between

León and Granada, a rivalry that dominated Nicaragua's politics for the first one hundred years of its existence as an independent entity. León labeled itself "liberal"; Granada labeled itself "conservative"; but ideology — particularly the question of church – state relations — was not at the root of the rivalry. In a society in which the concepts of shared or balanced power and compromise were almost totally alien — Herrera's administration being a notable exception — what really stood between the two cities was the question of who would possess absolute power.

After the dissolution of the Central American Union in 1838, Nicaragua's civil war continued. An American scholar and diplomat, John L. Stephens, traveled through Central America in 1840 and recorded his impressions at some length.[24] His visit to Nicaragua impressed him with the richness of the country and its abuse by its people: "The resources of this distracted country are incalculable. Peace and industry would open fountains which would overflow with wealth."[25]

Stephens was shocked by the cruelty and callousness he saw. He noted the arduous work of poor women lugging water near Masaya and commented: "The Spaniards found [Masaya] a large Indian village, and as they immediately made the owners of the soil their drawers of water, they did not feel the burden; nor do their descendants now."[26] Of a battle involving Nicaraguans in Honduras he observed, ". . . the records of civil wars among Christian people nowhere present a bloodier page. No quarter was given or asked. After the battle, fourteen officers were shot in cold blood, and not a single prisoner lived as a monument of mercy."[27] Similar brutality when Nicaraguans fought Nicaraguans was apparent to Stephens when he visited León and saw the total destruction of an area once occupied by an army from Granada.

Nicaragua's chronic and bloody instability was compounded by a resurgence of British interest in the Atlantic coast, importantly because of Nicaragua's potential as in interoceanic canal site. The long-standing alliance between the British, on the one hand, and the Indians and blacks, on the other, led to a British attempt in 1848 to set up an independent Miskito Indian republic — "Mosquitia." The Nicaraguans, however, signed a contract for a canal with the United States in 1849, which led to strong u.s. opposition to British intentions and, in 1850, to the Clayton – Bulwer Treaty, by the terms of which the United States and Britain agreed that they would not seek exclusive power to control a canal nor would they seek "dominion" in Central America. The Nicaraguans, although humiliatingly not a signatory of the treaty, were gratified by its negotiation.[28]

The Nicaraguan civil war continued into the mid-1850s. ("Sad to say, but after thirty years of war, the same bloodthirstiness and the same inhuman cruelty existed as at the outset," says Gámez.)[29] As their fortunes took a turn for the worse, the leaders of León looked to American mercenaries for help. The notorious American adventurer William Walker arrived in Nicaragua in 1855. A year later, he had made himself president, thereby succeeding in what no one before him had been able to do: unifying the Central Americans — against him. With Costa Rican President Juan Rafael Mora playing an important role, Walker was forced out of Central America in 1857. He returned in 1860 to Honduras, where he was captured and executed.

Through their link with Walker, the Nicaraguan Liberals were totally discredited, and the Conservatives held power continually from 1857 to 1893. Peace did not mean prosperity, however, at least for the large majority of Nicaraguans. The Nicaraguan oligarchy was the principal beneficiary.

Divisions within the Conservative ranks offered an opportunity to Liberal strongman José Santos Zelaya in early 1893, and he seized it. Zelaya was installed later in the same year and effectively ruled the country as dictator for sixteen years. He brought about a number of reforms, e.g., in education, separation of church and state, and in transportation. Agriculture flourished, particularly the production of coffee, which had been introduced to Nicaragua in the middle of the nineteenth century.

Zelaya is a hero — a precursor of Sandino — to today's Sandinistas, partly because of his reforms, partly because he was overthrown with the support of the United States. Zelaya had antagonized the United States by courting Great Britain and Japan, by invading Honduras, and by cancelling some American concessions in Nicaragua.

Mendieta, no great admirer of the United States, saw Zelaya quite differently:

> Zelaya's regime of autocracy, of rampant favoritism, of insatiable greed, of libertinism, of deceit, and of unlimited contempt for every virtue, every elevated idea, and every noble sentiment, was the best pretext Anglo-American imperialism could have wanted to infiltrate Nicaragua, take control of its economic life, and conclude by dominating it.[30]

The United States intervenes

The Conservatives returned to power when a u.s.-supported revolution against Zelaya succeeded, but the Liberals continued to threaten Conservative control, and in 1912, Conservative President Adolfo Díaz asked the United States for military protection. The u.s. Marines arrived soon thereafter, initiating a twenty-one-year period during which the United States was the ultimate arbiter of power.

The principal motives on the u.s. side for the intervention were strategic, not economic. The United States was concerned that another power might build a canal in Nicaragua (construction of the Panama Canal was well advanced; it opened in 1914). It was also concerned about its strategic position in the Caribbean, both because of its stake in the Panama Canal and because of increasingly ominous war clouds over Europe. There was an element of American evangelism as well, which in part influences u.s. policy toward Latin America to this day.

The intervention has profoundly affected relations between the two countries. It was a humiliating and indelible reminder to the Nicaraguans of their failures and impotence, and it is still highly charged with emotion, particularly for Nicaraguan youth. The intervention was also highly controversial in the United States, and pressure built for the withdrawal of the U.S. forces.

Two events occurred in the later years of the intervention that were destined to influence history profoundly: the creation, under U.S. military auspices, of the Nicaraguan National Guard in 1927, and the almost simultaneous emergence of Augusto César Sandino as a guerrilla leader opposed both to the Conservative government and to the presence of American troops in Nicaragua. Sandino's anti-Americanism may have been overstated by subsequent Nicaraguan and other Latin American observers. Richard Millett has observed that "often he expressed respect for the American people" and that Sandino believed "the United States should establish an American military government in Nicaragua until the 1928 elections."[31] But he successfully fought off a large U.S. Marine force and became the symbol of restored dignity for Nicaragua — and for Latin America.

U.S. motives in encouraging the creation of the National Guard were explained as follows by Dr. Dana G. Munro, former U.S. chargé d'affaires in Nicaragua and later minister to Haiti:

> The establishment of non-partisan constabularies in the Caribbean states was one of the chief objectives of our policy from the time it became clear that the customs collector [Americans in charge of customs operations] wouldn't assure stability by themselves. The old armies were or seemed to be one of the principal causes of disorder and financial disorganization. They consumed most of the government's revenue, chiefly in graft, and they gave nothing but disorder and repression in return. We thought that a disciplined force, trained by Americans, would do away with the petty local oppression that was responsible for much of the disorder that occurred and would be an important step toward better financial administration and economic progress generally.[32]

Anastasio ("Tacho") Somoza García, whose good English had ingratiated him with the American officers who led the Guard in the early days,[33] was named as the first Nicaraguan chief of the Guard. With the departure of the Americans in 1933 — a symbol of Franklin Roosevelt's Good Neighbor Policy — Somoza García became Nicaragua's most powerful man. Sandino was murdered in ambush in 1934, presumably on Somoza García's orders. Two years later, Somoza assumed the presidency in a coup and formally inaugurated a dynasty that was to endure for forty-three years.

Somoza García was assassinated in 1956, and his son Luís Somoza Debayle took over. Luís was the most modern and liberal of the three Somoza chiefs of state, and measurable social progress occurred during his seven years in power. He made good on his pledge to leave government in 1963, after which the widely respected René Schick was elected and served until his death in 1966. At this point, Luís's brother Anastasio ("Tachito") Somoza Debayle took over and was effectively in charge until ousted by the Sandinista revolution in July 1979.

The Somozas were not the worst dictators in Latin American, nor necessarily Nicaraguan, history. Charles L. Stansifer has said of Somoza García:

> Of all the dictators of the Caribbean area during the 1930's and 1940's, Somoza was perhaps the most interested in social and economic measures. Dividends such as he provided help to explain a degree of popular satisfaction with the Somoza government and an acceptance of the loss of political and press freedom.[34]

Luís Somoza Debayle's "dictatorship" was so benign by Nicaraguan standards as to evoke the 1829 – 33 administration of Dionisio Herrera. A clear reversion occurred when Tachito arrived on the scene, but he was probably less brutal and more concerned with economic and social development than is generally appreciated. Above all, Tachito, and his father before him, were preoccupied with preserving themselves in power and enriching themselves. When Tachito was ousted, roughly half of Nicaragua's people were illiterate. Had he dedicated to popular education a fraction of the hundreds of millions he and his cronies milked from the Nicaraguan economy, illiteracy would have been substantially eradicated. And if he had followed Luís's lead by genuinely encouraging pluralism, Nicaragua would almost surely look very different today.

The Sandinistas: a new anguish

Instead, the endless Nicaraguan tragedy continues. The Sandinistas are genuinely concerned with the well-being of the Nicaraguan masses and with national dignity. But they are obsessed with the belief that the United States is at the root of Nicaragua's problems. This obsession is partly understandable, given the nature of u.s. involvement in Nicaragua, particularly in this century (although, as Mark Falcoff has pointed out, the u.s. relationship with the Somozas was far from uniformly supportive).[35] But the Sandinistas tend to ignore a history of frequent greedy *caudillos*, instability, and bloodshed that goes back to 1522. They are to some extent prisoners of that tragic history, just as they are of Marxist ideology. They have turned their backs on their commitments to pluralism and nonalignment and have driven the revolution toward Marxist authoritarianism. To escape the American "infection," they have jumped into the open arms of the Cubans and the Soviets. And to preserve themselves in power, they have resorted to many of the same human rights abuses employed by Somoza — and many other Nicaraguan and Spanish caudillos since Gil González.

Lamenting the course of the Sandinista revolution, Alfonso Robelo, a member of the original revolutionary junta and now an opposition leader, had this to say twenty-two months after the Sandinista government was installed:

> . . . what the Nicaraguan people wanted after the sacrifice of 40,000 lives was the end of our sad history of 170 (sic) years of independence without, to this day, having produced one change of power, from one party to another, without the use of force . . . by revolution, or by coup d'etat, or by foreign intervention, or by some kind of insurrection . . . . This revolution could have brought democracy like that known by other Latin American countries, as indeed it is known by our neighbor, Costa Rica . . .[36]

What explains the endless Nicaraguan tragedy? I want to present the analyses of two Nicaraguans, one briefly, one in some depth. Miguel D'Escoto, a Maryknoll priest who is currently Nicaragua's foreign minister, wrote the introduction to Richard Millett's *Guardians of the Dynasty*, published in 1977. In that introduction, he identifies three principal causes "of the seemingly endless nightmare which Nicaragua has experienced since its independence in 1821" (the nightmare, of course, started long before then):[37]

1. "The rivalry between the cities of León and Granada, as well as the hatred and vindictiveness with which the political parties representing each of these two cities treated one another at least up until 1927, is the single most tragic trait in Nicaraguan history."[38]
2. Nicaragua's "strategic" location.[39]
3. United States intervention, which "got stability all right — but it is only the deceptive lull that accompanies the death of democratic institutions and portends future revolutions."[40]

Mendieta's view

Salvador Mendieta is a striking exception to Jean François Revel's somewhat hyperbolic observation that "Latin American civilization may be the first ever to avoid self-criticism entirely."[41] Mendieta, a Nicaraguan, was a student of Central American history and a dedicated proponent of restoration of the Central American Union, to which end he founded a political party. The 1971 Encyclopedia Britannica has this to say of him:

> Two great writers sprang from Nicaragua during [the second half of the nineteenth century]. Ruben Darío became recognized as one of Latin America's greatest poets. Salvador Mendieta (1879 – 1958) was a distinguished diagnostician of his own region's ills, who dedicated his life to the rebuilding of the Central American Union. Both men were critical of the new interest taken in isthmian affairs by the United States once the decision was made to build the Panama Canal.[42]

Mendieta's principal work, *La Enfermedad de Centro-América* (*The Sickness of Central America*), was written in 1906 – 7, first published in 1912, amended in 1934, and published again in 1936. The first volume describes Central America; the second diagnoses the Central American "sickness;" and the third prescribes "therapy." Mendieta's antipathy toward the United States notwithstanding, there is virtually no mention of the u.s. impact on Nicaragua or Central America.

Mendieta perceives a number of qualities in Central Americans that disturb him deeply, qualities that in his view explain Central America's chronic instability and underdevelopment. Among these are laziness, a lack of initiative, a lack of moral courage, and an alienation from truth.[43] He also perceives a number of positive qualities, among them physical courage, generosity, and lively intelligence. Mendieta believes that people are products of their culture and that both can change. His purpose in writing *La Enfermedad de Centro-América* was clearly to start a process that, through introspection and objectivity, would change Central American culture, thereby altering the course of Central American history.

Mendieta dedicates much of his second volume to an analysis of the roots of Central America's problems. At the outset, he identifies himself as "a fervent lover of Spain and everything Spanish."[44] He then follows the same line of analysis as Rangel and Gámez in reaching the conclusion that Central America's sickness has been caused by a cultural infection from a Spain that was increasingly sick itself during the conquest and the colonial period.

Like Rangel and Gámez, Mendieta speaks of "the most grave error of the expulsion of the Jews;"[45] "the other most grave error of expelling the Moors;"[46] a Catholic Church that was "a formidable political, economic, and social power" but "not a moral institution;"[47] an environment in which "faith substituted for intellectual curiosity;"[48] and "the Catholic conception that work was a curse."[49] Laziness was sanctified by "a series of beliefs, institutions, and antieconomic laws," and thrift was an alien concept, practiced only by the Basques and the people of Galicia (*gallegos*), both from the north of Spain.[50]

Mendieta considers the impact of the Indian and African cultures on Nicaragua and concludes that they were overwhelmed and corrupted by Spanish culture, particularly through institutions that enforced slavery or semislavery. Like so many others, Mendieta perceives slavery as the ultimate destroyer of attitudes conducive to progress: it nurtures laziness, lying, and cowardliness in human beings.

In summary:

While Europe in the midst of the cruelest sufferings caused by continuing wars was giving birth to religious freedom and was thereby renewing the spirituality of the world, Spain was blinding itself in its fierce intolerance, and the Inquisition, the Jesuits, and the monks, in the closest alliance with

increasingly despotic royal power, were chloroforming the energetic Spanish people, forcing their minds to close, paralyzing their will, and snatching
away their liberties to the point of converting them into a drowsy, weak,
bunch of paupers. . . .[51]

The colonial experience made things worse. Municipal autonomy, which
had existed in Spain before the conquest, was now passé as concepts of
centralism dominated the approach of the Spanish mor⸲rchs. Centralization
for the colonies meant that many decisions had to be referred back to Spain
at a time of extremely slow communication; initiative was stifled and bureaucracy was nurtured. Yet in some spheres, and for some people, great
power was within reach.

As Spain's decay progressed, graft and other forms of corruption became increasingly prevalent. "The kings, in their struggle to keep themselves
afloat financially, trafficked in — and degraded — everything: justice, jobs,
decorations, military ranks, etc."[52] The abuses tended to be magnified in
the colonies. Governors and other high officials held great power through
their authority to establish *encomiendas* and name other officials. There was
nothing to prevent them from favoring relatives and friends, and nepotism
flourished. The systems of justice and administration were similarly corrupted.

The recipients of the *encomiendas* had virtual absolute power over their
fiefdoms and over the human beings who resided on them. In this environment of moral decay, corruption, and abuse of power, it is not difficult to
understand how the institution of *caudillismo* prospered.

Mendieta's third volume — *Therapy* — is a 678-page prescription for
a cultural revolution. Mendieta continually returns to his list of weaknesses
and strengths and prescribes detailed approaches to eliminate the former
and reinforce the latter. He addresses all the principal institutions of Central
American society one by one, e.g., the education system, the military,
government, the system of justice. But his principal concern is with child-
rearing: writing seventy-five years ago, he anticipates what contemporary
social scientists (e.g., McClelland) have tried to illuminate about inculcation
of attitudes toward work and achievement in the young. For example:

To combat inconstancy, which is a common source of economic failure, explain to the child the inevitable . . . relationship between time and human
enterprise, and particularly in those kinds of undertakings that depend on
science, experience, constancy, and tenacity; explain to him that beginnings
are difficult; that by starting and not finishing things, one loses time, energy, and experience; and because of that, it is necessary to study with
prudence, attention, and sufficient time the project we propose to undertake, taking into account our likes and dislikes, our talents, our needs, our
aspirations, and the demands of the society in which we propose to start
the project.[53]

He pleads for the inculcation of a sense of the child's role in society and the need for social responsibility:

> . . . make [the children] understand that the man or woman isolated from society is helpless; [make them understand] how dependent we are on one another, and how necessary the cooperation of all human beings is if we are to achieve on earth the goals of justice, truth, well-being, love, and beauty. . . .[54]

Costa Rica's progress

Its name, which was given to it by Columbus and means "rich coast," notwithstanding, Costa Rica was by far the poorest country in Central America, and probably in all of Latin America, when it achieved independence in 1821. It had little gold and relatively few Indians — 27,200 in 1522, according to the most reliable, although probably understated, estimate[55] — and these few Indians were often hostile to the Spaniards. They were also courageous and skillful fighters. As a result of Costa Rica's poor resources and inaccessibility, it was not until 1564 — forty-two years after Gil Gonzáles arrived in Nicaragua — that Cartago, the first permanent settlement in Costa Rica, was established.

Archbishop Thiel's data tell a great deal about Costa Rica's early history: the decline of the Indians, the small number of Spaniards, and the rapid increase of mestizos and mulattos. (See Table 3.)[56]

With little gold and few Indians, the system of *encomienda* never really took root. For Spaniard, Indian, black, and mixed blood alike, life in colonial Costa Rica was a struggle for survival.

> The colonists could not establish a privileged class. Rather, they had to focus their attention — and their efforts and those of their families — on

Table 3.

Year	Spaniards	Indians	Negroes	Mestizos	Mulattos	Total
1522	—	27,200	—	—	—	27,200
1569	113	17,166	30	—	170	17,479
1611	330	14,908	25	25	250	15,538
1700	2,146	15,489	154	213	1,291	19,293
1720	3,059	13,269	168	748	2,193	19,437
1741	4,687	12,716	200	3,458	3,065	24,126
1751	7,807	10,109	62	3,057	2,987	24,022
1778	6,046	8,104	94	13,915	6,053	34,212
1801	4,942	8,281	30	30,413	8,925	52,591

the immediate necessities . . . longer-term economic or social activities were out of the question.[57]

In 1719, the governor of Costa Rica sent a report to the Spanish king containing the following:

> . . . in the entire province there is not one barber, surgeon, doctor, or pharmacist; neither in the capital nor in other towns is food sold on the streets or in the plazas; everyone has to grow their own food, including myself, for otherwise one would perish."[58]

"This same misery established the bases of our democratic system,"[59] in the view of Eugenio Rodríguez Vega, a view shared by most analysts of Costa Rican history. Costa Rica's poverty and the small number of Indians discouraged the evolution of plantation agriculture. It also discouraged the evolution of a military class. As Samuel Stone, a Costa Rican political scientist, observes, "The colonists who constituted the base of Costa Rican society were very different from the typical Latin American colonist . . . in this province, manual labor was not so looked down on as in the other countries of the Isthmus . . . . The Costa Rican colonist was above all a farmer . . . ."[60]

Two other explanations

Two other explanations for Costa Rica's democracy and relative prosperity concern the antecedents of the Spanish colonists: (1) a disproportionate number of colonists came from traditionally progressive northern Spanish provinces, and (2) a disproportionate number were converted Jews.

One hears in Central America that many of the settlers of Costa Rica came from Galicia, Catalonia, and the Basque country, northern Spanish provinces that have tended to be more democratic and progressive than Andalucía, Castile, and Extremadura, whence came the large majority of conquistadors.[61] Mendieta, for example, says the following:

> . . . Galicia . . . has the same array of characteristics . . . as the average Costa Rican from the interior. These characteristics engender excellent qualities of discipline, moderation, tenacity, and love of the land. But they do not encourage the great enterprises which demand audacity or vast intellect.[62]

The research of Archbishop Víctor Sanabria Martínez into the antecedents of the Spaniards who colonized Cartago, on the other hand, suggests that the composition of those who came to Costa Rica was not significantly different from the overall pattern of Hispanic America: of a sample of 242 people, 75 (31 percent) came from Andalucía, 44 (18 percent) from Castile, 25 (10 percent) the Basque provinces, and 17 (7 percent) Extremadura.[63]

That the Basque figure was somewhat higher than normal is unlikely to have made much difference, since it accounted for but 10 percent of the total. Archbishop Sanabria's analysis addresses only the early years of migration, however. It is possible that subsequent waves *were* disproportionately from the north of Spain, and further research of the archives is necessary before this theory can be discarded.

Gonzalo Chacón Trejos published the essay *Costa Rica es Distinta en Hispano América* (*Costa Rica is Distinctive in Hispanic America*) in 1969. In it, he argues that the majority of the first settlers of Costa Rica "were descendants of Jews converted to Catholicism who had lived in Spain oppressed by hatred, contempt, and disgrace, and persecuted and spied upon with merciless fury."[64] The extent of their loss of prestige was implicit in the name they were given by the Spaniards: Marranos — "pigs."

Chacón compares the Marranos who came to Costa Rica with the Pilgrims and Sephardic Jews who settled in North America. He attributes Costa Rica's "hostility to militarism, aversion to violence, and love of order, peace, equity, and justice"[65] to the ethos brought to Costa Rica by the Marranos. He draws an analogy to Antioquia in Colombia (mistakenly, since there is no evidence of large numbers of Marranos among the early Antioqueños, as Everett Hagen[66] has pointed out).

The evidence Chacón adduces to support his theory is a list of 118 Costa Rican surnames that he claims are of Sephardic origin. The list comes close to a *Who's Who in Costa Rica*, including several presidents and business leaders.

Samuel Stone, in *La Dinastía de los Conquistadores*, after wondering why other than persecuted Spaniards would want to come to so godforsaken a place as Costa Rica in its early years, adds one other piece of evidence:

> A Costa Rican historian [Carlos Monge Alfaro] makes a curious comment in this respect: for a long time the colonists gave such a bad example of Christian life that at the outset of the 18th century, the Bishop of Nicaragua excommunicated all the inhabitants of [Costa Rica], observing that they made a point of staying away from towns where there was a church.[67]

Stone concludes, "This theory deserves more thorough study and could, if confirmed, change substantially the accepted interpretation of the development of Costa Rican society."[68] There we leave the theory to return to the continuation of our review of Costa Rican history.

Costa Rica proceeds to independence

Costa Rica continued to be a sleepy backwater through the seventeenth and eighteenth centuries. Cacao production began to flourish at Matina on the Atlantic coast in the mid-seventeenth century, but its success soon attracted English and Zambo (mixed Miskito Indian and black) pirates who attacked ships carrying cacao from Costa Rica to Panama and invaded the Matina area from their Nicaraguan strongholds at the time of the cacao harvest. Cacao reserves also attracted Spanish colonial administrators who established a variety of restrictions and taxes, some of them confiscatory. Harassed cacao growers gradually turned to smuggling, often with the help of the English and the Zambos. Production stagnated.[69]

Through the first two decades of the nineteenth century, the principal economic activity in the Central Plateau and on the Pacific coast was cattle production. Truck farming was also practiced, and a variety of foodstuffs was exported to Panama. Tobacco was grown successfully around San José as a Spanish government monopoly; as a result, the economic and political balance began to shift to San José from Cartago. The shift was completed as Central America moved toward independence. Cartago remained loyal to the Crown, and San José led the republicans.

Largely because of its remoteness, Costa Rica avoided much of the chaos and bloodshed that swept over the other Central American countries in the years after independence was achieved. This tranquillity attracted Guanacaste province, which seceded from Nicaragua in 1824 to join Costa Rica (see page 39).

The itinerant American diplomat John Stephens visited Costa Rica in 1840, just before his trip to Nicaragua (see page 40), and had this to say:

> The State of Costa Rica enjoyed . . . a degree of prosperity unequalled by any in the disjointed confederacy. At a safe distance, without wealth enough to excite cupidity, and with a large tract of wilderness to protect it against the march of an invading army, it had escaped the tumults and wars which desolated and devastated the other states.[70]

Stephens describes a visit to Alajuela in the Central Plateau:

> It was Sunday, and the inhabitants, cleanly dressed, were sitting on the piazzas, or, with doors wide open, reclining in hammocks, or on high-backed wooden settees inside. The women were dressed like ladies, and some were handsome, and all white. A respectable-looking old man, standing in the door of one of the best houses, called out "Amigo," "friend," and asked us who we were, whence we came, and whither we were going, recommending us to God at parting; and all along the street we were accosted in the same friendly spirit.[71]

By the time of Stephens's visit the Costa Rica coffee boom was in its early stages, and doubtlessly contributed to the prosperity he perceived. While there had been some experiments with coffee in the late eighteenth and early nineteenth centuries, and while the city governments of San José and Cartago had tried to promote coffee in the early 1820s, it was not until a German, Jorge Stiepel, succeeded in exporting a few sacks to Chile in 1832 that coffee really caught on.[72] Within a few decades, as it became apparent that the Central Plateau was ideally suited to production of high-quality coffee, the new crop came to dominate the Costa Rican economy, importantly influenced its social and political structure, and showed promise of vindicating Columbus's choice of names.

Of the early Costa Rican presidents, some were strongmen (e.g., Braulio Carrillo, who governed from 1835 to 1842) while others were committed democrats (e.g., José María Castro, who served in 1848 – 49 and again from 1866 to 1868). But almost without exception, they concerned themselves with economic and social progress. Carrillo, for example, ran an efficient and honest government and promoted coffee production; Castro expanded the education system.

The increasingly powerful coffee growers forced Castro's resignation in 1849 and installed one of their own, Juan Rafael Mora, who served for ten years as the first of a line of "coffee presidents." It was Mora who led the Costa Rican army to decisive victories over William Walker in 1856, this notwithstanding what Gámez described as "the natural repugnance that military service inspired in the Costa Ricans."[73]

The coffee oligarchy's hold on the country continued into the twentieth century. But whereas coffee production elsewhere in Central America tended toward concentration in the hands of a few extremely rich families, in Costa Rica an important small-producer sector was preserved (about half of Costa Rica's coffee is produced on small farms):

> The large coffee growers got rich quick, and thanks to their political power, they were able to appropriate the best [unoccupied] coffee lands, without, however, threatening the survival of the small coffee farms. To satisfy the growing demand of the London market, the large coffee growers were obliged to buy the production of the small growers and mix that coffee with their own . . . in this manner, links of interdependence were forged between large and small growers.[74]

The large producers had the political and economic power substantially to eliminate the small coffee farms, as happened in Guatemala and El Salvador. But while some acquisitions did take place, resulting in, among other things, migration of the dispossessed from the Central Plateau to Guanacaste Province, a substantial small-farm subsector has endured. I am sure this is partly because of the economic benefits to both large and small producers alluded to by Stone. But, as Guatemala and El Salvador demonstrate, the rich *can* get richer by acquiring additional land. My theory is that also contributing to the preservation of Costa Rica's small coffee farms have been (1) restraint on the part of the large growers, akin to *noblesse oblige*, born of the unusual sense of identification of one Costa Rican with another, and (2) also a product of this mutual sense of identification, an effective political pluralism that disperses power well beyond the elite.[75]

The "coffee presidents" generally continued progressive social policies. Primary education was recognized as a responsibility of the state in 1869 and was made obligatory in the 1880s. In 1889, direct popular voting was instituted. Major programs in public health were initiated in the first years of this century. And major investments were made in the construction of roads and, particularly, railroads.

A railroad from San José to the Atlantic coast was begun in 1871 to facilitate the export of coffee. The construction, which took nineteen years to complete, was contracted to John Meiggs, an American with railroad construction experience in the Andes. Meiggs's nephews, Henry and Minor Keith, oversaw the project, which was comparable in difficulty and danger to the building of the Panama Canal. According to one source, 5,000 lives were lost,[76] and it was necessary to import thousands of English-speaking blacks from the Caribbean to complete the job. Many of them stayed on when a new opportunity for employment appeared.

Minor Keith, an entrepreneur in the Schumpeterian sense, realized that the railroad could be used to export bananas, which were being grown in small quantities on the Atlantic coast. His idea stimulated the production of a crop destined to rival coffee as Costa Rica's most important export. Keith's initiative was also instrumental in the creation of the fabled United Fruit Company.

The coffee oligarchy continued to dominate Costa Rican politics during the first four decades of this century, but its influence was exercised through benevolent and highly respected presidents, particularly Cleto González Víquez, who served from 1906 to 1910 and again from 1928 to 1932, and Ricardo Jiménez, who served three terms: 1910–14, 1924–28, and 1932–36.

Social problems related in part to the Great Depression led to the election in 1940 of the populist reformer Rafael Angel Calderón Guardia, marking the end of the domination of the presidency by coffee interests. With the support of the scholarly and progressive archbishop Víctor Sanabria, Calderón established a social security system and a forward-looking labor code, including a minimum wage structure and encouragement of collective bargaining. This did not endear him to the coffee establishment, which was further outraged when he established an alliance with the Costa Rican communists. Much more than the coffee establishment was antagonized by widespread corruption and, particularly, by Calderón's efforts to annul the results of the 1948 elections, which he lost. Calderón's hopes of preserving himself in power were frustrated by a group of young Turks led by José Figueres.

Figueres and his followers established a new party, the National Liberation Party (PLN), which has dominated Costa Rican politics ever since. While the PLN in its early years was largely an extension of Figueres's personality, it has evolved into a durable, generally left-of-center party — Costa Rica's first major political organization to be bound together more by ideology than by personality. The PLN has brought Figueres (twice), Francisco Orlich, Daniel Oduber, and, most recently, Luis Alberto Monge to the presidency during its thirty-one years of existence. Three non-PLN candidates won the presidency during this period, including José Joaquín Trejos, whose election in 1966 put Costa Rican democracy to the acid test. He beat Oduber, the candidate of the incumbent party, by a few thousand votes. There were some threats of violence, but power passed peacefully to the winner.

All is not positive, but . . .

In part because the histories of its neighbors are so much more troubled, their achievements so far behind those of the Costa Ricans, there is a tendency to romanticize the Costa Rican experience. In fact, a number of valid criticisms are often leveled at Costa Rica, frequently (and refreshingly) by Costa Ricans themselves.

There has been a strong flavor of paternalism in Costa Rican politics and, indeed, in Costa Rican human relationships in general. The Costa Rican oligarchy has been accused, with reason, of callousness toward the needs of the masses. The majority National Liberation Party has wooed the masses through costly, inefficient, and paternalistic social programs, e.g., food supplements for poor families. The social programs have, in turn, contributed to chronic budget deficits, which have combined with high petroleum and low coffee prices in the last few years to plunge Costa Rica into its worst economic crisis since the Great Depression. Some are concerned that Costa Rica will follow oversocialized Uruguay back into authoritarianism.

Paternalism also permeates relationships between employers and employees. Except among the banana workers and a few other groups, the labor movement has not come close to achieving the power it wields in Western Europe, North America, Japan, or some other Latin American countries, e.g., Argentina and Mexico. Partly as a result of a weak labor movement, income distribution is highly skewed toward the upper classes, although it is probably more equitable than in Mexico and Venezuela.[77]

We also must be mindful that the Costa Rican per-capita GNP, while by far the highest in Central America, is still roughly one-sixth of the average in the advanced democracies of the West.

Some Costa Ricans believe the quality of Costa Rican life has deteriorated:

> . . . the *nation of brothers* has been divided into a number of groups in conflict, and everything is worse than it was for their grandparents. . . . The people are less courteous, less moral, less honest, and less self-confident. They are materialistic and lazy, they love luxury and waste. There is chaos and disorder in the cities and lack of respect for authority and order. . . . True patriotism is eroding, and the country sells itself to foreigners. The most beloved values and traditions of the society are being disregarded and destroyed.[78]

These criticisms have a familiar ring: the same litany is heard in virtually all countries that have experienced rapid development. And while there is much truth and much to be genuinely concerned about in the litany, the fact remains that most Costa Ricans are substantially better off than they were ten, twenty, or thirty years ago. Indeed, it can be argued that Costa Rica's peaceful democratic revolution has achieved more for its people than Fidel Castro's authoritarian revolution has achieved for Cuba.[79]

Nicaragua, Costa Rica, and culture

Nicaragua and Costa Rica are neighbors. Both are well endowed with natural resources, but Nicaragua has an advantage in this regard. Yet Nicaragua's history is a tortured and chaotic one, while Costa Rica's is one of fairly steady progress and stability.

Our recounting of the early history of the two countries suggests a probable explanation: Nicaragua is in the mainstream of Hispanic-American culture, while Costa Rica's special circumstances as a Spanish colony, with a colonial experience in some ways reminiscent of the New England colonies, led to significant modifications of that culture.

One could argue that Nicaragua's underdevelopment relative to Costa Rica reflects the costs of Nicaragua's historical relationships with the outside world, first with the British, then with the Americans. While it is true that the British harassed the Costa Ricans in the seventeenth and eighteenth centuries, particularly in the cacao region of the Atlantic coast, the depredations they visited on the Nicaraguans were far more costly and sustained. Nicaragua's potential as a trans-isthmian canal site also attracted the special attention of the British and the Americans. And, of course, Nicaragua experienced the trauma of a prolonged U.S. military intervention, which further undermined the self-confidence and dignity of a people whose tragic history had left them with little of either.

Yet a reading of Nicaraguan history — to say nothing of Mendieta — leaves considerable doubt that the country's evolution was determined by external forces. The continuous threads of authoritarianism, polarization of politics, and economic exploitation of the masses by the oligarchy, from 1522 until well into the twentieth century, appear to have been little influenced from the outside — except by Spain during the colonial period. No one will ever know what the course of recent Nicaraguan history would have been had the United States not intervened in 1912. But if past performance is any indicator, it might not have been very different from what actually has happened.

But perhaps the strongest support for the cultural interpretation of Nicaraguan history comes from the similar patterns of political, economic, and social evolution in other Hispanic countries discussed in subsequent chapters: the Dominican Republic, Argentina, and Spain itself.

Costa Rica's remoteness, its small Indian population, and its early
poverty forced a colonial life style which was very different from that in
the other colonies — and attracted a quite different kind of colonist. Because
Costa Rica was poor, the Spaniards paid it relatively little attention, which
protected it from many of the corrosive and suffocating effects of Spanish
colonial administration. The *encomienda* and *hacienda* systems did not adapt
well to Costa Rica's special circumstances, which saved Costa Rica from
the morally corrupting effects of plantation agriculture. Colonists were by
self-selection different from the conquistadors: they had to work the land
themselves if they were to survive, and survival was a pressing issue for
virtually everyone.

Poverty and isolation fertilized the soil from which Costa Rican democracy sprang. They also nurtured a kind of individualism — or perhaps
more accurately, a modified traditional Spanish individualism — that cher-
ished liberty and a sense of equality but also may have contributed to some
negative national tendencies.[80]

Returning to the thesis of this book, and specifically Figure 1, on page
5, the one factor that distinguishes Costa Ricans from Nicaraguans (and
indeed from most other Hispanic Americans) is the Costa Rican's identification with other Costa Ricans. The Biesanzes put it this way: ". . . the
nation of brothers of years gone by continues to be one big family in many
respects. You still frequently hear people saying, 'everyone is a cousin of
everyone.' "[81]

The sense of family is doubtlessly reinforced by Costa Rica's relative
racial homogeneity. Stone shows the following breakdown in a table headed
"Ethnic Composition of Central America:"[82]

	Indians	Whites	Blacks	Mixed Blood
Costa Rica	1%	80%	2%	17%
Guatemala	60%	5%	—	35%
El Salvador	11%	11%	—	78%
Honduras	10%	2%	2%	86%
Nicaragua	5%	17%	9%	69%

The racial composition in Nicaragua has probably been more an obstacle
to national unity than the table would imply, because the Nicaraguan elite
has largely been white.

In any event, there is ample evidence that Costa Ricans have felt a
stronger bond to their countrymen than have Nicaraguans. That bond is
reflected in Costa Rica's long-standing emphasis on public education and
public health; in its more vigorous cooperative movement; in a judicial
system notable by Latin American standards for its impartiality and ad-

herence to fundamental concepts of due process; and above all in the resilience of its politics, its capacity to find peaceful solutions, its appreciation of the need for compromise.[83]

Had Central America been peopled exclusively by Costa Ricans in 1824, the federation would have stood a much better chance of holding together. Similarly, the Central American economic integration movement, which looked so promising in the early and mid-1960s, might still be flourishing had Costa Rican values and attitudes prevailed in the region.

The responsiveness of the Costa Rican system to internal political pressure was noted by Mitchell A. Seligson in a recent article in the *British Journal of Political Science*:

> . . . in Costa Rica land invasions of the early 1970's were directly responsible for a sharp change in government policy towards land reform. As a result, the pace of reform, which had almost come to a complete halt by the late 1960's, was dramatically speeded up. Similarly, as a result of strikes in the banana zones, major improvements were made in salaries, housing and work conditions. Unfortunately, elsewhere in Latin America peasant mobilization does not usually result in benefits for those involved.[84]

Its atypical history notwithstanding, Costa Rica remains a country strongly influenced by Spanish culture. Costa Rica's unique colonial experience did not transform Spanish culture; it modified it. There are consequently a number of important parallels between Nicaragua and Costa Rica. For example, *machismo* and *marianismo* (belief in the moral and spiritual superiority of women) strongly influence relations between the sexes and child-rearing practices in both countries. The significance and influence of the Roman Catholic Church are comparable, although somewhat greater in Nicaragua. And the complex of factors (e.g., paternal authoritarianism, a tendency to think more in the short term than the long) that influences entrepreneurial activity and attitudes about work is roughly the same. While Costa Rica is ahead of Nicaragua economically, its level of development is much closer to Nicaragua's than to that of the United States.

At the root of Costa Rica's economic lead over Nicaragua is the same set of values and attitudes that explains its greater social and political development. These are the values and attitudes that flow from a common leveling experience, one that has strengthened the identification of Costa Ricans with one another. High levels of literacy and public health are one manifestation. Political stability, with all that means for economic growth, is another.

That common leveling experience triggered a process of cultural change that is self-reinforcing. In an article comparing Costa Rica and Nicaragua, James L. Busey observes, "Previous stability lays the ground for understanding which makes possible future stability; previous chaos and resultant hatreds arouse deep bitterness which makes more difficult the task of es-

tablishing stable, constitutional government."[85] And, we might add, the task
of development.

NOTES

1. This figure reflects the impact of the insurrection that overthrew Anastasio Somoza.
   The figure for 1978 was $840 (*World Development Report 1980*).
2. From *World Development Report 1980; World Development Report 1981* shows Nicaragua at
   90%, which is patently overstated, although important progress on the illiteracy problem was made during the Literacy Crusade mounted by the Sandinista government in
   1980.
3. U.S. Department of State sources.
4. José Dolores Gámez, *Historia de Nicaragua*, p. 85.
5. *Ibid.*, pp. 85 – 86.
6. *Ibid.*, p. 128.
7. *Ibid.*, pp. 128 – 29.
8. *Ibid.*, p. 129.
9. *Ibid.*, p. 130; Gámez subsequently mentions that the Indians were often branded.
10. Padre Las Casas wrote *A Very Brief Account of the Destruction of the Indies* in 1544. It had
    a profound impact in Spain and elsewhere in Europe and contributed importantly to
    the "Black Legend" of Spanish cruelty in the New World.
11. Lewis Hanke, *The Spanish Struggle for Justice in the Conquest of America*, pp. 177 – 78.
12. *Ibid.*, p. 6.
13. Salvador Mendieta, *La Enfermedad de Centro-América (The Sickness of Central America)*,
    Vol. II, p. 41.
14. Gámez, *Historia de Nicaragua*, p. 134.
15. Octavio Paz, in *The Labyrinth of Solitude*, thinks that the religious embracing of the In-
    dians by the Spaniards had significant and positive psychological impact on the former,
    unlike the alienation of the Indians of New England who were "cruelly denied . . . the
    possibility of belonging to a living order . . . by the Protestants." Gámez, Mendieta,
    and Rangel — and Las Casas — would have trouble with Paz's view.
16. Murdo J. MacLeod, *Spanish Central America — A Socioeconomic History 1520 – 1720*, pp.
    50 – 56.
17. Gámez, *Historia de Nicaragua*, p. 224.
18. *Ibid.*, p. 226.
19. *Ibid.*, p. 290.
20. *Ibid.*, p. 333.
21. *Ibid.*, p. 370.
22. *Ibid.*, p. 422.
23. *Ibid.*, p. 425.
24. John L. Stephens, *Incidents of Travel in Central America, Chiapas and Yucatan*.
25. *Ibid.*, Vol. II, p. 29. Among the places Stephens visited was the Masaya volcano,
    which prompted a cultural comparison (Vol, II, p. 13): "I could not but reflect, what a
    waste of the bounties of Providence in this favoured but miserable land! At home, this
    volcano would be a fortune; with a good hotel on top, a railing round to protect chil-
    dren from falling in, a zigzag staircase down the sides, and a glass of iced lemonade at
    the bottom."
26. *Ibid.*, Vol. II, p. 8.
27. *Ibid.*, Vol. I, p. 423.
28. Gámez (p. 544) says, ". . . the treaty freed us from the English government" and (p.
    550) "The American government came generously to our aid." A few years later, how-

ever, the Nicaraguans were indignant when the British and Americans tried to clarify the border between Nicaragua and Costa Rica and segregate "Mosquitia."

29. *Ibid.*, p. 59.
30. Mendieta, *La Enfermedad de Centro-América*, Vol. II, p. 336.
31. Richard Millett, *Guardians of the Dynasty*, p. 63.
32. *Ibid.*, p. 41; the quotation is taken from a letter Munro wrote to Millett in 1965.
33. There is a strikingly close parallel between the careers of Somoza García and Rafael Leonidas Trujillo in the Dominican Republic, including the way those careers were launched. (See Chapter 4.)
34. In Helen Delpar, ed., *The Encyclopedia of Latin America*, p. 569.
35. Mark Falcoff, "Somoza, Sandino, and the United States: What the Past Teaches —and Doesn't," pp. 51 – 70.
36. From a speech in Managua before the Ibero-American Chambers of Commerce on May 18, 1981; quoted by *La Prensa*, pp. 1, 8, the following day.
37. Millet, *Guardians of the Dynasty*, pp. 4 – 6. D'Escoto's Sandinista colleagues place far more emphasis on the third cause, and u.s. imperialism in general, than does he. See, for example, Jaime Wheelock Román, *Imperialismo y Dictadura (Imperialism and Dictatorship)*.
38. *Ibid.*
39. *Ibid.* D'Escoto quotes *New York Times* correspondent Harold Norman Denny, who wrote, in 1928, "It has been Nicaragua's fate, often an evil fate like that of a woman too lovely, to be desired by many nations." I put "strategic" in quotes because, in my view, Nicaragua's strategic significance largely ended with the construction of the Panama Canal.
40. *Ibid.* One wonders which democratic institutions D'Escoto had in mind.
41. Jean-Francois Revel, "The Trouble with Latin America," pp. 47 – 50.
42. *Encyclopedia Britannica*, 1971, Vol. 16, p. 473.
43. With respect to the alienation from truth, Octavio Paz speaks of the omnipresence of the lie in Mexican culture in *The Labyrinth of Solitude* (p. 40): "Lying plays a decisive role in our daily lives, our politics, our love affairs, our friendships. . . ."
44. Mendieta, *La Enfermedad de Centro-América*, Vol. II, p. 35.
45. *Ibid.*, p. 38.
46. *Ibid.*, p. 70.
47. *Ibid.*, pp. 41 – 42.
48. *Ibid.*, p. 48.
49. *Ibid.*, p. 46.
50. *Ibid.*, pp. 46 – 47.
51. *Ibid.*, p. 60.
52. *Ibid.*, p. 115.
53. *Ibid.*, Vol. III, p. 357.
54. *Ibid.*, p. 340.
55. Archbishop Bernardo Augusto Thiel, *Monografía de la Población de la Republica de Costa Rica.*
56. This table, deriving from Thiel's data, appears in Samuel Stone, *La Dinastía de los Conquistadores*, p. 55. The sharp decline in the number of Indians from 1522 to 1569 reflects the consequences of disease, enslavement for export to Panama and Peru, and migration to avoid the Spanish.
57. Carlos Melendez, *Historia de Costa Rica*, p. 67.
58. Quoted in Eugenio Rodríguez Vega, *Apuntes para una Sociología Costarricense (Notes for a Costa Rican Sociology)*, p. 20.
59. *Ibid.*
60. Stone, *La Dinastía de los Conquistadores*, pp. 67 – 68.
61. For an interesting examination of the composition of Spanish emigrants to the New World, see George M. Foster, *Culture and Conquest*.

62. Mendieta, *La Enfermedad de Centro-América*, Vol. I, p. 311.

63. Stone, *La Dinastía de los Conquistadores*, p. 56.

64. Gonzalo Chacon Trejos, *Costa Rica es Distinta en Hispano America*, p. 10.

65. *Ibid.*, pp. 24 – 25.

66. Everett E. Hagen, *On the Theory of Social Change*, Chapter 5.

67. Stone, *La Dinastía de los Conquistadores*, p. 71.

68. *Ibid.*

69. MacLeod, *Spanish Central America* contains an interesting chapter (18) on Costa Rican cacao.

70. John L. Stephens, *Incidents of Travel*, Vol. I, p. 359.

71. *Ibid.*, p. 351.

72. In *La Dinastía de los Conquistadores*, Stone refers to Stiepel as "the first [coffee] 'entrepreneur,' in the Schumpeterian sense of the word" (p. 79).

73. Gámez, *Historia de Nicaragua*, p. 486.

74. Stone, *La Dinastía de los Conquistadores*, p. 38. The symbiosis between large and small producers led to the formation of coffee cooperatives with membership drawn from both classes. Costa Rica is far ahead of the other Central American countries in cooperative membership, in part because of the coffee experience. But it is far behind Western Europe and North America in this respect.

75. I have been unable to document this theory with the writings of people who have studied Costa Rica. However, Stephen Sellers, an anthropologist who has written extensively about Costa Rica, believes there is probably some validity to the theory.

76. Karen, Mavis, and Richard Biesanz, *Los Costarricenses (The Costa Ricans)*.

77. According to The World Bank's *World Development Report 1981*, Table 25, pp. 182 – 83.

78. Biesanz, *Los Costarricenses*, p. 664.

79. See Lawrence Harrison, "Costa Rica Shows a Better Way," *The Boston Globe*, page 11, April 27, 1982.

80. Eugenio Rodríguez Vega in *Apuntes para una Sociologia Costarricense* (pp. 27 – 56) mentions timidity, political *personalismo*, the absence of popular art, and the reluctance to get involved in cooperative activity all as a consequence of Costa Rican individualism.

81. Biesanz, *Los Costarricenses*, p. 664.

82. Stone, *La Dinastía de Los Conquistadores*, p. 28; the source is Preston E. James, *Latin America*.

83. The Biesanzes translate the English "compromise" with the Spanish "transacción" (e.g., *Los Costarricenses*, p. 70). Most bilingual people do not find "transacción" adequate.

84. Mitchell A. Seligson, "Trust, Efficacy and Modes of Political Participation: A Study of Costa Rican Peasants," pp. 75 – 98.

85. James L. Busey, "Costa Rica and Nicaragua Compared," pp. 565 – 85.

4

The Dominican Republic and Haiti

In 1776 Adam Smith observed, "The French colony of St. Domingue [now Haiti] . . . is now the most important of the sugar colonies of the West Indies, and its produce is said to be greater than that of all the English sugar colonies put together."[1] At the same time, the Spanish colony of Santo Domingo, on the same island, was abysmally poor.

Today, Haiti is one of the poorest countries in the world, with a per-capita GNP of $270 in 1980, 23 percent literacy, and a life expectancy of fifty-three years. (See Table 2.) Since independence in 1804, it has been ruled by a virtually unbroken chain of autocrats, many of them despots, most of them corrupt. The Dominican Republic, in contrast, is a middle-income country: its 1980 per-capita GNP was $1,160; 67 percent of Dominicans are literate; and life expectancy is sixty-one years. Since the 1965 revolution, the Dominican Republic has moved steadily, if painfully, toward democratic stability after almost one hundred fifty years of political turmoil dominated by caudillos. It is today one of the more promising democratic experiments in Spanish America.

The Dominican Republic and Haiti share the island of Hispaniola. The Dominican side, to the east, is about the size of Costa Rica. Haiti, to the west, is about one-half as large. There are today about six million people in each country, which means that Haiti's population density is twice the Dominican Republic's. Haiti and El Salvador, at about 550 people per square mile, are the two most densely populated countries in the hemisphere, excluding some of the smaller Caribbean islands.

The Dominican Republic's land resources are greater than Haiti's, particularly if measured against the number of people they support. Haiti's land endowment was sufficient, however, to support the extraordinary economic success of eighteenth-century Saint Domingue. Erosion, principally the result of overpopulation, has taken a terrible toll since then. Indeed, Haiti has lived the Malthusian prophecy.

The Dominican Republic also has an advantage in mineral resources. It currently produces gold, silver, ferronickel, and bauxite. In recent history, however, only bauxite has been commercially mined for more than fifteen years, and the value of bauxite exports has not exceeded $20 million per year.

Bauxite is the only mineral mined commercially in Haiti. The amounts have been generally less than on the Dominican side.

In any event, while the Dominican Republic has some advantage in resource endowment, that advantage is insufficient to explain the dramatic difference in the patterns of development during the past two centuries. What does explain it? Evidence points strongly toward cultural factors.

The colonial period: slavery and neglect

There are several striking parallels between the histories of the Dominican Republic and Nicaragua. After early intense interest in both countries, Spain turned its attention to other parts of the New World more richly endowed with precious metals, particularly Mexico and Peru. Both thus suffered from centuries of Spanish neglect. Both also experienced repeated pirate attacks, in part because of Spain's neglect. The history of the two countries since independence has been marked by political chaos interrupted by dictatorships. American Marines occupied both early in this century, and particularly durable and notorious dictatorships soon followed their departure.

Dominican history diverges sharply from Nicaraguan history, however, in a continuing search for a protector. This phenomenon is clearly related to the facts that (a) the Dominican Republic shares an island with Haiti, and (b) for most of the first half of the nineteenth century, the Haitians dominated, even terrorized, the Dominicans.

Columbus discovered and named Hispaniola — the Spanish isle — in December of 1492. The island was then inhabited by the Taino Indians, whose ancestors came from northeastern South America. The Tainos were a primitive tribe, particularly in comparison with the Aztecs, Mayas, and Incas. They fished and hunted, and their agriculture was based on cassava and corn.

The first Spanish settlement, populated by members of Columbus's first crew, was annihilated by the Indians. But Columbus returned on his second voyage with seventeen ships and established a permanent Spanish presence at Isabella, on the north coast. The Isabella settlement barely survived outbreaks of yellow fever and syphilis, shortages of medicine and food, and repeated conspiracies against Columbus and his lieutenants by the *hidalgos* — lower level nobles — "who had come to Hispaniola in search of riches and who considered below their station obligatory work with their hands side-by-side with common people."[2]

From another source we learn that

> . . . many of the settlers were utterly useless, inefficient men, who joining the expedition without the slightest knowledge of any vocation or trade, had expected they were simply to pick up gold as they wanted, while lead-

ing a life of indulgence and idleness . . . many of them were the dregs of
the population of Spain . . .[3]

The search for gold was the colony's raison d'être, and it required a
lot of manpower. The Spaniards soon dominated and effectively enslaved
the Indians. " . . . Columbus very soon discovered that he could save money
by giving his workers slaves instead of their salaries."[4] The institution through
which the subjugation occurred was the *repartimiento*, essentially the same
as the *encomienda* system discussed in the previous chapter.

As in Nicaragua, the Indians were decimated by overwork, physical
cruelty, and diseases introduced by the Spaniards. Suicide was common.
Moya estimates that there were 600,000 Indians when Columbus discovered
Hispaniola. Sixteen years later, in 1508, there were 60,000. Ten years later,
notwithstanding the importation of an additional 40,000 from neighboring
islands, the number had dropped to 3,000. Father Las Casas undertook a
crusade to protect the Indians, but it was too late. As the number of Indians
dwindled, the importation of African slaves increased.

The mines, which were the economic basis of the *repartimientos*, were
rapidly depleted. Growing conditions were found to be ideal, however, for
sugar cane, which was introduced in 1506. The *repartimientos* evolved into
plantations as agriculture overtook mining as the principal source of riches.
Tobacco and cattle production also flourished. Santo Domingo, which had
been founded in 1496, grew into a handsome and bustling city, principally
because of the sugar industry. It "had become noted for the splendour of
its houses and the regularity of its streets, while its port was the most busy
one in the New World."[5] The University of Santo Domingo, the first in
the hemisphere, was established in 1538.

But Spanish mercantilism, heavy taxes on production, peculation by
colonial bureaucrats, and accumulation of wealth by the Church weighed
heavily on agriculture, much as they did in Nicaragua. Even the richness
of Hispaniola's land resources could not assure profitability in the face of
these depredations, and by 1540 the boom was over. Spanish settlers had
been migrating to Mexico and Peru, where precious metals abounded, after
the Dominican mines were exhausted. The outflow accelerated when the
sugar boom ended. Those who remained increasingly engaged in contraband
trade, particularly of cattle hides.

Poor and neglected, Hispaniola was a sitting duck when Sir Francis
Drake led a British force against Santo Domingo in 1586. Drake took the
city and pocketed a substantial ransom. The British attacked Hispaniola
again five years later, and their warships disrupted Spanish shipping to and
from the island. Migration from Hispaniola was further stimulated by the
British attacks.

English, French, and Dutch privateers, who preyed on Spanish shipping with some encouragement from their governments, settled on the island

of Tortuga, off the northwest coast of Hispaniola, in 1630. The pirates employed long oar-propelled boats called *frei-botes* and soon became known as "freebooters" or "fillibusters." Some hunted animals on Hispaniola for their hides and meat and became known as "buccaneers" because of their habit of smoking meat over small fires called "boucans."

The forays of the fillibusters and buccaneers were highly disruptive, and in 1635 the Spanish attacked Tortuga. They failed to follow up an initial victory, and the fillibusters and buccaneers, the largest number of whom were French, strengthened their hold on the island. In the mid-seventeenth century, the French assumed control of Tortuga and fought off the Spaniards, who were also occupied with defending themselves against the British. The French then began to populate the western third of Hispaniola — what was to become Haiti. French control of "St. Domingue" was confirmed in 1697 by the Treaty of Ryswick, which ended a decade of warfare between Spain and France.

While French St. Domingue was emerging, ". . . the Spanish colony of Santo Domingo continued submerged in a sea of misery that, in more than one sense, mirrored the decadence which had affected Spain for decades."[6] Conditions on the Spanish side were so bad that, according to a census taken in 1739, the total population was about 30,000. Burgeoning prosperity on the French side, based initially on sugar and cattle, stimulated growth on the Spanish side, particularly in cacao and cattle production. "This commerce was what enabled the Spanish colonists to break out of the lamentable state of misery in which they were trapped during the entire seventeenth century."[7] The naming by the Spanish government in 1737 of an intelligent colonial administrator, Don Pedro Zorrilla, also helped. Zorrilla opened the ports to other than Spanish ships, thereby further stimulating production.

By 1783, the population on the Spanish side approximated 80,000. On the French side, which had been dubbed "the Queen of the Antilles," 1789 data showed a total of 520,000, of which 452,000 were slaves and 28,000 free mulattos. St. Domingue boasted 400 sugar plantations and 3,400 indigo farms, as well as numerous cacao, cotton, coffee, and tobacco farms.[8] The relationship between master and slave was far more cruel in St. Domingue, however; in Santo Domingo, "master and slave relied upon each other for company and support, and the chains were in this way gradually lightened."[9] The Spanish side was well on its way to becoming a mulatto society.

Haiti's bloody independence

Stimulated by the American and French revolutions, many of the whites of St. Domingue sought independence from France while preserving the slave system. The ideas of the Enlightenment led in 1790 to an uprising of the mulattos, which was put down by the whites. An insurrection of slaves that followed in 1791 was suppressed by whites *and* mulattos with appalling cruelty.

The slaves soon responded with a massive uprising in which the cruelties of the whites were repaid in kind. The plantations that made St. Domingue the richest of colonies were devastated, and surviving whites sought refuge in the cities. The mulattos, however, who still identified themselves with France, ended up in control of the black armies. When the British, who were at war with the French and in alliance with the Spanish, sent troops from Jamaica to St. Domingue, the fabled Toussaint L'Ouverture, who had fled from St. Domingue and become a general on the Spanish side of the island, was persuaded to return to lead the mulatto/black forces now under French control. The British and Spanish were defeated, and the Spanish side of the island was ceded to the French by the Peace of Basle in 1795. The French failed to consolidate this cession, mainly because of the continued presence of British troops in St. Domingue (they remained until 1798). A French garrison, however, did remain in the city of Santo Domingo.

By the time the British departed, Toussaint was in control of St. Domingue. The slaves were forced to return to the plantations as paid laborers, and whites were promised security and opportunity. The economy started to recover from the shock of the mulatto and black uprisings. In 1801 Toussaint forced the remaining Spanish out of Santo Domingo and unified the island — except the city of Santo Domingo, where the French garrison remained — under his generally effective and enlightened control. Peace was short-lived, however, as Napoleon fixed his attention on the island, sending a force of 58,000 men in early 1802 to reestablish French sovereignty. A series of bloody battles ensued which ended in an uneasy peace. In an act of treachery, the French then kidnapped Toussaint and removed him to a prison in France in 1803. He died soon thereafter.

Upon hearing of Toussaint's fate, the blacks rose up again under his successor, Jean-Jacques Dessalines. The roughly 8,000 French who survived the carnage — and a virulent yellow fever epidemic — departed late in 1803. The Republic of Haiti, the first black nation, declared its independence in January 1804, under Dessalines, who named himself governor general for life.

In 1805, Dessalines and his second-in-command, Henri Christophe, invaded what had been the Spanish side but was now under nominal French control. They laid siege to Santo Domingo but retreated, leaving a broad swath of death and destruction, when French warships appeared on the scene.

The French garrison that had been installed in Santo Domingo city in 1795 was finally expelled in 1809 by the Spanish colonials with the help of the British, and the eastern side of the island again became a Spanish

possession. The Spanish government was as neglectful, however, as it had
been before 1795:

> While the creoles of Venezuela, Buenos Aires, Nueva Granada and Mex-
> ico . . . were mobilizing themselves to fight the Spanish, the Dominicans
> were delivering themselves once again to the tutelage of a Spain that was
> almost as much in ruins as its colony on Hispaniola. . . . The Spanish aid
> that those who had fought to oust the French received . . . amounted to
> 100,000 pesos . . . scarcely enough to feed and clothe the troops without
> mentioning other needs.[10]

Dominican independence comes and goes

The Spanish colony proclaimed its independence from "España Boba"
(I can't resist translating this as "inane Spain") on November 30, 1821.
There was little Spanish resistance. Independence, which included a nominal link to Colombia, lasted just a few weeks, however. The Haitian president, Jean Pierre Boyer, marched on Santo Domingo early in 1822 and
encountered virtually no opposition. The entire island was unified under
Boyer's rule, which endured until 1843.[11] But the Dominicans increasingly
chafed under Boyer's arbitrary and at times despotic government (among
other provocations, he closed down the University of Santo Domingo), and
when he was overthrown in 1843, a new opportunity presented itself to
Dominican nationalists. Under the leadership of Juan Pablo Duarte, an
independent Dominican Republic was proclaimed on February 27, 1844.

Speaking of the period between 1843 and the early 1870s, Samuel
Hazard observes, ". . . we look in vain . . . for any period of six consecutive
years of peace and tranquillity for the inhabitants of the Spanish part of St.
Domingo. Nothing but conspiracies, revolutions, and civil wars, in which
Hayti, by constant incursions, added to the troubles of her neighbor."[12]

The Haitians attempted to reassert their control in 1844 but were
defeated by General Pedro Santana, who soon was named president of the
Dominican Republic. The Haitians attacked again in 1849; once again Santana, who had resigned the presidency a year earlier, defeated them. There-
upon he named himself dictator. But he was unable to secure the recognition
of the United States and was replaced in the same year by Buenaventura
Báez. Báez was pressed by some of his countrymen to seek annexation by
the United States as the best means of assuring security from Haitian attacks.
But he demurred because of the continued existence of slavery in the United
States.

Santana was elected president in 1853 and repelled another Haitian
attack in 1856, but he became increasingly unpopular, partly because of a
scheme he promoted to lease the Bay of Samaná to the United States for a
naval base. So Báez returned in 1857, only to be ousted in 1858 by a coalition
that included Santana, who was again named president. Apparently over-

whelmed by fear of the Haitians, Santana unilaterally delivered his country to Spanish rule in May 1861 in an act that ever since has given special meaning for Dominicans to the Spanish verb for deliver, *entregar*.

The Spaniards were no more enlightened colonial administrators than they had been before, and after two years of brutal efforts to suppress repeated Dominican uprisings, they had had enough. On March 3, 1865, independence was restored, and Báez was back in the presidency soon thereafter. With the end of slavery in the United States, Báez promoted annexation by that nation. A public official in Puerto Plata put it to Hazard this way during Hazard's 1870 visit: "We have no money; we have not enough people in the island to make it prosperous; we are liable to attack from Hayti at any moment they may have a revolution there; and, therefore, for our own safety we want annexation."[13]

Notwithstanding the support of President Ulysses S. Grant, annexation was rejected by the u.s. Senate. Charles Sumner, chairman of the Senate Committee on Foreign Relations and creator of the phrase "good neighbor," led the opposition and had this to say:

> Kindness, benevolence, assistance, aid, help, protection, all that is implied in good neighborhood, this we must give freely, bountifully; but [the Dominican people's independence] is as precious to them as ours is to us, and it is placed under the safeguard of natural laws which we cannot violate with impunity.[14]

Otto Schoenrich saw it differently in *Santo Domingo — A Country with a Future*:

> . . . the United States thus deliberately rejected an opportunity to obtain control of a most important strategical position and to secure peace and prosperity to the Dominican people.[15]

The game of presidential musical chairs continued to the accompaniment of conspiracies, *coups d'état*, and revolutions — in the year 1876 alone there were *four* presidents — until the arrival on the scene of Ulises ("Lilis") Heureaux in 1887. Heureaux established a harsh and enduring dictatorship that gave him total control of the country for twelve years.

The parallels between Heureaux and Rafael Leonidas Trujillo, who came to power thirty years later, are striking. Schoenrich described Heureaux as a combination of "ability and unscrupulousness, courage and cruelty, resolution and cunning,"[16] all of which are apt for Trujillo. The sexual prowess of both was legendary: of Heureaux, Schoenrich reports that "an isolated town gloried in the distinction of being the only place in the Republic where the president did not have a mistress."[17] The parallel with Trujillo extends to Heureaux's demise in 1899 in a conspiratorial assassination.

The Dominican Republic experienced deepening financial problems during the second half of the nineteenth century and increasingly resorted to loans from European countries and the United States. By 1905 payments on these loans were all in default, and Dominican President Carlos Morales asked the United States government to administer the Dominican customs, which were in chaos because of mismanagement and graft. Since then, the United States has played a dominant role in Dominican history.

Morales's efforts to establish himself as a dictator were successfully opposed by Ramon Cáceres, whom many Dominicans consider to have done more for his country than any other president.[18] Cáceres concerned himself with the education and health of his people and treated his opponents in a conciliatory, democratic manner. He also pursued fiscal reform vigorously. Cáceres was assassinated in 1911; he died in the American embassy, where his driver had taken him.

The United States intervenes

The United States was deeply involved in mediating among groups contending for power following the Cáceres assassination. But a stable solution was not achieved, and in 1916, with the consent of President Juan Isidro Jiménez, 1,800 U.S. Marines landed. Soon thereafter, in the face of growing Dominican opposition, the United States declared the Dominican Republic under U.S. military administration.

Behind the U.S. intervention were the same motives that explain similar actions in Nicaragua (1912) and Haiti (1915): (1) concern that European powers would seize on chronic political and financial instability to the detriment of the U.S. strategic position at the time of the First World War (the Panama Canal was of particular concern), and (2) what Sumner Welles has described as "the role of the evangel . . . to reform . . . the conditions of life and government of the independent peoples inhabiting the sovereign republics of the American hemisphere."[19] The first motive was, of course, the principal one.

The U.S. military government endured for eight years. As time passed, the Dominicans became increasingly unified in their opposition to the intervention, at least in part because of the clumsiness — for example, few of the U.S. military spoke Spanish — and in some cases cruelty of the occupying forces. Welles observed: "The fear of infringement of their independence has in practice proved to be the one great compelling force which at moments of national danger could have fused local jealousies, political rivalries, and selfish ambitions into true patriotism, into the overwhelming determination to preserve the national liberties of the Dominican Republic intact."[20]

Several Latin American countries took up the cause of the Dominicans, and the intervention became an increasingly hot political issue in the United States. Among many others, labor leader Samuel Gompers campaigned for withdrawal of the u.s. forces. In the 1920 election campaign, Warren Harding attacked the Democrats for the intervention. Nonetheless, it was not until mid-1924 that the last marine left.

The intervention was not without benefits for the Dominican Republic. Major educational reforms were instituted, and within a two-year period school enrollment increased from 18,000 to 100,000. Health and sanitation were measurably improved. Roads were built, harbors were improved, and the electricity and communications systems were expanded. The financial picture improved dramatically.

The u.s. military also established the *Guardia Nacional*, a constabulary led principally by American military officers. The lore of the Latin American and u.s. Left explains the creation of the *Guardia* as part of an insidious design to install a dictatorship subservient to u.s. interests, in much the same way as, it is alleged, was done in Nicaragua. In both cases, however, there is overwhelming evidence that the constabularies were established as apolitical security forces committed to the preservation of order in the democratic societies the u.s. military were supposed to leave behind, consistent with the evangelical mission. The United States can be rightly accused of extreme naiveté in creating the *Guardia*, but not of cynical manipulation.

Trujillo, the second intervention, and the Dominican "miracle"

In any event, one of the few Dominicans who became a *Guardia Nacional* officer (in 1919) was Rafael Leonidas Trujillo. By the time the Americans left in 1924 he had risen to the top of the institution. In 1927 he was made a brigadier general. In 1929, a coup engineered by Trujillo was thwarted only because of the intervention of the u.s. Legation. A year later, Trujillo outmaneuvered the incumbent Dominican president, Horacio Vásquez, who sought asylum in the u.s. Legation. Trujillo became president in 1930.

Robert D. Crassweller, whose book *Trujillo — The Life and Times of a Caribbean Dictator* is the definitive treatment of Trujillo, quotes Juan Bautista Alberdi in explaining Trujillo's rise to power:

> Everywhere when an orange tree reaches a certain age, it produces oranges. . . . Wherever there are Spanish republics formed out of former colonies, there will be dictators when the development of affairs reaches a certain point.[21]

Trujillo was the quintessential Spanish American dictator: cunning, amoral, cruel, ruthless, greedy — Heureaux resurrected and made even more voracious. He amassed enormous wealth during the thirty-one years he ran the country.

Trujillo ravaged the Dominican Republic. He built himself an economic empire larger even than that of the Somozas. He corrupted and gutted institutions that were pitifully weak to start with. But his cruelest legacy was his intimidation of his people: they were conditioned to be sycophants, to look to the *jefe*, the *patrón*, for everything; to regard themselves as impotent. A dependency mentality is one of the threads of Spanish culture that has most impeded progress in Hispanic societies, as has already been pointed out. Trujillo carried it to its corrupting, dehumanizing, humiliating extreme.

Trujillo was assassinated in 1961, apparently with the complicity of the U.S. government. Five turbulent years followed, during which the United States was profoundly involved in Dominican politics: first, to prevent Trujillo's son Ramfis from assuming power; then to set up the elections of 1962, which were won by Juan Bosch; then to try to maintain Bosch in power (the military ousted him in September 1963); then, through a massive military intervention, to prevent the "constitutionalists," a coalition running across the spectrum from center to extreme left that called for Bosch's return, from ousting the military;[22] then to set up a centrist provisional government under the distinguished statesman Héctor García Godoy, then to set up the elections in mid-1966 that brought Joaquín Balaguer to power.[23]

The eighteen years since the 1966 elections are sometimes referred to as "the Dominican miracle." Balaguer, who had been one of Trujillo's puppets, was a far cry from a modern Western leader. He largely ignored his responsibility for developing the institutions that could have enhanced political stability and social progress. His administrations were overcentralized,[24] initiative was suppressed, and sycophancy continued to pay while he was president. But he was resourceful and wise in keeping balance among contending political factions and in controlling the military. He pursued a simple but effective economic strategy emphasizing public and private investment, which contributed to the Dominican Republic's achieving one of the highest growth rates in the world from 1966 to 1978. And he did not enrich himself.

In 1978, after three terms as president, Balaguer was defeated by Antonio Guzmán, the centrist candidate of the Dominican Revolutionary Party (PRD), which Bosch had left several years before because he decided he no longer believed in democracy. As the vote count proceeded, the military, seeing the handwriting on the wall, attempted to thwart the outcome of the election, but were dissuaded by the timely intervention of President Jimmy Carter.

In an action for which his compatriots will always be indebted to him, Guzmán chose not to run again in 1982.[25] Salvador Jorge Blanco, from the moderate left wing of the PRD, defeated Balaguer easily and was inaugurated on August 16, 1982, with the country facing serious economic problems, largely as a result of worldwide recession.

The economic miracle was over, at least for the time being. But the political miracle continues.

The cultural burden

The Dominican Republic has done well since the time it was dominated, first economically, then militarily and politically, by its neighbor. By most indicators of development, it may now be something like half a century ahead of Haiti. But it may be half a century behind the developed countries of the West.

How to explain the gap between the Dominican Republic and the developed West? John Bartlow Martin, a liberal journalist who was named ambassador to the Dominican Republic by John F. Kennedy in 1962 and was withdrawn as a symbol of protest after Bosch was overthrown, asks himself what went wrong in his book *Overtaken by Events*. He sets up four possible explanations:

1. Geography (which he rejects).
2. Race (which he rejects).
3. (attributed to Carlos Fuentes) "That the United States system derives from the Reformation, with its emphasis on individuality and conscience, while the Latin American system is rooted in the Counter-Reformation, with its feudal authoritarianism and hostility to new ideas."[26]
4. (related to the third) ". . . that the British came to North America to plant colonies and rear families and build, while the Spaniards and Portuguese came to Central and South America to conquer and kill, to extract and exploit."[27]

Martin is not convinced by the third and fourth explanations: "I know of no single thesis that will answer the question why so many Latin American nations and people have lived in turmoil so often in the past."[28] But he makes some observations that lend credence to the cultural explanation:

> More was involved in Bosch's fall — Dominican society, Dominican tradition, Dominican institutions, Dominican history. A Dominican's responsibility seldom extends beyond his own tribe of cousins to the wider community — to his neighborhood, to his town, to his country. . . . So a tribal people faced a national election in today's complex world; and after the election the contending forces lapsed back into the pursuit of tribal, not national, interests.[29]

> Nor did Dominican democracy have the support of effective free and voluntary institutions — labor unions, professional societies, cooperatives, service clubs. We in the United States seldom realize how much strength our society derives from them. They assist enormously in adjusting differences; they provide safety valves for extremism and conduits for a dialogue among men who disagree.[30]

Several scholars have emphasized the Spanish imprint on Dominican culture. The Dominican writer José Ramón López, who focuses on nutritional shortcomings as the basis of underdevelopment, also traces a litany of national faults to "the ignorant soldier and the criminal freed from prison" who came to Santo Domingo during the early years. "Government, for them, was the arbitrary order which had to be blindly obeyed. Wealth was obtained through battle and conquest; work was for the slave; and commerce was for the Jew, who had just been expelled from the peninsula."[31] The faults include:

- a totally inadequate education system
- corrupt, abusive government
- the unbridled power of "the chief" ("*el jefe*")
- corruption of electoral institutions
- lack of respect for the law
- lack of respect for human life
- an "unconscionable individualism"[32]

Howard Wiarda also sees Spanish culture at the root of the Dominican Republic's — and indeed Latin America's — problems:

> Much of the history of Latin American all the way to the present may be understood in terms of the institutions and behavioral patterns that Catholic, feudal, authoritarian, patrimonial Spain carried with her to the Western Hemisphere. . . . What were, in effect, dying feudal-medieval institutions in much of the rest of Europe were transferred almost intact to Latin America where they not only received a new lease on life but actually thrived and persisted.[33]

In Wiarda's view, in which one hears echoes of the views of Salvador Mendieta, the intense centralism of post-fifteenth-century Spain has been perpetuated in Latin American dictatorships:

> The overriding importance first of the Crown as *the* symbol of authority and legitimacy . . . and after independence of the *caudillo* and later the state has, in the Latin American context, tended to militate against the growth of local government and initiative, modern interest associations, governmental checks and balances, party politics, delegation of authority, or any of the other intermediary structures that have grown up in the North American – Western European tradition.[34]

The profoundly paternalistic, dependent mindset of the Dominican has been noted by several scholars. Gerald F. Murray, an anthropologist, studied the impact on lumber mill workers and slash-and-burn farmers of a Balaguer decision to prohibit the felling of trees in an important watershed.[35] The mountaineers worshipped Balaguer and refused to accept his responsibility for the decision, which was highly prejudicial to them. Murray observes that, "The mountain dweller sees himself as humble, hard working,

obedient, poor, resigned to whatever comes from 'above,' be it from God . . .
or from the government . . ."36 and, "The participants in a *caudillo* system
are to a large degree locked psychologically in the system."37

The dependency mindset affects, in varying degrees, virtually all Dominicans, including *caudillos*. For obvious historical reasons, insecurity has
become a national complex. A difficult problem arises, and the instinctive
response, tragically, is often, "We Dominicans are not able to solve the
problem. We need help from outside." After returning from his field work,
Murray received a letter from a La Loma *campesino* which contained the
following:

> Our only hope is for . . . the government of the United States to do some-
> thing for the poor Dominicans, because here there's no hope that anybody
> is going to do anything for us . . .38

Murray also stresses the general absence of trust, the campesino belief
in Balaguer being more an expression of the current of paternalism in the
Dominican psyche. Kenneth Evan Sharpe also comments on the dependency
mindset of the Dominican campesino ("Many [campesinos] wondered if there
were any way out of their dilemmas — except through the grace of God,
El Presidente, or a rich patron.") and then observes that "another barrier
deeply embedded in the culture and reinforced by everyday experience was
a distrust of each other and of outsiders . . ."39

Mistrust dominates the Dominican's view of his government — and
with reason. André and Andrée Corten note:

> The corruption of public administration, the *"macutéo"* [a Dominican word
> for graft that derives from the same Taino root as the Haitian word for
> bag, *macoute*], the diversion of funds are tendencies typical of various Latin
> American countries. Honesty is rare in administration and provokes the
> hostility of all those who are accustomed to corruption, considering it ap-
> propriate to a certain status and certain level of prestige. . . . Public admin-
> istration, including the state enterprises and the armed forces, have an
> institutional structure that is closer to a system of financial entitlements
> than a capitalist or socialist state.40

Malcolm T. Walker adds:

> Once in office, some people consider it their prerogative to exploit the posi-
> tion to their own personal advantage. The judge and other court officials
> are open to bribery and the poor do not expect to receive justice.41

Mistrust of the system, and the expectation that fair play and justice
will not prevail, extend to the educational system. Wiarda observes that
"Distinguished academic achievement is not often rewarded, for such as-
criptive criteria as family and personal connections are still frequently more

important than merit in determining the Dominican's place in the society and his possibilities for advancement."[42]

The parallels between Banfield's Montegrano and the Dominican Republic should by now be apparent. As we see from Walker's comments on child-rearing in the Dominican mountain city of Constanza, the patterns of child-rearing in Montegrano and Constanza are strikingly similar:

> A baby in the household never wants for attention. If he cries, he is carried; throughout the day he is hugged, kissed, and fondled . . .[43]

> To obtain conformity from children, parents rely on threats and promises, sarcasm and ridicule. Threats are rarely carried out, and quite early in life the child learns to be equally skeptical of promises. Parents and others commonly make all manner of promises to the child that they do not feel bound to keep, and they also lie and exaggerate to one another and to children as well. Constanceros place little value on truth, and at an early age children learn to become adept liars.[44]

> Even at the risk of making value judgments, it does strike one that Constanza men are emotionally immature; in large measure this immaturity stems from the nature of the socialization of the male. . . . Boys . . . are treated with extreme indulgence. . . . More often than not, adults give into the demands of young children, but there is little consistency in their treatment of male children.[45]

> In his own eyes and in the view of the community, the father is the figure of supreme importance in the home. All members of the family seek to please him. His moods are catered to, and his decisions, in theory, are final.[46]

> As in other cultures with a strong Mediterranean background, the machismo . . . of the male is extremely important. . . . Fathers like to see manliness in their sons; displays of aggression and rage appear to be taken as an indication of this quality . . .[47]

The Dominican world view, then, contains a number of elements, many deriving from Spanish culture, that get in the way of progress. The society is highly paternalistic and authoritarian: it encourages strong feelings of dependence and impotence among its members, a psychological environment in which *caudillos* flourish. The individual derives a sense of stability and belonging only from the family; those outside the family are to be mistrusted if not feared. A government position is more a license than a trust. Justice and fair play do not prevail.

This world view works against the development of the sense of affiliation and the ideas of cooperation and compromise on which political harmony and stability depend. It also works against the entrepreneurial instinct, which needs free rein and incentive and which may depend on stimulating and supportive child-rearing. The values and attitudes that flow from this world view stand in the way of progress, and they are inculcated in the children early on. But the way children are raised may aggravate the problem by inflicting psychological and emotional wounds that both prevent the person from realizing his potential and leave him incapacitated to deal with his personal and social responsibilities.

"The Dominican problem is a problem of consciousness," Frank Moya Pons observed in 1982:

> Our society has always been, including now, essentially a rural and peasant society, a traditional society, a village society, dependent and poor, from which political and institutional forms have evolved that have been based on primary interpersonal relationships, on the ties of the extended family, and, naturally, on relationships of dependency and service based on the patron/client model . . . and *caudillismo*. . . . In this kind of society . . . its members develop the notion that, since resources are so limited, only someone who steals from others can break out of poverty. . . . The entrepreneur, the innovator is rejected.[48]

Explaining the "miracle"

If the Dominicans' cultural burden is so heavy, it can be reasonably asked, "How can you explain the Dominican economic and political miracles since 1966?"

The economic miracle occurred between 1966 and 1978. It has been followed by sustained recession, importantly reflecting worldwide conditions (e.g., low world prices for sugar, the Dominican Republic's principal export) but also an economic strategy that had essentially run its course. The twelve-year boom responded to Balaguer's promotion of public and private investment, the latter emphasizing mining (major ferronickel and gold operations began during this period) and tourism. In recent years, there have been no significant new mineral finds, and tourism has leveled off.

Thus, the Dominican economic miracle is not unlike that of Brazil, which experienced similarly high growth during the same period, also principally as the result of a successful economic strategy. In Brazil's case, the strategy emphasized exports, and although the Brazilian economy has cooled off notably in recent years, its export orientation is likely to serve it well in the future — as have similar strategies in Korea, Taiwan, Hong Kong, et al. over more than two decades.

The long-term prospects for the Dominican economy are not as bright, in part because the Dominican Republic is so much smaller than Brazil, but also because it has not yet refocused its economic strategy on exports.

The political miracle could turn out to be far more durable. To be sure, political stability and democratic evolution — particularly following on the heels of the revolutionary chaos of 1965 — helped nurture the economic miracle, and a continuation of the political miracle is likely to engender further economic benefits. But whereas economic performance will almost surely be subject to cyclical trends, the process of democratization could proceed without a serious hitch, as it has in Costa Rica since 1948 and in Venezuela since 1959. To repeat the words of James L. Busey (p. 56), "Previous stability lays the ground for understanding which makes possible future stability . . ."

What then explains why a country, which had known throughout its history only political turmoil, authoritarianism, and institutional debility, suddenly shifts to a sustained and apparently deepening democratization? I would suggest five basic causes:

1. *Good leadership* — Hector García Godoy, Joaquín Balaguer, Antonio Guzmán, and Salvador Jorge Blanco all have played an important role in nurturing the democratic experiment.
2. *The traumatic effects of the 1965 revolution and u.s. intervention* — The revolution left moderate elements across the political spectrum more prone to conciliation and compromise. The intervention revived feelings of nationalism that had been essentially dormant since the withdrawal of the u.s. Marines in 1924.
3. *A constructive post-revolution u.s. role* — The United States government provided very substantial economic support, especially during the years immediately following the revolution, which made it much easier for the Dominicans to stabilize their economy and get a development program moving. The United States also provided staunch moral support, culminating in President Carter's intervention against the Dominican military during the 1978 election count.
4. *A highly responsible, professional, and democratically oriented Dominican press* — El Caribe and Listín Diario are two of the best newspapers in Latin America. The editors of both are strongly committed to democratic processes.
5. *Favorable economic conditions* — Good politics facilitates good economics, as noted above. But good economics also facilitates good politics. The big question right now is whether the nascent political experiment can survive prolonged bad times.

The political and economic miracles notwithstanding, the Dominican Republic remains a country with a troubled past and many deeply rooted problems in the present, aside from the prolonged recession. The problems are typical of Spanish-American countries: relatively low per-capita income (at the lower range of the "middle-income" countries), highly inequitable income distribution, substantial illiteracy, pressing health problems, and a military institution in which the concept of civilian control is still not deeply rooted, despite the efforts of Hector García Godoy, Joaquín Balaguer, Antonio Guzmán, and Salvador Jorge Blanco during the past eighteen years. And it is far from clear that civilian politicians will exercise the necessary restraint and flexibility to permit democratic institutions to root themselves deeply and securely.

The past eighteen years leave one hopeful. But the one hundred forty-four years of history between the Dominican Republic's first independence and the 1965 revolution leave one anxious about this country's agonizing search for its identity, for unity, for peace, and for progress.

Haiti after independence

Our recounting of the history of the Dominican Republic has included the relevant events in Haitian history through the achievement of independence in 1804 under Dessalines. Dessalines proclaimed himself emperor and set up a system that essentially divided the Haitian people into two categories: laborers and soldiers. Almost all laborers worked the land, in conditions only slightly improved over the days of slavery. The state replaced the French plantation owner; the *liane*, a thick, pliable vine, replaced the whip. James Leyburn observes in his classic, *The Haitian People*, that both Dessalines and the French plantation owners looked upon the poor blacks as "cattle."[49]

Dessalines' autocratic manner alienated many of his black followers as well as the mulatto elite, and in October 1806 an insurrection broke out that led to his assassination. For the next thirteen years, Haiti was effectively two countries: the North, ruled by Henri Christophe; and the South, governed by Alexandre Pétion until his death in 1818 and then by Jean Pierre Boyer.

The contrast between the systems employed in the North and South was striking. Christophe, a black who named himself king and established a system of nobility, built upon Toussaint's and Dessalines's restoration of plantation agriculture. He leased state-owned plantations to entrepreneurs who operated within policies established by the state, e.g., one-quarter of the total crop was distributed among the workers. The workers were bound to the land and were effectively serfs. Their lives were highly regimented by Christophe's authoritarian and paternalistic system. But they produced. The North grew increasingly prosperous.

Christophe, with the help of foreign advisors, many of them British, was an economic and administrative innovator. Pétion, a mulatto, was a social innovator. While his agrarian reform, which divided up the large plantations into small farms, was an economic disaster, it bore some of the characteristics of progressive twentieth-century land and other social reform schemes. Those who did not receive land were assured of family garden plots. Farmers who employed field hands had to provide them with medical care. The aged and infirm were guaranteed their houses and gardens. Expectant mothers stopped work in the fourth month of pregnancy but continued to receive pay. Nursing mothers remained at home until their children were weaned.

But production dwindled steadily as the South evolved toward the small-farm subsistence poverty that has characterized Haiti ever since. As the experience of colonial New England and more recently Japan and Taiwan has demonstrated, small farms can be productive. But this has not been Haiti's experience. Leyburn, contrasting the economic decline of Pétion's South with the boom in Christophe's North, concludes that what was missing was coercion. That may be so. But there was also something missing from the Haitian peasant's view of the world and himself that led him to settle for subsistence.

Pétion died in 1818 and was succeeded by Jean Pierre Boyer, also a mulatto, who followed Pétion's policies. When Christophe committed suicide two years later, Haiti was reunified under Boyer. Boyer then broke up the northern plantations into small farms, and the entire country moved toward subsistence agriculture. Leyburn observes, "During [Boyer's] twenty-five-year presidency, the mass of Haitians became so indifferent to pecuniary inducements that little work could be got from them beyond that required to produce necessary food."[50]

Haitian fears that the French would attempt to retake the former colony, which had obsessed Christophe (he built the fabled Citadel to defend against precisely that eventuality),[51] weighed heavily on Boyer. In 1825, he further impoverished his country by buying Haiti's security through an indemnity of 150 million francs to be paid to the French over five years.[52]

The caste system became firmly entrenched under Boyer, although it was not by his design. The mulatto elite was literate and convinced of its natural superiority. Boyer's efforts to promote blacks into government posts were frustrated by the fact that so few blacks were literate. There were, after all, *no* public schools when Haiti gained independence in 1804. For most blacks, upward mobility was possible only through the army. Boyer did little, however, to expand educational opportunities for blacks. What is particularly interesting is that subsequent black chiefs of state, too, did little for education.

Boyer was overthrown in 1843, and a prolonged period of political instability ensued. Leyburn observes that only one of the twenty-two heads of state between 1843 and 1915 served out his prescribed term.[53] Politics was dominated by the racial issue, and the blacks, often through their influence in the army, dominated politics: mulatto presidents were in office for but eight of those seventy-two years.

The most durable of the chiefs of state was Faustin Soulouque, who acceded to the presidency by virtue of a stalemate in the senate following which his name surfaced on a whim. Soulouque, whom Leyburn describes as "an ignorant, entirely unillustrious black general,"[54] showed a wholly unexpected and perverse talent for wielding power and soon had himself crowned as Emperor Faustin I. He was overthrown in 1859 after "a 12-year nightmare."[55]

Of the chiefs of state after Soulouque, Leyburn says, "Some . . . were mildly progressive, many were indifferent; still more were actually harmful; but the lives of the mass of peasants were not often touched by presidential vagaries."[56] Political instability was accompanied by financial instability, and Haitian governments increasingly depended on foreign loans to bail themselves out.

Another U.S. intervention

In the early years of the twentieth century, French and German interests were competing with American interests — particularly the National City Bank — for a dominant position at a time of particularly flagrant financial mismanagement by the Haitian government. The U.S. State Department grew increasingly concerned that Germany might intervene militarily in Haiti because of Haiti's strategic significance: Haiti commands the Windward Passage, and there is a large deep-water harbor at Môle Saint Nicolas abutting the Passage.

These concerns were further aggravated by Haiti's descent into political chaos under President Guillaume Sam. On July 28, 1915, almost a year after the outbreak of World War I, 330 U.S. sailors and marines landed in Port-au-Prince, inaugurating a military occupation that lasted nineteen years.

Robert Rotberg observes, in his book *Haiti — The Politics of Squalor*: "Considered as an intervention, the occupation of Haiti was of a piece with the virtually simultaneous American takeover of Nicaragua and the Dominican Republic."[57] The principal U.S. motive was a strategic one, again importantly related to concerns about defending the Panama Canal. A lesser factor was the Yankee evangelism alluded to by Sumner Welles in his treatment of the Dominican occupation.

Rotberg summarizes the consequences of the occupation well:

[The United States] occupied, pacified, and administered, introduced new methods of solving old problems, suggested and provided an array of technological innovations, added significantly to the fragile and fragmentary infrastructure, improved medical and educational facilities, sought to develop the country in a general way, and, like colonial powers nearly everywhere, strove diligently to make the pattern of life in its subject dominion conform as closely as possible, and certainly in external aspects, to the cultural expectations of the dominant society. . . . Haiti certainly absorbed and reacted to American initiative in a particularly Haitian manner; it is also evident that the nature of the occupation contributed in a number of ineradicable ways to the tensions and the methods of manipulating Haitian society.[58]

Among the consequences Rotberg had in mind were the return to power of the mulattos; the destruction of the army and the creation of a small constabulary in its place; and the reinforcement of authoritarianism in the minds of the Haitian people.

As in the Dominican Republic and Nicaragua (especially with regard to Augusto César Sandino), the u.s. intervention increasingly became a rallying point for nationalism in Haiti. One expression of this nationalism was a new awareness of Haiti's African antecedents, as well as an identification of occupied Haiti's condition with the condition of colonial Africa. A group of Haitian intellectuals calling themselves *noiristes*, among them François Duvalier, propagated these concepts of *negritude*.

In 1930, the mulatto Stenio Vincent was elected president. Vincent's negotiation of the departure of the u.s. marines benefited from Franklin Roosevelt's enunciation of the Good Neighbor Policy; the last marine departed in August 1934. An American overseer of the budget remained until 1941.

Leadership: from bad to worse

Vincent continued in power, which he exercised in an authoritarian and self-serving manner, until 1941, when the rubber-stamp legislature elected him to an unconstitutional third term. The United States showed its displeasure, and Elie L. Lescot was elected instead. Lescot had been Haiti's ambassador to the United States and was a respected, experienced, and sophisticated professional. He was on Trujillo's payroll, however, and it was with the *generalísimo*'s funds that he bought his way to the presidency, where "he was transformed, like so many of his predecessors and successors, from a cautious diplomat into a megalomaniacal president; like Vincent, he regarded the occupation of Haiti's highest office as sanction for unbridled personal and presidential license, for authoritarianism and intolerance, and for a disregard of the constitutional stipulations to the contrary."[59]

Lescot was ousted by a military coup in 1946. He was succeeded by Dumarsais Estimé, a black reformer and friend of Duvalier, whom Estimé named to several important posts, including secretary of labor and public health. Estimé committed himself to major reforms in health, education, and public administration. He also expressed respect for freedom of speech, freedom of the press, and the rights of the political opposition. As Rotberg observes, however, Estimé "succumbed to the national disease which afflicted most occupants of the presidential office."[60] He became intolerant of criticism, authoritarian, and paranoiac. He also convinced himself that he was indispensable to his country and decided to succeed himself, the constitution notwithstanding. This precipitated a coup by the same military men who had ousted Lescot. One was Paul Magloire, an "amiable, hard-drinking, pleasure-loving officer,"[61] who became president (with 99 percent of the votes).

While Magloire supported several measures that facilitated economic development, and indeed the Haitian economy did show some improvement during his term in office, he succumbed to another manifestation of Haiti's presidential disease: self-enrichment. Magloire and his cronies stole and spent so blatantly that he lost much of his support. When, in Rotberg's delicate words, Magloire "indicated that he might try to avoid vacating the presidency when his term expired,"[62] his remaining support collapsed, and on December 12, 1956, he went into exile, taking with him, according to some estimates, $12 million to $28 million.

In the subsequent ten months there were five separate governments. On October 22, 1957, François Duvalier was elected president.

"Papa Doc" Duvalier arrived at the presidency with an impressive reputation: philosopher and member of the *negritude* movement; sociologist; public health specialist trained at the University of Michigan;[63] humanitarian; experienced government official and political leader. His fourteen years in power are characterized by Rotberg as "tyranny, rapacity, and an all-encompassing, disfiguring dictatorship which has surpassed all of its Third World counterparts in singlemindedness of purpose, tenacity, and lack of redeeming social and economic features."[64] The ferocity, brutality, and corruption with which Duvalier pursued his single purpose — to retain dictatorial power — have been catalogued by several authors, including Bernard Diederich and Col. Robert Heinl. Graham Greene's novel *The Comedians* trenchantly conveys the oppressive gloom, fear, and desperation of life under Papa Doc.

Duvalier died of a stroke on April 21, 1971. He was succeeded by his nineteen-year-old son, Jean Claude, who soon proclaimed himself president for life. Under the tutelage of several members of Papa Doc's inner circle, "Baby Doc" has survived for thirteen years as of this writing. His has been a less malevolent dictatorship than his father's, and some economic progress has taken place, in part because Haiti's wage structure, the lowest in the hemisphere, has attracted a number of employment-intensive industries, and in part because Haiti's plight as one of the poorest countries in the world has attracted the interest of development assistance donors.

But the evidence strongly suggests that Baby Doc is motivated by the same lust for absolute power — and wealth — that motivated his father. There is no evidence that he or his advisors have any real concern for the well-being and progress of the Haitian people.

A West African/slave culture

Haiti and the Dominican Republic make an interesting contrast. During the past two centuries they have reversed roles. St. Domingue was the richest French colony and perhaps the richest of all the New World colonies at a time when Spanish Santo Domingo was little more than a primitive backwater. As an independent country, Haiti terrorized and dominated the Dominican Republic for several decades. Today, the Dominican Republic is a middle (albeit lower-middle) income country, fairly typical of former Spanish colonies, but embarked on a promising experiment in democratic development. Haiti is among the poorest of the poor and governed by rulers

contrast

and a system more appropriate to the seventeenth century. The quality of life does not improve for the large bulk of the people. As wretched as life is for most Haitians, it could actually be deteriorating, importantly because of the Malthusian phenomenon.

Rayford W. Logan has made an effort in the concluding chapter of his book *Haiti and the Dominican Republic* to explain Haiti's decline. He cites ten factors:

1. the destructive effects of slavery
2. devastation of St. Domingue's economy during the thirteen years of war leading up to independence
3. "class-caste-color" strife
4. the large indemnity Haiti paid to France to insure its independence
5. the Haitians' hatred and fear of whites
6. Haiti's early ostracism, particularly by the pre-Civil War United States, which feared that Haiti's example would trigger an uprising of black slaves in the South
7. Haiti's fear that U.S. annexation of the Dominican Republic would result in the return of slavery to Haiti
8. the failure of the United States to effect any profound and durable changes during the nineteen-year occupation
9. overpopulation
10. the flight of trained Haitians to the North American mainland and elsewhere.

While all these factors are relevant, they seem to me to miss the basic point: there is something going on in the minds of the Haitians that impedes progress and facilitates the perpetuation of a stagnant, exploitative, repressive system.

The mindsets of three groups have to be considered: the mulatto elite, the black elite, and the black masses. We also have to consider some values and attitudes common to all groups.

To this day, the mulatto elite reflects many of the values of the nineteenth-century French plantation owners. It considers itself innately superior by virtue of the color of its skin. It views the blacks as not entirely human and doubts "the wisdom, even the possibility, of enlightening the masses."[65] It disdains manual labor: "The elite do not work with their hands. This is the cardinal rule of Haitian society."[66] It is Francophile. It is fundamentally aristocratic and antidemocratic. There is little room for noblesse oblige.

The black elite, which has governed for more than half of Haiti's one hundred seventy-eight years of independence, should have been the engine of social progress for the black masses. But this has not happened. Almost without exception, black chiefs of state have been as indifferent to the needs of their people as the mulatto presidents. On several occasions in Haitian history — the governments of Christophe, Soulouque, the six consecutive black presidents from 1879 to 1911, Estimé, Magloire, and the Duvaliers — it has been within the power of black leaders to do the one thing most likely to assure progress for their people: to educate them. They have not done so. Why? Leyburn may not have been wide of the mark when he quoted W. S. Gilbert: "When everyone is somebody, then no one's anybody."[67] As we shall see, there is evidence that the radius of identification of Haitians in *all* classes is largely confined to the family.

In *Life in a Haitian Valley*, Melville J. Herskovits examines the cultural currents that have contributed to the world view of the Haitian peasant. He concludes that West African values, attitudes, and institutions — particularly from the region of Dahomey (now Benin)[68] — have indelibly influenced the Haitian. Some examples:

- high levels of discipline: "In all this vast territory [West Africa] law and order reigned, and regimentation of behavior under kings and priests was the rule. . . . Discipline rules within the family as well as outside it and is exacted from the earliest days in the life of a child."[69]
- continuity of slavery: "In Dahomey . . . members of the ruling class were wealthy landowners who carried on large-scale production, utilizing great numbers of slaves . . . not only was the slavery to which the negroes were brought in the New World familiar to them as an institution, but work on plantations was not unknown to them."[70]
- women's roles: polygyny is common both in Benin and Haiti; women are almost exclusively responsible for marketing agricultural products.
- the profound influence of magic in religion: the roots of "Voodoo" (most scholars refer to it as "Vodun") are in Dahomey.

Leyburn observes that "Vodun is a true religion . . . it is a set of beliefs and practices which claim to deal with the spiritual forces of the universe and attempt to keep the individual in harmonious relation with them as they affect his life."[71] Vodun profoundly influences the way the Haitian peasants — and indeed many members of the elite[72] — see the world.

Vodun focuses the adherent's attention particularly on the present but also on the ancestral past. "It is a daily strength for daily needs," says Leyburn.[73] It is little concerned with the future. It explains the events that affect people's lives as the consequence of actions, often capricious, of a pantheon of hundreds of spirits called *loa*. At the heart of the religion is the requirement that the adherent propitiate the *loa*, particularly the one or ones who take special interest in him, as evidenced in ceremonies in which adherents achieve a trance-like state and are "mounted" by a *loa* who speaks through the "mounted" person. The propitiation often takes the form of animal sacrifices.

Magic is an important element of Vodun. It is practiced by Vodun priests — the male *houngans* and the female *mambus* — but particularly by

magic specialists called *bocors*. The magic can be good, as in the case of
healing through the use of "magical" potions (many of which probably
contain herbs and other plant medicinals that in fact do have curative prop-
erties). It can also be bad, as in the case of the *ouanga*, which brings "illness,
misfortune, or even death to an enemy."[74]

Vodun is not a religion that concerns itself with ethical issues: ". . .the
notions of sin and a moral law . . . are alien to Vodun,"[75] says Leyburn.
Above all, Vodun helps the Haitian survive the rigors and menaces of an
existence where survival is continually at stake. It provides him with a system
that explains worldly phenomena; through his propitiation of his *loa* he has
some sense of being able to control events affecting him; and because spec-
tacle, dancing, and feasting are central to Vodun, it is one of the few sources
of diversion in his life.

Vodun is thus one of the principal allies of the Haitian peasant in his
fight for survival, along with the extended family and hard work, particularly
by the Haitian woman.[76] But it is irrational, it propagates the view that
existence is essentially static and the world unchangeable, and it consequently tends to lock the Haitian into the status quo. One finds it hard not
to agree with Alexandre Bonneau's judgment rendered in 1862: "The shock-
ing phantasmagorias of fetishism paralyzed the development of the African
race for six thousand years. . . . The Haitian people need to break with
their past."[77]

Herskovits notes the influence of French culture as well, but it was a
French culture transmitted largely by "the flotsam and jetsam"[78] of French
society: convicts, escaped criminals, deserters, and women of the streets
made up a large part of the early French population of St. Domingue
(remarkably like the early Spanish colonists in Santo Domingo). French
culture was further distorted by the institution of slavery. Herskovits adds
his voice to the chorus of observations about the debilitating effects of
slavery:

> It is common knowledge that slavery not only affects those who are held in
> bondage, but deeply influences the master-class as well. In Haiti the role
> played by the institution of slavery in the formation of the character and
> personalities of Creole [i.e., Frenchmen born in St. Domingue] children
> brought up in a setting of servility, cupidity, brutality, and terror must
> have been of the utmost importance . . . from earliest infancy they were
> spoiled by their parents and servants; their least wishes were gratified, and
> their least complaints immediately rectified so as to make them petty ty-
> rants in their households. This tyranny was most often exercised over the
> family slaves.[79]

The slaves suffered from the excesses of the Creoles, but they also
were infected by that mistreatment and by what they observed. Herskovits
concludes, "What was bequeathed [by the French] to the Haitians . . . were

those aspects of French civilization which . . . are partly responsible not only for the graciousness, the hospitality, and the generosity of the Haitian today, but also for the less pleasant aspects of the culture . . ."[80]

While the caste system has clearly been a major obstacle to national integration and progress, a number of values and attitudes shared by the entire society also get in the way of progress.

Haiti is a country in which the extended family largely describes the radius of trust. Rotberg observes, "Nearly all Haitians share the attitudes of rivalry, suspicion, and intrigue that are so particularly apparent in rural life. . . . To persuade rural and urban Haitians to cooperate, or to concert their efforts to a mutually desirable end, is difficult and usually unrewarding."[81] While family life is far from idyllic (again Rotberg: "The extent of vitriol, invective, bitterness and discourtesy toward one's compatriots, relatives, or mistresses surpasses imagination."[82]), it is clear that Haitians do identify their own interests with those of family members. But those beyond the family are usually mistrusted and feared.

Shortly after I arrived in Haiti in 1977, I set up a meeting for all the Haitian and American members of the USAID staff. The purpose was to discuss the direction of our programs: I wanted to find out how much support they had, what criticisms there were, and what ideas for new directions might surface. The session was dominated by the Haitian employees, who vented their feelings on a number of issues transcending my agenda, e.g., their concerns about being second-class citizens within a u.s. government mission where they were subordinated to Americans; their embarrassment at Haiti's political and economic failures as a nation; their difficulties even in getting along with one another. The emotionally charged discussion reached a climax when one of the most respected Haitian employees observed, "Our fundamental problem is that we don't care enough about one another." Another Haitian responded, "But we do within our families."

The word "paranoia" recurs in analytical writings on Haiti. Rotberg observes, ". . . there are states of mania and depression and paranoia, the magnification of imagined slights, and a kind of sullenness that seems to be as much a product of healthy apathy as of fear."[83] There are obvious historical roots to Haitian paranoia: as the first independent black nation, it was virtually ostracized for decades, particularly, until the u.s. Civil War, by the United States, which feared the example of a slave uprising. Skin color has also contributed to paranoia: most Haitians — black and mulatto — are convinced that inferiority *does* attach to color.[84] And, as we shall see, child-rearing practices may also be relevant.

Rotberg draws an interesting parallel between Haiti and Sicily. Internal communications in both are difficult because of jagged mountain ranges. Both have suffered from acute erosion and declining agricultural productivity. Both have known extraordinary violence, brutality, and corruption. But it is the parallel in world views that is particularly interesting, and reminiscent of Banfield's Montegrano:

. . . passive obedience [is] the norm. . . . Admiration was reserved for those who knew how to defend and enrich themselves by their own strength and influence. . . . Both have also been closed societies in which becoming a man of respect and achieving status have traditionally seemed aspirations more important than mutual activity directed at the furtherance of the commonweal . . . both . . . have depended upon their relations with a local boss, a "big man" . . . suspicion predominates in such societies, and association with others is anathema.[85]

Rotberg quotes Dantès Bellegarde, a Haitian who wrote critically of his own society in 1901:

Everyone has two faces — one for those above him and one for those below. Flattery is preferred to frankness. A friend is abandoned as soon as he is no longer useful. Those in power also appear to have lost any ability to discriminate, for they are taken in by all manner of lies, they give favors to those who deceive them, and they are angry with those who are too proud to sink to the indignities of flattery . . .[86]

It is also Rotberg who suggests that child-rearing practices, some of them similar to those in the Dominican Republic, contribute to Haiti's political problems and the cultural/psychological obstacles they reflect:

. . . most Haitians seem to rear their children in a manner that is traumatic and conducive to later conflict. . . . Haitian children are highly indulged and learn to expect immediate and intense physical gratification, but lack the concurrent satisfaction of . . . ego-sustaining and ego-developing nurturance . . . Haitian children become deficient in . . . basic trust. The Haitian boy is unready for justice, stunted in his appreciation of the meaning of moral responsibility . . . he despairs of his own potency as an autonomous individual. . . . Because of the harsh ways in which he is forced to grovel before authority, he begins to think of himself as inferior and inadequate and rejects the impulses toward cooperation and mastery . . . at the age of seven or eight, according to Herskovits, hitherto totally dependent, he is suddenly encouraged to become completely independent . . . when he disobeys . . . he is faced with . . . tantrums and severe corporal punishment. He rapidly learns to submit totally, to repress his aggressive, masterly responses, and never to express independent autonomous resistance to authority . . . he learns helplessness and despair.[87]

The insight of Placide David, a Haitian in exile writing in 1959, is particularly poignant:

Our souls are like dead leaves. We live in indifference, are silently malcontent . . . the most flagrant violation of our rights and the most outrageous abuse of authority provokes among us merely submission.[88]

The only hope: cultural change

The foregoing analysis of Haiti's history describes a static society "caught firmly in the grip of a viselike social structure," to use Rotberg's phrase.[89] But Haiti, for all its isolation, is not impervious to external cultural currents. The u.s. occupation reinforced the inferiority feelings of Haitians, but it also helped both to unify them and to expose them, for the first time on a national scale, to a different way of seeing the world. The opening up of Haitian culture has been accelerated by the communications explosion and, particularly, by the migration of hundreds of thousands of Haitians to the United States and Canada. They are not only a major source of income for their families who remain in Haiti; they are also a source of information about the outside world and contribute to breaking the cultural molds that have locked Haitians into poverty.

The phenomenon of the Haitian boat people is not only a flight from desperate poverty. After all, Haitians have been living at the edge of survival since slaves were first brought to St. Domingue. It is also a flight to opportunity, and the phenomenon depends on the awareness of people that opportunity exists. This awareness is now widespread in Haiti. Those who migrate learn to see the world very differently. But even those who stay are affected.

The elite subculture is also changing. Their children are increasingly exposed to the United States and Canada, either because they are educated there, do business there, or both. The racial revolution in the United States is felt in Haiti, as is the racial tolerance of Canada. The Haitian elite is increasingly uncomfortable with its traditional racism and with its own responsibility for Haiti's backwardness.

Haitian culture is changing. But it remains the principal obstacle to progress. I conclude this chapter with excerpts from a recent article in *The Baltimore Sun*, based on an interview with an American Baptist missionary, Dr. Wallace Hodges, who had spent more than twenty years in the town of Limbé, some twenty miles from Cape Haitian:[90]

> [Dr. Hodges] has developed a theory as to why Haiti . . . is one of the poorest [countries] in the world.
>
> It is a theory based on culture, not race; on belief, not ability. It puts the blame for Haiti's plight squarely with the "voodoo spirits" that still hold dominant influence over the lives of these people.
>
> Haiti, Dr. Hodges says, "has a special vision of the world," created by its African roots and tempered by its experience of slavery . . .
>
> "Haitians see the nature of events much differently than we do," he said.
>
> The basic difference is that the Judeo-Christian tradition makes man responsible for his destiny. "By internalizing guilt we hold ourselves responsible for what happens, and what to do about it."
>
> In contrast, the Haitian externalizes his guilt. He attributes every-

thing, the good as well as the bad, to the spirits. Since this limits his responsibility . . . it also limits his potential.

At its simplest, it means that if a Haitian steals a jug of milk from Dr. Hodge's hospital, he has no shame because he believes he was given the opportunity by the spirits.

On a more complex level, it means that there is a limit to the "intensification" of Haitian society: to how organized that society can become, how advanced its agriculture can be.

"A child is made to understand immediately that he is surrounded by these menacing forces, and that everything that happens is due to them. He is raised to externalize evil and to understand he is in continuous danger.

"People believe that the real reason Haitians want to leave is that they are afraid of the government. That is superficial. They are afraid of each other. You will find a high degree of paranoia in Haiti . . ."

NOTES

1. Adam Smith, *Wealth of Nations*, p. 538.
2. Frank Moya Pons, *Historia Colonial de Santo Domingo*, p. 54. Most of my treatment of early Dominican history derives from this book.
3. Samuel Hazard, *Santo Domingo Past and Present with a Glance at Hayti*, pp. 25, 34.
4. Moya Pons, p. 55.
5. Hazard, *Past and Present*, p. 49.
6. Moya Pons, *Santo Domingo*, p. 201.
7. *Ibid.*, p. 255.
8. Figures in this paragraph derive from Moya Pons, *Santo Domingo*, pp. 303 – 314 passim, and Hazard, *Past and Present*, p. 105.
9. Hazard, *Past and Present*, p. 103.
10. Moya Pons, *Santo Domingo*, p. 405.
11. Interestingly, up to 1843, not one country had extended recognition to the black nation. This was one of the factors that alienated the Spanish side.
12. *Ibid.*, p. 247. By the count of Otto Schoenrich in his *Santo Domingo: a Country with a Future*, p. 334, there were twenty-three successful revolutions in the Dominican Republic between 1844 and 1914.
13. *Ibid.*, p. 189. Haitian attacks on the Dominican Republic during the first half of the nineteenth century have left indelible scars on the Dominican psyche. In late 1965, during the first weeks of Hector García Godoy's provisional presidency, I was invited to an informal evening meeting of Dominican technocrats to discuss reconstruction and development priorities following the 1965 revolution and U.S. intervention. After a few minutes of desultory discussion of the announced subject of the meeting, talk shifted to "The Haitian problem," and that was all that was discussed for the rest of the evening.
14. Quoted in John Bartlow Martin, *Overtaken by Events*, p. 23.
15. Otto Schoenrich, *Santo Domingo*, p. 64. Lest we give too much credence to Schoenrich's judgments, I quote the last paragraph (p. 395) of Schoenrich's book, published in 1918 during the U.S. Marine occupation: "The curtain has gone down upon the epoch of revolution, conspiracies, civil wars and destruction. That period belongs to the past as definitely as the era of freebooters and pirates. A new era has begun for beautiful Quisqueya [the Taino name for Hispaniola], in which, under the protection of the Stars and Stripes, it is destined to enjoy a greater measure of freedom, progress and prosperity than its inhabitants have ever dreamed."

16. *Ibid.*, p. 72.
17. *Ibid.*
18. Cáceres was the grandfather of Hector García Godoy, who was widely admired for the intelligent and effective job he did bringing a divided nation together.
19. Sumner Welles, *Naboth's Vineyard: The Dominican Republic 1844 – 1924*, p. 917. Welles goes on to editorialize: "All sense of proportion was lost." It can be argued that the same evangelical streak has continued to influence U.S. policies toward Latin America, e.g., in the Alliance for Progress, in the Carter administration's emphasis on human rights, and in the Reagan administration's emphasis on free enterprise.
20. *Ibid.*, p. 900.
21. Robert D. Crassweller, *Trujillo: The Life and Times of a Caribbean Dictator*, p. 39.
22. The U.S. government was afraid the extreme left would control a "constitutionalist" government, which is why Lyndon Johnson ordered the intervention. Had Juan Bosch returned to the Dominican Republic from exile in Puerto Rico, he might have overcome U.S. fears. After all, how could we oppose the return to power of the president whom the Dominican people had chosen in the 1962 elections that we had worked so hard to set up? But Bosch, afraid for his safety, chose not to return.
23. Dependency-theory conventional wisdom has it that the U.S. worked for Balaguer's victory. In fact, U.S. Ambassador John Hugh Crimmins and several members of the U.S. mission (including myself) were rooting for Bosch.
24. Balaguer personally approved virtually every expenditure made by the Dominican government. When then Undersecretary of State Nicholas Katzenbach visited Santo Domingo a few years after the revolution, Balaguer said to him, "I spend almost all my waking time, seven days a week, running a small country. What I can't understand is how it is humanly possible for President Johnson to run the United States."
25. He tragically committed suicide just a few weeks before turning over power to Jorge Blanco.
26. Martin, *Overtaken by Events*, p. 724. Juan Bosch restates this thesis in his *Composición Social Dominicana*, Colección Pensamiento y Cultura, Santo Domingo, 1970, p. 9. "We became a country of the West, not of the most developed models of Europe, but of the Spanish model. Spain transmitted to us everything it had: its language, its architecture, its religion, its dress and its food, its military tradition and its juridical and civil institutions; wheat, livestock, sugar cane, even our dogs and chickens. But we couldn't receive from Spain Western methods of production and distribution, technique, capital, and the ideas of European society, because Spain didn't have them. We knew the evangel but not the works of Erasmus."
27. *Ibid.*, p. 725.
28. *Ibid.*
29. *Ibid.*, p. 719.
30. *Ibid.*, pp. 719 – 20. One is reminded of the opening pages of Banfield's *The Moral Basis of a Backward Society*.
31. José Ramón López, *La Paz en la República Dominicana (Peace in the Dominican Republic)*, p. 102.
32. *Ibid.*, p. 123. Like Mendieta, López called for a campaign to stress cooperation.
33. Howard J. Wiarda, *Dictatorship, Development and Disintegration*, Volume I, pp. 17, 19.
34. *Ibid.*, pp. 19 – 20. Wiarda emphasizes that, in the Dominican case, below the white, clearly Hispanic culture, there is a complex and mystifying combination of Spanish and Afro-Haitian cultures which, on the one hand, has been used by the elite to rigidify social stratification but represents, on the other, a massive threat to the position of the whites. The popularity and charisma of the PRD's José Francisco Peña Gómez, who has Haitian antecedents, is a case in point.
35. Gerald F. Murray, *La Loma: Paternalism in a Caribbean Community*.
36. *Ibid.*, p. 73.
37. *Ibid.*, p. 177.

38. *Ibid.*, p. 179.
39. Kenneth Evan Sharpe, *Peasant Politics: Struggle in a Dominican Village*, pp. 133, 179.
40. André and Andrée Corten, *Cambio Social en Santo Domingo (Social Change in Santo Domingo)*, pp. 76, 77.
41. Malcolm T. Walker, *Politics and the Power Structure: A Rural Community in the Dominican Republic*, p. 107.
42. Wiarda, *Dictatorship*, p. 137.
43. Walker, *Politics and Power Structure*, p. 105.
44. *Ibid.*, p. 108.
45. *Ibid.*, p. 107.
46. *Ibid.*
47. *Ibid.*
48. From a speech entitled "Raices del Problema Dominicano" ("Roots of the Dominican Problem") delivered at the American Chamber of Commerce in Santo Domingo on October 27, 1982.
49. James G. Leyburn, *The Haitian People*, p. 41.
50. *Ibid.*, p. 65.
51. No one has yet adequately explained how the Citadel was going to deter a French attack on Haiti. It was built on top of a remote northern mountain. Its only military utility was to withstand a siege — it could have supported and protected several thousand soldiers for an extended period. But there would have been nothing to prevent the French from moving around it to take control of the country. It was an extraordinary feat of construction, but hundreds and perhaps thousands of Haitians lost their lives building it.
52. The French subsequently reduced the indemnity to 60 million francs payable in thirty years.
53. Leyburn, *The Haitian People*, p. 89.
54. *Ibid.*, p. 91.
55. *Ibid.*
56. *Ibid.*, p. 93.
57. Robert Rotberg, *Haiti: The Politics of Squalor*, p. 109.
58. *Ibid.*
59. *Ibid.*, p. 168.
60. *Ibid.*, p. 174.
61. Herbert Gold, "Caribbean Caudillo: Magloire of Haiti" (quoted in Rotberg, p. 183).
62. Rotberg, *Politics of Squalor*, p. 185.
63. He did not do well in his studies, did not receive a degree, and was not asked back.
64. Rotberg, *Politics of Squalor*, pp. 197–98.
65. Leyburn, *The Haitian People*, p. 41.
66. *Ibid.*, p. 4.
67. *Ibid.*, p. 81.
68. Interestingly, the indicators of progress for Haiti and Benin are quite close to one another:

	Haiti	Benin
Per-capita GNP	$270	$310
Adult literacy	23%	25%
Life expectancy	53 years	47 years

69. Melville J. Herskovits, *Life in a Haitian Valley*, p. 23.
70. *Ibid.*, p. 26.
71. Leyburn, *The Haitian People*, p. 134.

72. A mulatto colleague in the USAID mission in Port-au-Prince, who held a master's degree from a U.S. university, once told me there is no Haitian — himself included — who wholly rejects Vodun.

73. Leyburn, *The Haitian People*, p. 165.

74. *Ibid.*, p. 160. During my two years in Haiti, the son-in-law of our cook, an educated young man with a good job and recently married to our cook's attractive and educated daughter, took sick and became convinced that the illness was the result of a *ouanga* placed on him by a jealous male acquaintance. He was treated in one of Port-au-Prince's better hospitals, but no threatening disease was diagnosed. He also sought the help of a *houngan*. Neither was of any avail. He died absolutely convinced he had been irretrievably cursed.

75. *Ibid.*, p. 144.

76. Leyburn, *The Haitian People* (p. 201) quotes Sir Harry Johnston's observations in 1910: "The women are the best part of the nation. They are splendid, unremitting toilers . . . such industry . . . should make Haiti one of the richest countries in the world. . . ." (from *The Negro in the New World*, pp. 196 – 97).

77. Quoted by Leyburn, p. 141, from *Haiti: Ses Progres — Son Avenir*, Paris, 1862, pp. 24 – 25.

78. Herskovits, *Haitian Valley*, p. 35.

79. *Ibid.*, pp. 41 – 42.

80. *Ibid.*, p. 47.

81. Rotberg, *Politics of Squalor*, pp. 17, 18.

82. *Ibid.*, p. 4.

83. *Ibid.*, p. 4.

84. Leyburn, *The Haitian People*, p. 83, observes that most Haitians prefer white priests because "colored baptism will not stick."

85. Rotberg, *Politics of Squalor*, pp. 7 – 9.

86. From *Dessalines a Parlé*, Port-au-Prince, 1948, pp. 303 – 4, quoted in Rotberg, p. 18.

87. *Ibid.*, pp. 19 – 22; Herskovits's treatment of child-rearing (pp. 99 – 101, 122 – 127) lends credibility to Rotberg's analysis.

88. Placide David, *L'Heritage Colonial en Haiti*, Madrid, 1959, pp. 210 – 211; quoted in Rotberg, p. 23.

89. Rotberg, *Politics of Squalor*, p. 5.

90. Wallace Hodges, "Poverty Linked to Voodoo Spirits," *The Baltimore Sun*, November 15, 1981.

5

Barbados and Haiti

Barbados is the second most affluent Caribbean nation, after petroleum-exporting Trinidad and Tobago. According to a *World Development Report 1982* table[1] for countries with fewer than one million people, Barbados's per-capita GNP was $3,040 in 1980. Adult literacy was 99 percent, life expectancy seventy-one years.

Barbados is tiny — 166 square miles, about the size of Martha's Vineyard. Its population numbers about 250,000, making it one of the most densely populated countries in the world, with 1,506 people per square mile. (Haiti's population density is about 550 per square mile.)

Barbados has no commercially exploited mineral resources. Its soil is reasonably fertile, but the topsoil is shallow. The easternmost of the Caribbean islands, it sits in the middle of "Hurricane Alley."

While it had been inhabited by Arawak and Carib Indians, and visited by both Spanish and Portuguese explorers in the sixteenth century, Barbados was uninhabited when it was claimed in 1625 by an Englishman, John Powell, who was traveling from Brazil to England. Eighty English colonists returned in 1627, from which date the island has been continuously settled.

With the help of Indians imported from Guyana, the English planted food crops as well as cotton and tobacco. Agriculture prospered, and the population grew rapidly. Initially, Barbados was owned by a stock company, and the colonists, who were "tenants at will," were treated fairly. But when James I awarded Barbados to the Earl of Carlisle, the fortune of the settlers changed for the worse. Their condition was now closer to that of serfs, and they resisted Carlisle's policies and governors at every turn. The resistance forced Governor Henry Hawley to acquiesce in the establishment of a House of Burgesses in 1639. Some form of representative government has existed ever since.

When Philip Bell was appointed governor in 1641, there were 10,000 Englishmen, many of whom had fought for the revival of the English Parliament, which occurred in 1640 after an eleven-year lapse. Bell, "a wise, honest and just man,"[2] strengthened the House of Burgesses by assuring appropriate geographic representation and by empowering it to pass laws.

The English Civil War, which began in 1642, precipitated the migration to Barbados of large numbers from each of the contending factions: the Monarchists (or "Cavaliers"), and the "Roundheads," who supported Parliament. Governor Bell successfully avoided confrontation for several years, but by 1650 Monarchists had gained the ascendancy in Barbados, even as the Roundheads and Oliver Cromwell won out in England. Notwithstanding the conciliatory policies of Bell's successor, Francis Lord Willoughby, Parliament sent a fleet to subdue Monarchist Barbados. After an extended blockade, the fleet commander, Sir George Ayscue, succeeded in getting the support of moderate Cavaliers, which led Willoughby to capitulate. The surrender agreement, ratified by the English Parliament on August 18, 1652, confirmed some important rights to the Barbadians:

1. That liberty of conscience in matters of religion was to be allowed to all.[3]
2. That no taxes, customs, imposts, loans and excise should be levied on the inhabitants of Barbados without their consent in a General Assembly.
3. That all port-towns and cities under the English Parliament's power should be open to the people of the island and that trade should be free with all nations that traded amicably with England.
4. That the government of the island should be by a Governor, Council and Assembly, the Governor to be appointed by the States of England, the Council to be chosen by him and the Assembly to be elected by the freeholders of the island in the several parishes.[4]

A sugar economy

Until the late 1630s, tobacco had been the principal cash crop. It was grown with the labor of white indentured servants, who were assured of some money and a piece of land after working, virtually as slaves, for five or seven years. But when the higher-quality Virginia tobacco began to be produced in quantity, Barbados had to seek a new crop. The first sugar cane was introduced from Brazil in 1637. It was ideally suited to Barbados's soil and climate, and the sugar economy boomed, with land values increasing by as much as thirty-five times.

White indentured labor could not meet the demands of highly labor-intensive sugar production, and Barbadian planters began to import black slaves from Africa. The slaves came from essentially the same areas of West Africa as those brought to Haiti by the French. By 1645 there were 5,680 blacks in Barbados and 36,600 whites, of which 11,200 were smallholders (owners of small farms). By 1684, the number of blacks had grown to 60,000, while the number of whites had declined to about 15,000, as the profitability of sugar production carried land beyond the reach of freedmen and inevitably caused many smallholders to sell their land and emigrate. Treatment of the blacks by the whites was "probably . . . worse than in any other sugar colony,"[5] and the first slave uprising occurred in 1675. It was put down brutally.

A combination of the sugar boom and the political tranquillity brought about by the 1652 agreements produced what is sometimes referred to as Barbados's Golden Age. Prosperity lasted little more than a decade, however. The intense sugar monoculture resulted in the buildup of pests and exhaustion of the land. Drought aggravated the agricultural problem, and the island was ravaged repeatedly by epidemics of smallpox, yellow fever, and other diseases. In 1675, a major hurricane devastated Barbados. And wide fluctuations in world sugar prices took their toll.

But a number of sugar plantations continued to prosper and, with the franchise limited to property holders, the planters controlled the House of Assembly, which frequently was in conflict with the Crown-appointed governors. One such point of conflict was a 4½ percent duty on exports, payable to the Crown, which was imposed in 1663 and endured for 175 years. The House swallowed it but steadily pressed for an increase in its own powers (House members frequently referred to themselves as members of a parliament) and a concomitant diminution in the powers of the governor.

While the "plantocracy" was the dominant group among the whites, a middle class emerged composed of professionals, merchants, craftsmen, and farmers with medium-sized holdings. By the early eighteenth century, the middle class accounted for 25 percent of the total white population of about 20,000. The black slave population stabilized at about 60,000.

Slow but steady social progress

It was at this time that the first efforts to improve the conditions of the slaves occurred. George Fox, founder of the Quakers, had visited Barbados in 1671 and urged his followers to prepare their slaves for freedom. The first concrete steps occurred in 1710, eight years after another slave uprising was brutally suppressed. In 1710, Christoper Codrington, an affluent planter, died and bequeathed his holdings to an Anglican missionary organization, the Society for the Propagation of the Gospel, for the purpose of educating and making Christians of the slaves. (The slaves practiced an African religion similar to Vodun called Obeah, some residues of which persist to this day.) Bishop William Fleetwood gave the Society's Annual Sermon in 1711 and averred that the blacks "were equally the Workmanship of God with (the planters) . . . with the same faculties and intellectual powers . . . and bodies of the same Flesh and Blood, and Souls certainly immortal."[6]

The planters correctly viewed the Society as a threat to the plantocracy system and did everything they could to resist and undermine it. At the outset, the Society confined its concerns to the spiritual well-being of the slaves and did not promote reform of the system. The Christianizing of the blacks was to coexist with their slavery. But black participation in the Anglican Church inevitably led both blacks and whites to see one another and the world differently. "The slaves were given their first chance in British West Indian history to participate in a form of social organization in which they could attain a measure of social recognition and find some scope for individual talents and satisfy their desire for self-expression."7 The whites increasingly came to realize that the blacks were indeed human beings.

It was not long before English concern for the souls of the blacks evolved into a movement to abolish slavery throughout the empire. Among those whose voices spurred the movement were John Wesley, Thomas Paine, and Adam Smith. In 1772, the Chief Justice of England, Lord Mansfield, declared that all slaves in England must be recognized as free. In 1807, the slave trade was abolished.

The planters of Barbados were increasingly alarmed by these developments. Their only recourse to slow the momentum toward emancipation was to improve the living conditions of the slaves, thereby neutralizing one of the principal arguments of the abolitionists. The slaves were thus better fed and clothed, and in 1805 the House repealed an old statute that punished the murder of a slave with a fifteen-pound fine, substituting a law that made such a murder a capital offense. But the slaves, many of them now literate, were aware of the rapid movement toward emancipation in England and of the successful uprising in 1803 of the blacks in Saint Domingue. Their hopes were aroused, and they were increasingly mistrustful of the intentions of the planters. The result was the slave uprising of 1816, which resulted in the deaths of 390 blacks, more than half of them by execution after trial by court martial. One white lost his life.

Another threat to the plantocracy emerged at about the same time. As mentioned earlier, farmers with medium-sized holdings — sometimes referred to as the "ten-acre men" — were an important element of the middle class. They formed the Salmagundi party and started publishing a newspaper in 1818. In 1819 the Salmagundi won control of the Assembly, and the plantocracy shifted its attention from the threat of emancipation to the threat from the middle class.

Yet another group with growing influence in this increasingly pluralistic environment was formed by colored freedmen, who numbered more than 5,000 in 1829. Some were so successful they became members of the plantocracy, accumulating hundreds of acres of land. Others became successful merchants and craftsmen. Free colored women ran prosperous inns and taverns. But the majority were poor, and a statute that blatantly discriminated against all free colored people was on the books until emancipation. Interestingly, as in Haiti, the free mulattos disdained the blacks, much as did the agricultural elite.

Emancipation

The Emancipation Act was finally passed in August 1833, with an effective date of August 1834. The act legislated a transition period during which domestic servants were to be apprentices for four years and field workers for six. As apprentices, they received partial wages.

Slave owners in nearby Antigua ignored the apprenticeship clauses and moved forthwith to a full wage system. But, as Hoyos observes, "The apprenticeship system was rigidly and severely administered in Barbados from the outset. Friction was, therefore, inevitable and this embittered the relations between masters and apprentices."[8] As a result, the Assembly ended the apprenticeship system in 1838.

But the freed slaves had few options because land was so limited. In Jamaica, former slaves moved into the mountains and formed "new villages" away from the sugar plantations. While a few such villages appeared in Barbados, the large majority of newly freed blacks remained as paid workers on the plantations they had worked as slaves.

Emancipation produced a striking change of attitude among free colored people. Whereas before they in no way identified themselves with the slaves, after emancipation they assumed a tutelary responsibility for the blacks, at the same time that they were welding themselves into a unified group. The colored leaders "sought to build their own institutions within their group. They trained their followers in habits of hard work, sacrifice and self-help and, in all their efforts to promote their welfare, they demonstrated their attachment to representative institutions . . . after emancipation they took the recently liberated slaves under their wing and persuaded them to accept their habits, their life style and their philosophy."[9] The contrast with the Haitian elite is noteworthy.

Samuel Jackman Prescod was the principal colored leader. He edited the colored newspaper, and was the first colored man to be elected to the Assembly, in 1843. He quickly built an alliance with the white "ten-acre men" and was soon the leader of a Liberal Party contingent of nine in the Assembly.

Political liberalization was paralleled by expansion of educational opportunities. A Charity School for colored and black children was established in 1818. The first private school for colored boys was established the same year, and a similar school for girls opened its doors in 1825. A school for poor whites was started in 1819. Secondary schools soon followed. Codrington College was upgraded to the university level in 1875. As Hoyos observes, "the new system was unduly influenced by the demands of a class conscious society. Yet, by the facilities and improvements it offered, it provided opportunities, however limited by our present-day standards, for the upward social mobility of the people of Barbados."[10]

The political and educational ferment notwithstanding, the rich planters continued to dominate Barbadian politics, principally because the franchise was still linked to property. The only effective counter to the disproportionate influence of the oligarchy was the Crown, which, following emancipation, recognized that it would have to serve as the advocate of the former slaves and poor whites. The Colonial Office thus adopted a policy aimed at restructuring the legislatures of the West Indies within a Crown Colony system that would give the governor the power to assure balance in the legislature. By 1875, all the British islands except the Bahamas, Bermuda, and Barbados were Crown Colonies. At that time, there were about 105,000 blacks, 40,000 mulattos, and 15,000 whites in Barbados.

British efforts to establish the Crown Colony system in Barbados were stoutly resisted by the Assembly. But the Crown was supported by the Barbadian lower classes. Violence erupted in April 1876, in which eight people died and eighty-nine estates were damaged. A compromise ensued that expanded the franchise and assured that elected representatives would sit on the governor's council.

It was at this time that subsidized European beet sugar production threatened to wipe out Barbados's sugar industry, on which the island's economy depended totally. The prolonged beet-sugar-induced depression was aggravated by a drought in 1894 that brought in its wake several pests that attacked the cane. A hurricane devastated the already prostrated island in 1898.

Barbados's economy was saved by four consecutive external events: the Cuban insurgency under José Martí, which started in 1895 and pursued a scorched-earth policy, reducing Cuban sugar exports, which competed with Barbadian exports; the Spanish – American War, which reduced Cuban exports further and also seriously affected the Puerto Rican sugar industry; the elimination of beet sugar subsidies by European governments in 1903; and the construction of the Panama Canal, which attracted large numbers of Barbadian workers who remitted a good part of their pay to relatives in Barbados.

Diversification into cotton helped. So did the fledgling tourism industry. But emigration was still the only hope for many Barbadians. Many migrated to the United States.

Economic problems did not block social progress, however. Relief programs were instituted for the poor. A vital statistics system was established. And a rural water supply system was built.

Barbados experienced a major boom between 1914 and 1920. European sugar beet production was disrupted by World War I, world sugar prices skyrocketed, and the island enjoyed bumper crops. The bust came in 1921, and emigration once again accelerated. Many Barbadians depended on remittances from abroad. Economic problems contributed to pressures for political and social reform as they would again during the Great Depression.

Toward real democracy

The history of Barbados from the years after World War I to the present is marked by a steady evolution toward a more equitable society. When one looks at the distribution of political power sixty years ago and today, it is apparent that dramatic changes have been wrought. Some of the highlights along the way:

- 1921 — establishment of the income tax
- mid-1920s — important strides in public health, education, and social security
- 1924 — formation of the democratic socialist Democratic League and election of several of its members to the Assembly in subsequent years
- 1938 — formation of the Barbados Progressive League, led by Grantley Adams, some of whose ancestors were slaves, following in the footsteps of the Democratic League
- 1942 — liberalization of the franchise
- 1946 — liberal parties control a majority of seats in the Assembly; the plantocracy loses control
- 1951 — full adult franchise
- 1954 — Grantley Adams named premier
- 1958 — cabinet system of government inaugurated
- 1961 — Adams's party, now called the Barbados Labor Party (BLP), defeated by the further-left Democratic Labor Party (DLP); Errol Barrows, a black, becomes prime minister
- early 1960s — major social reforms
- 1966 — independence achieved
- 1976 — Barrow and DLP suffer overwhelming defeat at hands of J. M. G. "Tom" Adams (Sir Grantley's son) and BLP
- 1981 — Adams reelected

Political parties responsive to the principally black lower classes have thus dominated Barbadian politics for more than thirty-five years. They have built on a substantial base of social progress reaching back more than two hundred years to produce a society whose achievements in health and education are comparable to those of the developed countries. These liberal governments have also stimulated free-market economic development, particularly in tourism and manufacturing, which has brought high levels of prosperity to the island.

Explaining the striking contrast

Haiti and Barbados have several things in common. Both are island nations; they share essentially the same climate. Both have depended principally on one crop for extended periods, and have only moderate natural resource endowments. The large majority of their people have ancestral roots in West Africa. Both countries experienced long periods of enslavement of blacks. Both are today extremely densely populated.

There the similarities end. Haiti is one of the world's poorest countries, suffers from low levels of literacy, faces serious health problems, and has most often been ruled — as it is currently — by self-seeking autocrats who for the most part ignored popular needs and aspirations. Barbados is among the most affluent of the middle-income countries; its achievements in education and health rank it with the developed countries; and its democracy is both of long duration and responsive to the popular will.

How can one explain the vast differences between Haiti's and Barbados's development? The argument can be made that it has been much easier for Barbados to develop because it is so much smaller, in both population and area. There is probably some truth in this. A smaller country may find it easier to establish a national identity, and small size may help break down social barriers such as caste and clan. But Barbados has not developed very differently from Jamaica and Trinidad and Tobago, both of which are much larger in both population and area.[11]

My own belief is that Barbados's absorption of British culture over three hundred years is the principal explanation of its success. The liberalization of Barbadian society is closely linked to the liberalization of British society. Barbados's experience with representative government, however rudimentary and elitist, began in 1639. A link between taxation and representation was forged in 1652. Christopher Codrington's 1710 bequest for the education and Christianizing of blacks was the first of a series of acts of noblesse oblige leading to emancipation in 1834. Subsequently, the British parliament served as advocate for the freed slaves within a political system dominated by the plantocracy. Social reform proceeded apace throughout the nineteenth and twentieth centuries. Political dominance shifted from the affluent few to the predominantly black middle and lower classes in 1946, where it has remained.

It is not just "enlightened colonialism" that is in play.[12] It is not just the imposition by a colonial power of European institutions that results in elections, a free press, literacy, and public health programs. It is also the absorption by the colonized people of the colonial power's values and attitudes *over an extended period* that gives vitality and durability to the imported institutions. I stress "over an extended period" because the evidence (e.g., the u.s. occupations of Nicaragua, Haiti, and the Dominican Republic) is that brief colonial experiences make only a superficial imprint on culture and leave imposed institutions (e.g., the "*apolitical*" National Guard in Nicaragua) which soon revert to their precolonial condition.

What appears to have happened in Barbados is that British values and attitudes have largely supplanted the African culture of the slaves, which was modified, usually in destructive ways, by the experience of slavery in the New World. A colleague has referred to the Barbadians as "Afro-Saxons." I think it is more accurate to think of them as black Englishmen.

The combination of seventeenth- and eighteenth-century African culture with New World slavery bred a culture largely focused on survival in those places where it was sealed off from effective contact with more dynamic, progressive cultures — as in Haiti and the southern United States. Attitudes about work were negative or ambivalent. People outside the family were mistrusted; the obsession with survival in the present impeded thinking about the future, planning for it, sacrificing for it; irrational religions discouraged the development of the idea that human beings can importantly influence their destinies.

The same Protestant values that both contributed to and reflected British social and economic progress took root in Barbados. These values included fair play, cooperation, social responsibility, and achievement.

The Barbadian anthem includes the lines:

A pride that makes no wanton boast
Of what it has withstood;
That binds our hearts from coast to coast:
The pride of nationhood.[13]

George Hunte observes, "From pride stems that optimism which is the official creed of the islanders."[14] Hunte also quotes former Prime Minister Grantley Adams: "Cricket is the religion of Barbados." Hunte goes on to say, "For undoubtedly the cricketer who is circumscribed by rules approved by gentlemen is bound by standards of conduct which equate to 'playing the game.' The quality of Barbadian life and its codes of conduct owe as much to cricket as to any other single activity. The game of life follows the rules of cricket."[15]

Economic achievement

I have observed in earlier chapters that democratic stability, continuity, and freedom facilitate economic progress by providing an environment that encourages long-range planning and risk-taking. The "optimism" of which Hunte speaks is relevant in this connection. Yet Barbados is not noted for entrepreneurial activity:

Barbadians must accept the need to work for a living and whenever incentives are great enough may even work harder than most. The basic philosophy of the Barbadian, however, is that enough is as good as a feast and that when there is a choice between work for work's sake and work to satisfy human needs it is better to choose the latter alternative.[16]

On the other hand, English-speaking West Indians who have migrated to the United States have been high achievers. In a 1979 article in the *Wilson Quarterly*, Thomas Sowell pointed out that first-generation West Indian blacks earned 94 percent of the average U.S. family median income in 1969, compared with 62 percent for North American blacks. Second-generation West Indian blacks *exceeded* the national average.

Sowell also observes that the descendants of black freedmen ("free persons of color") in the United States, who numbered 488,000 in 1860, have done far better than the descendants of emancipated slaves. He attributes the substantially higher achievement of West Indian blacks and the descendants of American freedmen importantly to the degree to which their early circumstances encouraged self-reliance:

> In the West Indies, slaves grew their own food and sold the surplus in the market, while slaves in the United States were issued food or were fed from communal kitchens. In other words, even under slavery, blacks in the West Indies had generations of experience with individual rewards for individual efforts, in at least part of their lives. By contrast, slaves in the United States lived in regimented dependence. Paradoxically (given the greater brutality of West Indian slavery), post-emancipation race relations and job opportunities for blacks were better in the West Indies than in the United States.[18]

Sowell concludes:

> The real differences . . .are cultural, as further evidenced by their social separateness from each other even in an era of "black solidarity" rhetoric. That one group has a fertility rate above the national average while the other does not have even enough children to reproduce itself is indicative of fundamental differences in values and aspirations . . .in those schools where native black children have been successfully educated, the principal difference has been the attitude of parents and students — not physical plant, student-teacher ratios, or "innovative" methods.[19]

Galbraith makes the point in *The Nature of Mass Poverty* that at least to some extent, people who decide to emigrate from their homelands are more likely to be achieving risk-takers than those who do not. This may partially explain the high levels of achievement of West Indians in the United States. The self-selection phenomenon may also be relevant for Haitian immigrants to the u.s., although it can also be argued that the Haitian's fight for survival at home is so desperate that he is well equipped to advance when he finds himself in an open system where progress is possible. James Traub observed in a recent *Harper's* article:

> Certainly the most amazing vindication of immigrant values in the absence of skills is the tenuous success of the Haitians. Not all the Haitians in Brooklyn are illegal immigrants or boat people, but few of them speak English, many are illiterate even in French, and all are black. Like West Indians generally, Haitians have constructed an insular, small-scale economy that depends very little on the cooperation of the outside world for success. Haitians have brought with them from Port-au-Prince their own occupations — changing tires and cruising up and down the streets picking up people who are sick of waiting for the bus. Observers of the Haitians who lay down roots in Brooklyn are amazed, and almost appalled, by their capacity for sacrifice and their fierce determination. "I actually think these

people are going to make it," says Rene Williams, director of the Erasmus Neighborhood Federation . . .[20]

But the self-selection of emigrants doesn't explain the success of descendants of freedmen. The one explanation that applies equally to English-speaking West Indians and the descendants of freedmen in the u.s. is that the Afro-slave culture was substantially displaced by cultures more oriented toward progress than survival — British culture in the case of the West Indies, and u.s. culture, so strongly influenced by British culture, in the case of the freedmen.

Haiti's partly self-imposed isolation and Jim Crowism in the United States up to the 1960s had prevented attitudes more conducive to progress from penetrating the Afro-slave culture. Increasing Haitian contact with the outside, importantly as a result of emigration, is gradually changing the Haitian's world view. The change has been far more rapid for u.s. blacks since the breakthroughs of the 1960s.

It is difficult to avoid the conclusion that the British colonial experience in the Caribbean has been more beneficial for the descendants of West African slaves than has the experience — in some cases within British colonies — of those blacks who remained in West Africa. The average 1980 per-capita GNP of 21 West African countries with a population of 196.8 million was $680. In the same year, the average per-capita GNP for 11 former British colonies in the West Indies was $1,915. Moreover, literacy and life expectancy are much higher in the English-speaking Caribbean than in Africa.

While it is true that the three countries of the twenty-one that were British colonies — Nigeria, Ghana, and Sierra Leone — have a higher average per-capita GNP ($1,017) than the average of the twenty-one, the figure for the British colonies is skewed by Nigeria's oil and its size. What must be kept in mind is that the African slave experience in the British Caribbean started in the mid-seventeenth century. The English colonial experience in West Africa dates from the late nineteenth century.

I conclude this chapter with an anecdote. Toward the end of my second year as AID director in Haiti, I had dinner with a black Trinidadian friend who had been in Haiti for about the same period of time. We were both experiencing the frustration and emotional fatigue that most people who work in development in Haiti experience. I observed that the roots of both Trinidad's and Haiti's people were in West Africa, that both had suffered under slavery at about the same time. Yet the indicators of Trinidad's development are today so high that it is close to being labeled a developed country, while Haiti is among the poorest countries in the world. How did she explain it?

She paused for some time, then replied, in obvious discomfort, "It is very painful for me to say it, but I can think of no other explanation than the British."

NOTES

1. *World Development Report 1982*, p. 163
2. F. A. Hoyos, *Barbados: A History from the Amerindians to Independence*, p. 24. This book is the principal source of this recounting of Barbadian history.
3. This may have had something to do with the influx of Sephardic Jews into Barbados at about this time. Three hundred practicing Jews, most of whom had migrated from England, Holland, and Brazil, were recorded in Barbados's 1679 census. As with several other progressive areas of the New World — e.g., Costa Rica, Antigua, Jamaica, Mexico's Monterrey — Barbados's success is attributed by some to a disproportionate presence of Jews. The case has not been adequately documented, however. For more on the early Jewish colonists of Barbados see Wilfred S. Samuel, *The Jewish Colonists in Barbados in the Year 1680* (London: Purnell and Sons, Ltd., 1936).
4. Hoyos, *Barbados*, pp. 30 – 31.
5. *Ibid.*, p. 41.
6. *Ibid.*, p. 84.
7. *Ibid.*, p. 86.
8. *Ibid.*, p. 128.
9. *Ibid.*, p. 135.
10. *Ibid.*, p. 155.
11. Jamaica's population in 1980 was 2.2 million, about ten times as large as Barbados's and about 40 percent of Haiti's. Jamaica's area is 4,411 square miles, about twenty-five times the size of Barbados and about 40 percent of Haiti's area. Trinidad and Tobago's population in 1980 was 1.2 million; its area is 1,864 square miles.
12. In an article in the October 26, 1983, *New York Times* (page A19), Prime Minister Eugenia Charles of Dominica is quoted as follows:
    "Like many other leaders in the English-speaking Caribbean, she does not take a harsh view of Britain's former colonial domination. 'They didn't do too bad by us . . .They tried to educate us. They were narrow-minded at the time, but it's easy to see things with hindsight. They taught us lessons of democracy and freedom.' "
13. Quoted in George Hunte, *Barbados*, p. 171.
14. *Ibid.*
15. *Ibid.*, p. 173.
16. *Ibid.*, p. 171.
17. Thomas Sowell, "Three Black Histories," pp. 96 – 106.
18. *Ibid.*, p. 103.
19. *Ibid.*, p. 105.
20. James Traub, "You Can Get It if You Really Want It," p. 29. Rene Williams, who is a black American, is subsequently quoted as saying, "Even if you moved racism out of the way, values would have a large part." ("I'll probably get my head chopped off for saying it," she sighs.)

6

Argentina and Australia

Argentina is among the world's most richly endowed countries. With over one million square miles — 85 percent of India's area — it is the eighth largest country in the world. Its land is extraordinarily fertile: "The 200,000 square miles of pampa (the vast east – central plain) contain . . . some of the world's richest soil: alfalfa roots have been traced to a depth of 15 feet in stoneless dirt."[1]

The country is very sparsely settled with a population of about 28 million (India's is about 700 million), of whom about 15 million live in Buenos Aires. Population density is 26 per square mile. The people are predominantly European: more than 80 percent are of either Spanish or Italian extraction.

While its identified mineral resource endowment is moderate, Argentina has substantial oil and natural gas deposits and is able to supply the lion's share of its energy needs. Moreover, there is reason to believe that important unexploited mineral deposits may exist, particularly in the Andean region.

The words "enigma" and "paradox" appear often in the literature about Argentina. V. S. Naipaul observes, "The failure of Argentina, so rich, so underpopulated . . . is one of the mysteries of our time."[2] Early in this century, it was considered an advanced country, along with Western Europe and the United States. It has achieved high levels of literacy and public health. But Argentina's development has faltered in the past fifty years, during which military authoritarianism has dominated politics.

Today, after a prolonged period of political and economic chaos under military rule, Argentina is once again seeking stability and progress through an elected civilian president. Raúl Alfonsín follows military leadership that has been discredited by its inability to cope with deteriorating economic conditions, by its abuses of human rights, and by its costly and humiliating adventure in the Falkland Islands. The divisions within Argentine society have been so profound they have sometimes appeared to be irreconcilable, and although President Alfonsín is off to an impressive start, he faces enormous obstacles as he tries to guide his country along the democratic path.

The countries with which Argentina was grouped in terms of economic progress early in this century have attained per-capita GNPs generally four or five times Argentina's, and virtually all of them are viable democracies.

In Carlos Fuentes's words, Argentina has demonstrated a "constant inability to find a degree of synchronization between the bounty of its natural and human resources and the poverty of its political institutions."[3]

Australia bears several parallels with Argentina. It is large — almost three million square miles, making it the sixth largest country in the world — and, with about 15 million people, very sparsely populated. Much of Australia is desert, and its land resources are not nearly as rich as Argentina's. But it is blessed with mineral resources.

Australia is even more remote from Europe and the United States than Argentina, which is 7,000 miles from both New York and Paris.

Early in this century, Australia, which was first settled by the British late in the eighteenth century, was less developed than Argentina, which the Spanish first settled in the sixteenth century. Yet today, Australia is a stable democracy with a per-capita GNP four times Argentina's.

A review of the two countries' histories suggests that cultural factors are at the root of the divergent national experiences.

Argentina

Argentina's colonial history is similar in most respects to that of the Hispanic-American societies we have already discussed. The first settlements were established in the mid-sixteenth century by the same kinds of people — certainly not representative of the best elements in Spain — who first came to Santo Domingo and Central America. Their objective "was neither to colonize nor populate. . . . To farm, to build, to resign oneself, to persevere were all depressing and outside the set of values of conquest and domination. To work, to yield a little to the exigencies of nature was to be defeated, to be a barbarian. Thus was born a scale of false values."[4]

Buenos Aires was first permanently settled in 1580, but notwithstanding its excellent port and far better communications with Spain than Lima, it was to the latter that the Crown gave the trading monopoly, and Buenos Aires was for a long time nothing more than "a remote rim of the Spanish Empire."[5] It did, however, engage in contraband trade, which became a major factor in its later growth.

Peru was of far greater interest to Spain because of its rich gold and silver deposits. Early explorers, particularly Sebastian Cabot, believed precious metals would be found in abundance in what would one day be called Argentina ("silver land") whose principal river would be named Rio de la Plata ("silver river"). But the early explorers were wrong. Argentina's richness would spring from its soil, and agriculture was of little interest to the Spaniards.

Nor were there large numbers of Indians to subjugate and exploit, as there were in Peru and Central America. Scobie estimates there were 300,000 Indians when the colonists first arrived. The *encomienda* system was established, and cotton, rice, wheat, and corn produced by *encomienda* Indians were shipped to Peru. But there were not enough Indians either to make slave trade lucrative or to work extensive plantations. As in other Spanish colonies, the Indian numbers dropped precipitously as a result of the diseases introduced by the Spaniards, cruel treatment on the *encomiendas*, and fighting between colonists and those Indians who resisted Spanish domination. It was not long before black slaves were introduced.

The absence of large numbers of Indians had a leveling effect on the colonists as it did to some extent in Santo Domingo and particularly Costa Rica. Scobie speaks of "a more egalitarian type of society" and "reduced economic and social differences."[6] But increasingly, the vast, unexploited hinterland influenced the development of Argentina, in both an economic and a psychic sense. The pampa was Argentina's rich frontier, and the people drawn to it, the gauchos, tended to exhibit a "spirit of independence, of individualism . . . reinforcing the individualism inherited from the conquerors."[7] Whereas the frontier experience in the United States and Australia — and Costa Rica — contributed to democratization, the fertile soil of the pampa nourished the authoritarianism and the brutality of the conquistador.

Badly in need of money, the Spanish Crown sold land in large tracts to Creole settlers. The *encomiendas* thus were transformed into *estancias* (the equivalent of *haciendas* in other Spanish-American countries). The land was considered to have little value because, in the absence of significant numbers of Indians or black slaves, it was assumed that it could not produce much wealth. Thus the Crown sold very large tracts — tens or hundreds of thousands of acres. The resulting land tenure pattern, which has not changed significantly in some three hundred years, appears today as one of the most inequitable in the world. Those who came to own the land formed an aristocracy that largely dominated Argentine politics until the dictatorship of Juan Perón.

The geographic irrationality of forcing Argentina's trade through Lima finally resulted, after two hundred years of ever-increasing smuggling, in the establishment in 1776 of the vice-royalty of the Rio de la Plata, with its seat in Buenos Aires. The opening of Buenos Aires as a legal port led to a rapid increase in the production and export of livestock and by-products, and also in the population of the city:[8]

1750	17,000
1780	25,000
1800	50,000

Early in the nineteenth century, the total population of Argentina approximated 500,000. The large majority were Creole whites or mestizos.

Argentina was attacked in 1806 and 1807 by the British, who occupied Buenos Aires for a time. While the Creoles finally dislodged the British, they had a taste of truly free trade during the occupation that contrasted sharply with the constraints on trade imposed by the Spanish. (After Buenos Aires became a legal port, Spain had virtually exclusive access.)

Independence

Movement toward independence was accelerated by Napoleon's overthrow of the Spanish monarchy in 1808. This led to the deposing of the viceroy in 1810 and his replacement by a Creole-controlled junta. It was not until 1816, however, that independence was formally proclaimed, and it did not become a reality until 1824, when the Spanish departed from Peru.

From the outset, Argentina was a divided country. Those who lived in rapidly growing Buenos Aires — the *porteños* — had a vision of a unified, modern country, guided by the ideologies of the American and French revolutions, and under centralized administration from Buenos Aires. The people of the interior advocated local autonomy and their special brand of frontier individualism, which was soon dominated by *caudillos* and their gaucho bands. The differences, captured so trenchantly in Domingo Sarmiento's classic *Facundo — Civilization and Barbarism*,[9] were irreconcilable and led to repeated civil wars and a political chaos that "destroyed the grand vision of a modern nation which some Creoles had held, and denied the hope that Argentina . . . would become a vigorous, sovereign state."[10]

It took brute force to bring a degree of unity out of the chaos, and that force was wielded by Juan Manuel de Rosas — "Bloody Rosas" — who ruled with an iron first from 1829 to 1852. Unprincipled and reactionary, Rosas was "the *estanciero's estanciero* [the quintessential plantation owner] and the gaucho's gaucho."[11] He was the prototype of frontier barbarism: he murdered, bribed, and stole whenever it suited him, and concerned himself almost exclusively with preserving his power and enhancing his wealth. Argentina stagnated for a generation as "public education was practically abandoned; immigration nearly ceased; the distribution of public lands for colonization was halted, although vast tracts were acquired by Rosas and other *estancieros*, thus fixing more firmly the pattern of the *latifundio*, or great estate, as the dominant form of land ownership."[12]

Rosas was overthrown in 1852 by another *caudillo*, Justo José de Urquiza. Urquiza promptly called a constitutional convention that produced the durable Constitution of 1853, which closely parallels the Constitution of the United States. Buenos Aires had broken away from Urquiza's confederation before his election in 1854. Between 1854 and 1862 there was continual conflict between Buenos Aires and the confederation, which was terminated only by the accession to the presidency of Bartolomé Mitre, a *porteño*, an intellectual, and a fighter. The focus of insurrection now shifted to the provinces, and Mitre had to suppress revolts and resist Paraguayan incursions for much of the time he was in office.

Mitre was followed in the presidency by Sarmiento, who had spent much of his life as a teacher and writer. Mitre had appointed Sarmiento as ambassador to the United States in 1864, and his four years of service in Washington left him with a deep respect and admiration for the United States. His commitment to the modernization of Argentina was manifested in expansion of trade, construction of a railroad network, promotion of immigration, and heavy emphasis on education, all of which were consistent with his assertion, "We must *be* the United States."[13]

Much of the economic progress that made social progress possible during Sarmiento's administration was the result of foreign — particularly British — investment, particularly in railroads, a telegraph system, meat-packing plants, and port facilities. McGann observes, "British investment in and trade with Argentina were as significant as they were with Australia and Canada."[14] Interestingly, foreign capital, particularly British, was flowing in large quantities to the United States at the same time for investments — e.g., in the livestock industry — that accelerated the development of the American West.

Nicolás Avellaneda followed Sarmiento and continued the development policies of his predecessor. The flow of immigrants increased as did livestock production, particularly of sheep. Frozen meat was shipped to Europe for the first time. Economic progress nothwithstanding, Avellaneda had to suppress a revolt led by Mitre.

The golden age

A brief civil war erupted in 1880 between *porteños* and *provincianos* which resulted in Buenos Aires's becoming, for the first time, the true capital of the nation. The final link in the political structure was closed, and Argentina embarked on a period of fifty years of relative stability and progress — its Golden Age.

Except during the last sixteen years of the Golden Age, the traditional landed oligarchy and its Conservative Party controlled Argentine politics, manipulating the electoral mechanism as necessary to assure that control. For the most part, the policies of Mitre, Sarmiento, and Avellaneda were continued. Immigration and foreign investment were encouraged. Buenos Aires grew explosively:

1855	90,000
1880	300,000
1895	660,000
1914	1,500,000[15]

About 50 percent of the immigrants were Italians. Another 30 percent were Spaniards. The Italians, mainly from rural areas of Italy, tended to gravitate to the interior in search of land, which they rarely acquired because the oligarchy controlled so much and was not inclined to dispose of it. Land values soared as the rich land began to be more intensively exploited. Beef-cattle production was stimulated by the meat packing and freezing plants, and cereal production burgeoned:

Volume of Argentine Wheat Exports (tons)[16]	
1876	21
1890	327,000
annual average 1900 – 1914	2,285,000

While other countries that were getting rich on their agricultural resources (e.g., the United States, Canada) were also promoting industry, Argentina did not.

> . . . industry was neglected, if not positively deprecated, not only by the elite, but by the general creole populace, among whom the Spanish tradition, essentially anti-industrial, was strong.[17]

But Argentina's land resources were so rich, and the levels of foreign investment sufficiently high, that it was able to keep up, at least for a time, with the most economically dynamic nations of the world. Buenos Aires became one of the world's great cities, with spacious parks, wide avenues, and imposing public and private buildings, as well as an active cultural life.

It was not until 1912, however, that the Conservatives decided to risk their control of Argentine politics, a control they had exercised through restriction of suffrage and rigging of elections. The Radical Civic Union — essentially a middle-class party — had been established in 1891 and had worked persistently for an expanded franchise, along with other disenfranchised groups, principally from the working classes. Political stability was increasingly threatened by the large numbers of disenfranchised, and in 1912 Conservative president Roque Saenz Peña forced through his party a law establishing universal and secret suffrage for men. As a consequence, the founder of the Radical Party, Hipólito Yrigoyen, was elected to the presidency in 1916.

Of this turning point, Carlos Rangel has said, ". . . oligarchic democracy became chaotic democracy, full of inner contradictions, demagogical, ineffectual, incapable of holding in check the factions and the forces of disintegration that are characteristic of Hispanic societies."[18]

The Radicals had succeeded in achieving a peaceful revolution by opening up Argentine politics to the middle class and the masses. But they were unsuccessful in bringing about any significant social change, nor did they promote modernization of the economy. After a spurt of industrial investment during World War 1, Argentina fell far behind Europe and the United States. And the Radicals neglected development of energy resources.

The golden age ends

Until 1929, the leadership shortcomings of the Radicals were not so apparent because of continuing agricultural growth and high levels of foreign investment. The worldwide depression abruptly ended this fragile prosperity. In 1930, the seventy-eight-year-old and senile Yrigoyen was overthrown by the military. The Golden Age was over. Argentina's failure to build viable, progressive democratic institutions had finally caught up with its extraordinary natural wealth.

The military had formed an alliance with the aristocracy, but there were some significant policy differences between the Golden Age Conservatives and the new rightist coalition, which emphasized "authoritarianism, ultranationalism, and fascistic and Nazi concepts of militarism, elitism, and the corporate state."[19]

General José F. Uriburu led the coup d'etat and served as provisional president. Agustín P. Justo was fraudulently elected in 1932. One of his first acts was to put down a Radical Party uprising. Justo was succeeded by Roberto M. Ortíz, who was also elected fraudulently, in 1938, and who was replaced in 1940, because of failing health, by Ramón S. Castillo. Under Castillo, Argentina increasingly identified itself with the Axis.

In 1943, the military again intervened to prevent the accession to power of pro-British conservatives. But as Nazi Germany increasingly looked like a loser, the generals, including Juan Domingo Perón, who was made vice president in 1944, shifted their ground and finally, in March 1945, declared war on Germany and Japan.

The Argentine economy had made an impressive recovery from the shock of the early years of the Depression. With its export earnings drastically reduced and its ability to import thus curtailed, Argentina turned to domestic industry to meet its demand for manufactured products. By 1943, industry had overtaken agriculture as the principal contributor to GNP. The industrial spurt brought with it two important social changes: a rapidly expanding industrially based bourgeoisie and a rising urban proletariat that was fed by migration from the provinces, where land tenure patterns frustrated aspirations,[20] to Buenos Aires.

The rise of Perón

Perón, who had been named secretary of labor in 1943, wooed the burgeoning proletariat by encouraging them to organize, by pushing important new social security legislation, and by decreeing substantial pay increases. It became clear that Perón was working his way toward the presidency as the champion of the *descamisados* (the shirtless ones), and he was imprisoned following a coup in October 1945. But the *descamisados*, mobilized by, among others, Perón's mistress Eva Duarte, went into the streets, and Perón was released. Four months later he was elected to the presidency.

Peronism is "protest, despair, faith, machismo, magic, *espiritismo* [mysticism], revenge,"[21] in Naipaul's words. But Perón did have a vision of a new Argentina: economically — particularly industrially — dynamic, free of European influence, the leader of Latin America. It was in Perón's failure to bring about the realization of his vision that Naipaul's definition is apt.

Perón did succeed in shifting power from the oligarchy to the urban proletariat, the new bourgeoisie, and the army. The army became the overseer and administrator of the Peronist revolution. One of Perón's principal instruments for control of the economy was IAPI, the Argentine Institute for Trade Promotion, a state trading monopoly that bought surplus agricultural products and sold them abroad. IAPI set its purchase price as low and its sales price as high as it could, leaving a substantial profit margin, at least in the short run. This margin, along with foreign exchange reserves accumulated during World War II, permitted the nationalization of many foreign investments, including, in 1947 – 48, the British-owned railroads. The margin also permitted promotion of new industries and substantial wage increases for the working classes.

But agricultural pricing policy inevitably discouraged production — Argentina produced 33 million tons of grain in 1950 – 55; in 1939 – 44 it had produced 90 million tons — and the economy began to deteriorate in the late forties. The trend was aggravated by declining world prices and drought. Inflation accelerated as other key flaws of Perón's stewardship — e.g., corruption, a bloated bureaucracy (the number of public employees almost quintupled between 1945 and 1955), excessive state intervention in enterprise — became apparent. Perón attempted to reestablish economic equilibrium by increasing prices to agricultural producers, by resisting labor's demands, and by opening up oil exploration to American companies. He attempted to force discipline on Argentina by building up a tough police force that, like similar predecessor and successor institutions, often employed torture. But it was too late. In 1955, as Perón was threatening to arm his *descamisados*, he was overthrown by the military and sent into exile.

Perón left Argentina even more deeply divided than it was when he came to power. He had undertaken a campaign against the aristocracy *and* against the supporters of liberal democracy. He had dramatically improved the living conditions of Buenos Aires's proletariat, but the condition of the small farmers and rural poor remained essentially unchanged. To be sure, he had succeeded in putting together a powerful political coalition, but it was viewed as so threatening to non-Peronists that, ever since, they have been reluctant to legitimize the Peronists.

Included in Perón's highly costly legacy to his country was a military institution that became accustomed, during his dictatorship, to the idea that it was entirely appropriate for the military to intervene in the political process and administer the country.

But perhaps Perón's greatest disservice to his country was his perpetuation, through himself and his wife, of the symbol of the *caudillo*, the authoritarian ruler who bestows favors on his friends, destroys his enemies, enriches himself, and generally operates outside the framework of law. In such circumstances, human beings are encouraged to become sycophants and cult worshippers. Naipaul says of Eva Perón, "She is her own cult; she offers protection to those who believe in her. Where there are no reliable institutions or codes or law, no secular assurance, people need faith and magic."[22]

The military dominates

After Perón was deposed, the military, under General Pedro E. Aramburu, held power for three years, during which they crushed a Peronista revolt. Labor unrest was chronic and violent. But the military were committed to honest elections, and Arturo Frondizi, a Radical who had received Peronista support, was inaugurated in 1958. Four years later, inflation was galloping, Argentina was deep in debt, and unemployment and bankruptcies reached record highs. Frondizi provoked strong opposition when he extended oil exploration contracts to American companies. When he permitted the Peronistas to run in the 1962 provincial and congressional elections, he was imprisoned by the military. A civil war broke out among the military services later that year over the issue of Peronista political participation.

The Peronistas were permitted some participation in the 1963 elections, which were won, with only 26 percent of the popular vote, by Radical Arturo Illia. Illia pursued a nationalistic economic policy and rescinded the American oil company exploration concessions. But he was removed by the military in 1966, importantly because of growing Peronista strength. This time, the military decided to hold onto power, and Generals Onganía, Levingston, and Lanusse ran the country until elections were held in 1973. The victor was Hector J. Cámpora, a Peronist who soon resigned, paving the way for the return of Perón.

Perón was elected with more than 60 percent of the vote and was inaugurated on October 12, 1973. Eight months later he died, having done little to solve the acute political, economic, and social problems that plagued Argentina. He had clearly moved to the right during his eighteen years of exile, and many left-wing Peronistas were alienated by his policies. Many of the alienated turned to the left-wing terrorist *Montoneros*, who adopted the name of a group of fighters who played a big role in achieving Argentina's independence.

Perón's legacy to his country this time was his second wife, Isabel, a former cabaret dancer who, as vice president, succeeded him on his death. Her principal advisor was José López Rega, a mystic and soothsayer. Chaos reigned, partly as a consequence of increased *Montonero* activity, until the military intervened in March 1976, installing General Jorge A. Videla as president.

Having witnessed the Allende experience in Chile and the *Tupamaro* years in neighboring Uruguay, the Argentina military concluded that a combination of political and economic chaos and the growing strength of the *Montoneros* constituted a grave threat to the survival of their institution, and under Videla a no-quarter-given undeclared war was waged against the left. Due process had never been one of Argentina's strengths, and it was totally ignored in an indiscriminate military campaign of counterterror and torture.

In his movie *State of Siege*, which is a highly dubious treatment of the *Tupamaros's* kidnapping and execution of U.S. Public Safety Advisor Dan Mitrione, Greek film-maker Costa Gavras leaves the impression that the CIA introduced torture to the Uruguayan police as an instrument of counterinsurgency. The strong implication is that police forces in the United States are past masters at torture and that Latin American security forces have been corrupted by their association with their American advisors.

Naipaul, I believe, is much closer to the truth:

> Torture is not new in Argentina. And though Argentines abroad, when they are campaigning against a particular regime, talk as if torture has just been started by that regime, in Argentina itself torture is spoken of — and accepted — by all groups as an Argentine institution.[23]

In any event, thousands of Argentines were picked up by the security forces. Many were tortured. Many disappeared. Leading the attack on the human rights abuses of the Argentine military was the Carter administration. Relationships between the Argentine and U.S. governments became increasingly strained.

The Argentine economy continued to falter. During the 1970 – 80 decade, the rate of inflation averaged an annual increase of 130 percent, second highest in the world (after Chile). During the same period, industry grew at the rate of 1.8 percent annually, one of the lowest in the world.

Videla was replaced in 1981 by General Roberto Eduardo Viola. General Leopoldo Galtieri succeeded Viola after a brief period. With economic deterioration accelerating, in part because of worldwide recession, and with the military increasingly unpopular, Galtieri attempted to galvanize popular support for his government by occupying the Falkland Islands (the Argentines call them the Malvinas), a British colony since 1833. The British then ousted the Argentine occupying forces, Galtieri fell, and he was replaced by General Reynaldo Bignone, who, at the end of 1982, promised elections in 1983. The elections were won by Raúl Alfonsín, one of whose highest priorities was to bring military officers responsible for crimes to justice.

Explaining the Argentine 'failure'

In a 1981 article in the *Boston Globe*, reporter Stephen Kinzer quoted an unnamed Argentine writer: "Argentina is simply a failure as a country.

Everyone knows that something has gone very wrong here, and there is little prospect that it will improve."[24]

But what has gone wrong? Why have other sparsely populated, resource-rich countries, such as Australia, Canada, and the United States, achieved high levels of economic growth and democratic political stability while Argentina has foundered both economically and politically?

One explanation commonly encountered in academic circles in Latin America, Europe, and the United States is "dependency theory,"[25] an essentially Marxist-Leninist view of the world that explains the condition of poor countries "of the Periphery" as a consequence of their economic exploitation and political manipulation by the rich countries "of the Center."

Fernando Henrique Cardoso and Enzo Faletto, both schooled in the U.N.'s Economic Commission for Latin America (ECLA) and both Marxists, are two of the best-known prophets of dependency theory. Their book, *Dependency and Development in Latin America*, is required reading for courses on Latin America in many U.S. universities.

For Cardoso and Faletto, Argentina's relative poverty is explained by the fact that Britain and the United States, the countries "of the Center" that historically have had the most extensive economic relationships with Argentina, are relatively rich. But in addition to milking Argentina, the imperialist powers — first Britain, then the United States — have insinuated themselves into a dominant economic and political position within the country through their bourgeois lackeys, "a hegemonic entrepreneurial agro-exporting sector."[26]

Inevitably, for Cardoso and Faletto, ". . . imperialism turns into an active and metaphysical principle which traces out the paths of history on the sensitive but passive skin of dependent countries."[27] According to dependency theory, for reasons that are not clear, dependent countries are impotent — unable to defend their own interests and passive observers to their own rape.

Cardoso and Faletto note, as has Argentine economist Raul Prebisch,[28] the grand old man of ECLA and a principal Third World spokesman who is not a Marxist, that "peripheral industrialization is based on products which in the Center are *mass consumed*, but which are typically *luxurious consumption* in dependent societies. Industrialization in dependent economies enhances income concentration . . ."[29] Cardoso, Faletto, and Prebisch all explain this phenomenon — of capitalism's being an engine of progress in the Center but an obstacle to progress in the Periphery — as a consequence of imperialism. But the link between the suppression of the aspirations of the masses and imperialism is a murky one. In any event, for Cardoso and Faletto, "The important question . . . is how to construct paths toward socialism."[30]

It is difficult to reconcile dependency theory with Argentina's history. In fact, Argentina appears to be a case in point for the opinion of French intellectual François Bourricaud that "Dependency theory is an interesting ideology but its explanatory powers are extremely limited."[31] The most obvious explanation for Argentina's impressive growth during the fifty-year Golden Age (1880 – 1930) was the stimulation of the Argentine economy by exports of livestock products and grain to Europe, principally Britain, and by high levels of foreign investment, again principally British, in transport and finance. There is no other convincing explanation for Argentina's economic success during this period, and the beneficial effects of comparable European (and again especially British) trade with and investment in the United States, Canada, and Australia bear this out. The Argentine political scientist Guillermo A. O'Donnell, who ascribes some validity to dependency theory, is among those who believe that the role of foreign trade and investment was crucial to Argentina's economic success during the Golden Age.[32]

The declining role of foreign investment in Argentina and the very high levels of foreign investment in the early decades of this century are clearly indicated in Table 4.[33]

Table 4. Ratio of foreign capital to aggregate fixed capital, 1900 – 1955

Years	Domestic capital	Foreign capital	Aggregate fixed capital	Ratio of foreign to aggregate fixed capital (percent)
	(Millions of dollars at 1950 prices)			
1900	4,327	2,020	6,347	31.8
1909	7,716	5,250	12,966	40.5
1913	9,007	8,230	17,237	47.7
1917	9,537	7,980	17,517	45.6
1920	10,164	7,300	17,464	41.8
1923	11,961	7,100	19,061	37.2
1927	14,450	7,580	22,030	34.4
1929	16,639	7,835	24,474	32.0
1931	17,942	7,640	25,582	30.0
1934	18,559	6,920	25,479	27.2
1940	21,795	5,570	27,365	20.4
1945	23,394	4,260	27,654	15.4
1949	30,378	1,740	32,118	5.4
1953	33,279	1,870	35,149	5.3
1955	34,924	1,860	36,784	5.1

It is difficult to make a coherent case for undue British or u.s. influence in Argentine politics, at least during the past half-century. Argentina has not been passive or impotent during this period. As we have observed, Argentina sided with the Axis until it was clear they were losing. Perón pursued, for the most part, strongly nationalistic economic policies, including expropriation of the British-owned railroads. Frondizi's decision to permit American companies to explore for oil contributed to his downfall and was overturned by his successor, Illia. The u.s. was increasingly strident — from the Argentine government view, provocative and interventionist — in its criticism of human rights abuses in the 1970s, and its influence on the Argentine government virtually disappeared. And, in the wake of the Falklands debacle, it may be some time before the British or Americans have much influence in Buenos Aires.

The Cardoso-Faletto-Prebisch judgment that capitalism "of the Center" has failed to improve the living conditions of the lower social strata in countries "of the Periphery" has some important elements of truth in it. Lower-income people — say, the bottom 40 percent — have progressed far more in the capitalist economies of Western Europe, the United States, Canada, Japan, and Australia than they have in most Latin American countries. Their standard of living in the Western democracies would place the poor well up into the middle class in Latin America, where the poor live on a few hundred dollars per person per year.

Cardoso, Faletto, and Prebisch explain this phenomenon as a consequence of the impact of imperialism on dependent societies, partly because foreign companies take out profits, partly because of the link between the Latin American economic elite and the countries "of the Center," particularly the United States. But the explanation is not convincing. It exaggerates the profits of multinational corporations[34] and ignores the clear u.s. government preference for centrist, progressive, democratic governments in Latin America, at least since 1960.

In my view, the principal explanation is the failure of most Latin American countries, and most especially Argentina, to develop political systems that adequately reflect and further the interests of the poor. Capitalism has been an engine of widespread progress in Western Europe, Canada, the United States, Japan, and Australia because it has operated within effective democratic frameworks in which lower-income groups play a major role in the political process. Viable democracies, in turn, reflect value and attitude systems that attach importance to questions of equity and progress for the entire society. Labor movements are vigorous participants in all these countries; social mobility is far greater than in most Latin American societies; and governments often come to power that are beholden to the lower-income groups.

Where effective democracy has endured in Latin America, and Costa Rica may be the best example, economic growth has brought with it important benefits for the poor.

Some other views

Why have most Latin American countries failed to construct durable pluralistic political systems? Why is Argentina so often referred to as a divided or fragmented country, a political failure, its enormous natural endowment notwithstanding? McGann says, "If the people have failed . . . perhaps the reasons lie in their cultural personality and in their value system . . ."[35]

McGann's discussion of Argentine culture is reminiscent of Salvador Mendieta's diagnosis of Central America's ills, also of the several writers referred to in Chapter 4 who have analyzed the Dominican Republic from a cultural point of view. McGann catalogues elements of Argentine culture:[36]

- excessive egoism, reflected in a lack of consideration for others
- an excessive concern with *dignidad* and *machismo* ("important in the traditional societies of Spain and Italy; they were reinforced for the creole settlers in the hostile, isolated, New World environment")[37]
- excessive consciousness of status, of "being" rather than "doing"
- disdain for manual labor
- apathy, lack of commitment, withdrawal
- belief that one gets ahead only through "pull" or trickery
- institutionalized corruption — "a formalized, accepted, widely practiced disregard for or violation of the law and of moral standards through the use of bribery and influence in public and private occupations"[38]
- loyalty to one's extended family and to powerful patrons as substitutes for the law
- the absence of "civic culture"[39]
- "the owner – entrepreneur continues to be paternalistic and even autocratic in his relations with his employees . . . a Dickensian type of capitalism"[40]

McGann quotes the Argentine scholar Delfín L. Garosa:

Argentines are "imitative . . . habitually dissatisfied with their fellow men, their attitudes a mixture of impatience and inertia, people who are improvident, sentimental, full of self-love, and suspicious. Behind the pose of cynicism and sophistication, there is immaturity."[41]

Naipaul's searing observations about Argentine society in *The Return of Eva Peron* parallel those of McGann:[42]

Argentine political life is like the life of an ant community or an African forest tribe: full of events, full of crises and deaths, but life is only cyclical, and the year always ends as it begins.

The artificiality of the society shows: that absence of links between men and men, between immigrant and immigrant, aristocrat and artisan, city dweller and *cabecita negra*, the "blackhead," the man from the interior; that absence of a link between men and the meaningless flat land.

Where jargon turns living issues into abstractions . . . and where jargon ends by competing with jargon, people don't have causes. They only have enemies; only the enemies are real. It has been the South American nightmare since the breakup of the Spanish Empire.

A waiter in Mendoza said, "Argentines don't work. Everything we do is small and petty." An artist said, "There were very few *professionals* here. By that I mean people who know what to do with themselves. No one knows why he is doing a particular job. For that reason, if you are doing what I do, then you are my enemy."

Argentina is a land of plunder . . . and its politics can be nothing but the politics of plunder.

The political life of the country is . . . little more than a struggle for political power. There seems to be no higher good.

[Argentina] is like a sixteenth-century colony of the Spanish Empire, with the same greed and internal weaknesses, the same potential for dissension, the cynicism and sterility. *Obedezco pero no cumplo*, I obey but I don't comply: it was the attitude of the sixteenth-century conquistador or official . . .

. . . politics have to do with the nature of human association, the contract of men with men. The politics of a country can only be an extension of its idea of human relationships.

The insights of Tomás Roberto Fillol

The cultural roots of Argentina's chaotic politics and its faltering economy have been traced most comprehensively by an Argentine, Tomás Roberto Fillol, in his master's thesis at MIT, entitled *Social Factors in Economic Development*, presented in 1960. "The viewpoint taken in this book," says Fillol, "is that the basically passive, apathetic value orientation profile of the Argentine society must be regarded as the *critical* factor limiting the possibilities of steady, long-run economic development."[43]

Fillol's diagnosis of Argentine national character recapitulates some of the other writers we have cited, both in this and other chapters, and adds some new dimensions. He sees the Argentine as an easily corruptible, envious person who knows shame but not guilt. The Argentine emphasizes luck and supernatural forces as determinants of the future much more than planning and hard work. He is highly individualistic and avoids group action except when it benefits him directly. He is excessively motivated by concerns about dignity and manliness. He is more concerned with his inherited status than with achievement, and he has contempt for work. He expects career advancement to depend on whom he knows, not on merit. As a superior he is autocratic and does not delegate. As a subordinate he is submissive. The anxiety and rage built up by the subordinate are often taken out on *his* subordinates and on his children.

"Argentines emphasize present time," Fillol observes. "[They] do not *live or work for* the future; [they] *contemplate its image*."[44] He goes on: "Such an emphasis is inimical to conscientious planning for the future; to long-run economic, political, or social commitments; to the emergence of a collective sense of duty — especially of the sense of duty to do productive work; or to furthering the interest of, or unselfishly cooperating with, a group, an organization, or a community . . ."[45] Fillol quotes H. A. Murena: "*There is no community in Argentina.* We do not form a body, though we may form a *conglomeration*."[46]

The family is the only truly cohesive institution in Argentine society — "the *only* institution on which an individual can depend . . . the only institution towards which an Argentine feels obligation and (almost always) manifests loyalty."[47]

In Fillol's description of what might be described as Argentine family paranoia, one is reminded of Banfield's analysis of the family in Montegrano, which is particularly significant for Argentina because so many Argentines trace their roots back to Italy. But the description also reminds us of some of the other countries treated in this book:

> [The Argentine] is acutely aware that any advantage that may be given to somebody outside his family is necessarily at the expense of himself and his own family. He will value gains accruing to the community only insofar as he and his are likely to share them. Similarly, he will feel a deep imperative to preserve what he has gained or achieved for himself and his family. This automatically leads to nepotism in business and industry, family-run enterprises, reluctance to delegate authority and responsibilities, and unwillingness to dispense or share wealth with institutions other than one's own family.[48]

As we pointed out above, Fillol believes the frustrations, anxieties, and rage the Argentine experiences in his autocratic working environment are taken out on his children. Fillol employs analytical concepts, used by McClelland and others, that focus on people's emotional "needs," and concludes that Argentines have a high need for dependency and aggression. The symbol of the Argentine's need for dependency is the *caudillo*, quintessentially symbolized by Juan and Eva Perón. The need for aggression is apparent in the way children play, in Argentine driving habits, in politics, and in the home.

The Argentine, in Fillol's view, tends to be an autocratic father and an obedient son. Fillol's words evoke family socialization patterns in both Haiti and the Dominican Republic, as well as Banfield's Montegrano. The father "is apt to be arbitrary, inconsistent, and unpredictable in the treatment of his children. Such attitudes may inculcate in the child a feeling that he is not valued, that it is reasonable to handle interpersonal situations in terms of power, and above all, that the world around him is unmanageable, that its reponses to his actions are random, and thus that he is not responsible for such reactions or, indeed, for his behavior . . . suspicion is the reasonable attitude towards the world."[49]

Fillol believes these tendencies are reinforced by the son's[50] observation of how the father conducts himself and by his experience (e.g., in school, in work) growing up. He concludes that Argentines live in a rigid, static, self-perpetuating value system.

Observers often refer to Argentina as "European," a country of "European immigrants," which tends to deepen the mystery surrounding Argentina's problems. After all, Western European societies are generally successful, stable, and progressive. Fillol stresses that Argentina is *not* European; it is Spanish and Italian, and there is so much similarity between Spanish and Italian culture that there is not really much difference between Argentina and other countries of Spanish America when it comes to the way people see the world.

Fillol thus believes that immigration has made little difference to Argentina, that "its *dominant* [Hispanic] cultural characteristics remained basically unchanged, as witnessed by Argentina's history as an independent republic."[51]

The political history of the republic can best be depicted in terms of the Argentine national character. It is a tale of power, of struggle between "superiors" and "subordinates," of autocracy, of complete centralization of decision-making in the hands of the ruling hierarchy — a natural consequence of the need for dependency and need for aggression conspicuous in the majority of Argentines. By and large, whoever has been in a position of political power has made use of it for his personal benefit. The nation's problems have typically been solved by force and power — rarely by the cooperative, unselfish efforts of the individuals, communities, or institutions concerned.[52]

Notwithstanding the centuries-long persistence of those aspects of Hispanic culture that get in the way of progress, Fillol believes changes are possible that can increase Argentina's chances for a happier future. He points to the workplace as a setting in which changes can be introduced that will ultimately reverberate throughout the static culture, including the family. Foremost among such changes are the decentralization of authority and responsibility; encouragement of broadened participation in decision-making; development of cooperative skills by emphasizing teamwork; and sustained effort to link advancement with merit.

Fillol concludes that "steady, long-run economic development will hardly take place in Argentina unless there is a simultaneous change in the value orientation profile of the people."[53]

Australia

Australia has to be considered a successful country. Its per capita GNP of $9,820 in 1980, life expectancy of seventy-four years, and 100 percent adult literacy clearly place it among the world's developed countries. Its democratic institutions are deeply rooted and dynamic, and it has been a leader in social reform.

Australia's first immigrants were mostly British convicts.[54] The continent was not formally claimed by the British until 1770, when James Cook visited Botany Bay and named the surrounding area New South Wales. When the British lost the American War of Independence, they lost a dumping ground for convicts, as many as one thousand of whom had been shipped to the southern colonies each year. Australia was a logical substitute, and on January 26, 1788, more than one thousand criminals and their guards arrived at Botany Bay, near present-day Sydney.

The colony barely survived its first few years. The aboriginal Australians, who may have numbered about 300,000 (coincidentally, the same number of Indians estimated in Argentina when the Spaniards arrived), were peaceful and posed no problem. But the settlers knew little about agriculture, lacked discipline, and nearly starved. The leadership of the first governor, Arthur Phillip, was principally responsible for the colony's survival.

Early Australian society was rigidly stratified between those who came to the colony with their reputations intact (the military and civil administrators) and the "felonry." The former came to be known as "exclusionists," the latter, now free, as "emancipists." Russell Ward quotes John Hood's views, published in 1843: "Caste in Hindostan is not more rigidly regarded than it is in Australia: the bond and free, emancipist and exclusionist, seldom associate together familiarly."[55]

There were leveling forces at work, however. Life was rustic, and the rough-hewn manners of the emancipists tended to infect the exclusionists. An "oceanic tide" (Ward's words) of Bengal rum was an effective common denominator. So, too, was the fluidity of colonial society: many emancipists became successful businessmen. And during the first thirty years, men outnumbered women four to one, a condition propitious for the most powerful leveler of them all.

Children born in the colony, often in the most chaotic and dissolute family circumstances, were referred to as "currency" children, an analogy with the hodgepodge of currency that circulated. They were the first generation of true Australians, and, almost miraculously, they were dramatically different from their parents, both in appearance ("tall in person, and slender in their limbs, of fair complexion and small features")[56] and in character ("simplicity of character . . . little tainted by the vices so prominent among their parents . . . Drunkenness is almost unknown to them, and honesty proverbial").[57]

Ward believes that economic opportunity, which was significantly greater in Australia than in Britain, was the principal incentive for the currency youngsters to turn from the life-styles of their parents. But he also observes that conditions in the homes were so awful that children wanted to get out on their own as soon as possible. The children kept some of the better values of their parents, "such as group loyalty, or hatred of informers and of affected manners,"[58] but they otherwise appeared to be mutations. Ward concludes:

> From the most unpromising possible material there developed in a few short years the self-reliant progenitors of a free and generous people. By 1821 New South Wales had begun to be something much more than the miserable slave farm which had been founded thirty-three years earlier. Not only was a vigorous and self-respecting generation of native-born people growing up, but a new class of respectable free immigrants, not mainly dependent upon colonial civil or military establishments, had begun to make its appearance.[59]

It was at about this time that sheep were introduced to the extensive grasslands to the west of the New South Wales coastal range. The sheep prospered, and the easily accessible pasture lands were soon occupied by squatters. In the Australian context, the word "squatter" was applied to ranchers who raised livestock on vast tracts of land to which they had no title. As in Argentina and elsewhere, these large landholders came to constitute a politically powerful elite.

But simultaneously, a liberalizing political process was evolving that would effectively check the power of the squatters much as the Barbadian plantocracy was ultimately checked. An Australian has observed, ". . . even though livestock was the base of the economy during the 19th century, the ranchers never got to be the governing class."[60] This can scarcely be said for Argentina.

In 1823, the British parliament established a Legislative Council for New South Wales. The Council was strengthened in 1828, although the appointed governor still held very broad powers, principally by virtue of his authority to appoint Council members. Largely through the efforts of William Charles Wentworth, a "currency" man (his mother had been a convict) who started a newspaper in 1835, Parliament further strengthened the Council in 1842 by increasing the number of representatives from fifteen to thirty-six, of whom two-thirds were to be elected. The franchise was limited, however, to men who owned substantial property.

In 1850, this same representative structure was established by Parliament for all four Australian colonies then in being: New South Wales (where it had operated since 1842), Van Diemen's Land (which would become Tasmania), Victoria, and South Australia. And the franchise was extended, although it was not until 1856 that universal manhood suffrage and the secret ballot (the "Australian ballot") were introduced, in South Australia.

In 1855 and 1856, Parliament authorized the four colonies to write their own constitutions, all of which were influenced by the United States constitution.[61]

As in the u.s., the Australian frontier experience both increased the sense of nationhood and promoted democracy. In both countries the frontier (referred to in Australia as "the bush") contributed to a sense of pragmatism, a disposition toward problem-solving, and an appreciation for equality of opportunity. The frontier taught self-reliance, but it also taught the importance of cooperation, on which survival often depended. Perhaps the only significant difference between the Australian and the American frontier experience was the much greater collectivism stimulated by the former. The Australian concept of "mateship" was born on the frontier. How different the Australian and American experience from the barbarism of the Argentine pampa!

In 1851, two years after gold was discovered at Sutter's Mill in California, a major gold deposit was found in Australia on the western side of the coastal mountains, at Summerhill Creek, and another soon thereafter near Ballarat, Victoria. Australians left their regular jobs and flocked to the gold fields. They were soon followed by hordes of immigrants. With the exceptions of a brief and bloody uprising of miners antagonized by arbitrary government controls and some anti-Chinese riots sparked by American prospectors (Ward estimates there were about 40,000 Chinese and four or five thousand Americans in the gold fields), Australia absorbed the gold-rush pressures and people comfortably. According to Ward, Australia's population totaled 405,000 just before the discovery of gold. Ten years later, the total was 1,140,000.

The large majority of the immigrants were British, and mostly from the middle class. Australia suddenly found itself with a substantial number of educated people who knew a trade or profession and who were generally committed to liberal or even radical politics. They imparted additional momentum toward nationhood and added further impulse to the process of democratization: Ward quotes an Englishman of the post-gold-rush era as saying that Australian society was English "with the upper class left out."[62]

The generally liberal tenor of Australian politics at that time was reflected in repeated efforts, beginning in 1860 in Victoria, to help small farmers acquire land. The laws were frequently circumvented by the squatters, particularly at the outset. But while large farms and ranches remain a feature of contemporary land tenure patterns, one observer concludes that there has been a significant redistribution of land and that there is a large and influential body of smallholders.[63]

The evolution of the education system also followed a liberal path. The schools were the responsibility of religion in the early colonial days. But in 1851, South Australia ended subsidies to church schools, and free and compulsory education was enacted in Victoria in 1872, in South Australia and Queensland in 1875, and in New South Wales in 1880.

Political liberalization kept apace. Universal adult male suffrage was practiced in most of Australia by 1872 and throughout the country by 1900; universal female suffrage was in force by 1908; and members of all legislative bodies were being paid by 1900.

The economy was steadily diversifying. Cattle joined sheep on the extensive pasture lands. Cereal — particularly wheat — production became increasingly important. Large quantities of sugar were produced in Queensland and New South Wales. And important deposits of silver, lead, zinc, and then iron and coal were discovered and exploited. Substantial flows of British capital contributed to steadily increasing prosperity.

The labor movement also developed rapidly. As early as 1856, small craft unions had won the eight-hour day for members. The first intercolony trade union congress was held in 1879. By 1886, bush-workers in New South Wales, Victoria, Queensland, and South Australia were organized in highly effective unions. Ward believes that "Trade unionism in Australia was stronger than in any other country at the time."[64]

The Australian Labor Party made its debut with a bang in the 1891 legislative elections in New South Wales, winning thirty-six seats, which gave it the balance of power. Similar gains occurred in Queensland in 1893. From the outset, Labor politicians pursued a pragmatic line, eschewing doctrinaire socialism. Their objective was "to make the economy work more effectively and to protect less fortunate citizens from its untrammelled operations,"[65] and in this respect the Labor Party's orientation is similar to that of the Democratic Party in the United States. Labor's innovations included arbitration machinery for labor disputes, minimum working conditions and maximum hours, and new and more effective land reform schemes.

Nationhood and continued progress

The emergence of the Labor Party in the individual colonies was one more impulse toward nationhood. Technological advances in transportation and communications had facilitated contact among the colonies (albeit imperfectly — the railroad system, which by 1888 had joined Melbourne, Sydney, Brisbane, and Adelaide, suffered from the use of different gauges from one colony to the next). Above all, Australians increasingly sensed the mutuality of their interests, their identification with one another, their sense of belonging to the great island continent and not to Great Britain. In 1900, a constitution that was strongly influenced by the Constitution of the United States and that had been confirmed by popular referendum was ratified by the British Parliament. The new nation was born on January 1, 1901.

Australia was guided through its first decade as an independent country by Alfred Deakin, of the Protectionist Party, who, with Labor Party support, was prime minister during the periods 1903–04, 1905–08, and 1909–10. Deakin was a gifted leader who pursued liberal policies, but it was during his stewardship that a "White Australia" policy was established. The policy reflected the belief in white superiority generally accepted in the

West at the time, but it also reflected Australia's special concerns for the preservation of a high standard of living for its working class. The second-class status of Australia's aboriginal colored people was formalized by this policy.

Consistent with his party's name, Deakin also introduced, in 1906, a protectionist tariff policy requiring that Australian industry assure good wages and working conditions to its laborers. This led, in 1907, to the establishment of a minimum wage. The use of protectionism as an incentive to industrial development has been cited as one of the key reasons Australian industry has outperformed industry in Argentina, where tariffs are viewed principally as a means of obtaining public revenue.[66]

Under the leadership of Andrew Fisher, the Labor Party won the 1910 elections — the first labor party in the world to do so — and welfare-state legislation expanded. Coverage of old age and invalid pensions was extended, maternity allowances were introduced, government workers were given access to the Arbitration Court, a land tax was established, and a publicly owned bank, which has since become the central bank, was introduced. But Fisher also concerned himself with national development. He initiated construction of the first railroad across the desert to Western Australia, and he started work on the new federal capital at Canberra. He also strengthened the Australian army and navy.

Australia's forces fought bravely in World War I, particularly at Gallipoli, where their casualties were staggering: 10,000 Australians and New Zealanders (organized in the Australian and New Zealand Army Corps, whence ANZAC) lost their lives.

Labor lost control of the government in 1917, and anti-Labor governments, often coalitions of the Nationalist and Country parties (the former had earlier been called the Liberal Party and would later return to this name; the latter represented essentially rural interests), were in office from 1917 to 1941, with the exception of 1930 – 31. High tariffs were sustained, the government promoted industrial and agricultural research and development, and industry continued to grow, as did agricultural productivity.

When the Great Depression struck, Australia still was mainly an exporter of primary products, and it suffered more than most advanced countries, with unemployment almost reaching 30 percent. One consequence was the return of Labor to federal power, albeit short-lived. James Scullin became prime minister in 1929. Economic conditions did not improve, and Scullin was ousted in 1931 by a right-wing Laborite, Joseph Aloysius Lyons, who had helped to create a new anti-Labor party, the United Australia Party. Recovery was very slow, but Lyons remained in office until his death in 1939.

Lyons was succeeded by Robert G. Menzies, who was in office when World War II erupted. Australia declared war on Nazi Germany shortly after Britain did, and Australian fighting men reached the Mediterranean war zone early in 1940. Their reputation for bravery was strengthened by repeated rear-guard actions as the Germans moved eastward, for example, in Greece, Crete, and North Africa.

Menzies' first term was brief. The Labor Party, which was traditionally identified with Australian nationalism and a strong defense posture, was returned to power under John Curtin shortly before Pearl Harbor.

The Japanese bombed several Australian ports, and a midget submarine sank a ferry in Sydney Harbor. The Australian navy participated in the Battle of the Coral Sea, and the army defeated the Japanese on New Guinea. The Australian Ninth Division played an important role in the German defeat at El Alamein. By the end of 1942, the tide of the war had turned, and Australians, who had lived with the threat of imminent invasion, could breathe more easily.

As in the United States, the war was the ultimate cure in Australia for the lingering effects of the Depression. It precipitated a boom not only by eliminating unemployment but also by stimulating industrial development. Australia's only possible outside source of heavy armaments and industrial products was the United States, whose industrial base was under intense pressure from its own needs and those of Russia and Britain. Australia consequently had to depend mostly on itself. This spurred industrial diversification, which along with military demands, led to acute labor shortages. One consequence was a more liberal immigration policy and the arrival of two million "New Australians" between 1945 and 1966.

Robert Menzies returned to power in 1949, now as the head of the Liberal Party in coalition with the Country Party. The Soviet takeover of Eastern Europe produced the same kind of obsession in Australia that nurtured McCarthyism in the United States. Menzies' government passed a "Communist Party Dissolution Bill" that amounted to an assault on the Australian Communist Party and individual communists. The bill was declared unconstitutional by the High Court, and a subsequent attempt to amend the Constitution was defeated in a nationwide referendum. Ward observes that "the vast majority of Australians were almost as strongly opposed to Communism as were Americans at the same period; but they were apparently less ready to sacrifice traditional liberties in the name of opposing it."[67]

The economic boom persisted under the durable leadership of Menzies, who retired early in 1966 after more than sixteen consecutive years in office. But the Liberal – Country Party coalition remained in power for six more years. Agricultural production was increasingly diversified, and research led to steady increases in productivity. Essentially the same pattern of growth was experienced in the minerals sector. Significant oil finds reduced Australia's dependence on foreign suppliers, which had cost it dearly during World War II. "By 1965, relative to its population, Australia had one of the strongest and best-balanced economies in the world,"[68] in Ward's view.

The social revolution of the 1960s in the United States was paralleled in Australia by increasing concerns, particularly among young people, about the rights of aboriginal Australians and the "White Australia" immigration policies. Progress was made on both scores.

Australia's relationship with the United States had intensified to the point where concerns were frequently voiced about the Americanization of Australia, particularly with respect to growing u.s. investment. The United States had surpassed Britain in 1963 as Australia's principal foreign investor, and by the end of 1980, the u.s. total was more than $7.5 billion. (u.s. investment in Argentina at the same time totaled less than $2.5 billion.)

Partly as a result of the Liberal – Country Party coalition's support for the u.s. Vietnam intervention, the Labor Party, under Edward Gough Whitlam, returned to power in 1972, after an absence of twenty-three years. Labor enacted an ambitious reform program, including abolition of race as a criterion of immigration policy, a new deal for the aboriginal people, and significant movement toward equal rights for women.

Whitlam was turned out, however, late in 1975, largely because of economic problems associated with inflation. Malcolm Fraser was named prime minister for the Liberals. His stewardship was confirmed by elections in 1977 and 1980, as Australia groped its way through the intensifying worldwide recession. Economic problems led to a Labor victory in March 1983, with Bob Hawke replacing Fraser as prime minister.

Argentina and Australia

Australia is not paradise. Its history until fairly recently has been blemished by racist immigration policies and discrimination against its indigenous peoples. It clearly displays less social snobbery than Great Britain. But as in all human societies, Australia has its elites, and between them and the masses, at least some of the snobbery that the early colonial exclusionists felt for the emancipists is present today.

But Australia has to be viewed as a successful society, particularly by comparison with Argentina. Commonly used economic and social indicators clearly place Australia among the world's most advanced countries. Beyond that, its history has been one of dynamic progress toward a more humane, open, and just society. Along the way, it has established several precedents that have been followed elsewhere in the world: e.g., the secret ballot, the eight-hour workday, the election of a labor government.

How to explain the different paths followed by two countries with so much in common? Several scholars have examined this question with interesting results:

- The Harvard economist Arthur Smithies blames Argentina's problems principally on the irresponsible economic policies pursued by Perón.[69]
- Peter Cochrane, an Australian economist, finds an interesting Marxist explanation: "Australia was a special case . . . because the colonial structure came to sanction its industrial development. European cap-

italism not only threw out stagnation to other parts of the world; it also projected its own image to select countries such as Australia."[70]
· American political scientist Theodore Moran believes that the principal explanation resides in the differing ways the Australian Labor Party and the Argentine Radical Party managed power, and particularly tariff policy, after winning elections in the early twentieth century. In Australia, "there was no political exclusion for any group." In Argentina, ". . . the Radicals completely excluded the landed classes from the chance for success in democratic politics . . ."[71] Moran goes on to observe that the Argentine Radicals "did not build institutions of compromise" while the Australian Labor Party contributed to "building Australia's political institutions . . . [especially] the creation of ways of attempting to resolve conflicts."[72] "Subsequent economic growth led in Australia to political integration and in Argentina to political disintegration."[73]
· Aldo Ferrer (an Argentine) and E. L. Wheelwright (an Australian) perceive a pattern similar to Moran's but with deeper historical roots. "Both [countries] had a federal system, but in Australia the powerful landed interest was challenged from the very beginning. There was for example manhood suffrage and vote by ballot in most colonies by the 1850s; by 1891 there were 35 Labour members of Parliament elected to the New South Wales Legislative Assembly."[74] And, "It is clear . . . that Argentina has not been able to reach a dynamic balance between the social forces of its body politic, expressing them in the framework of democratic institutions, while Australia reached that situation [during the] last decades of the nineteenth century . . ."[75]

A number of other explanations are covered in *Argentina y Australia*, which captures the highlights of a seminar in late 1977 involving scholars from both countries. John Fogarty believes that large increases in agricultural productivity, the result of scientific research that started in the twenties, are important, but that Australia's mineral endowment is the principal explanation. John Hirst believes that the significant redistribution of Australian land, which has resulted in "a large and influential body of smallholders," is crucial. Hirst also believes that the Australian frontier experience was more beneficial than Argentina's, particularly in encouraging cooperation — the "mateship" factor. Many observers point to political stability and progress, particularly in terms of the ability of Australian society to involve all its sectors according to rules of the game accepted by all.
I find it difficult not to conclude that at the center of the explanation is Australia's success at building a well-integrated, pluralistic political system and in the process creating the concept of a nation to which the very large majority of Australians feel a strong allegiance. The system, in turn, has doubtless done more to liberate human creativity than has Argentina's. In Australia the radius of trust encompasses the nation. (Interestingly, at least

in the eyes of two Australian scholars, "The extended family . . . is not a prominent feature of Australian life."[76] That trust, along with a progressive vision of the responsibilities of a society to its people and vice versa, are the foundations of the Australian success, much as they are of Barbados's success.

Australian democracy, which reflects British culture modified by the leveling effects of Australia's peculiar geography and history, has helped confound Marx's prediction that the masses would become steadily more impoverished under capitalism. As in the United States and other Western-style democracies, the standard of living of manual laborers, urban and rural, has improved steadily. The same cannot be said for Hispanic America, where tens of millions shared highly unequally or not at all in the impressive economic growth of the first three post-World War II decades. And while Argentine urban workers benefited, particularly under Perón, rural workers remain a forgotten sector of the society.

I believe Raul Prebisch has failed to perceive that it is Argentina's political failure, rooted in its basically Hispanic culture, not its "dependency" on Great Britain and the United States, that principally explains the inequities — and, of course, the political instability — of Argentine society. The extent of these inequities is suggested by the following table, drawn from the World Bank's *World Development Report 1982*:[77, 78]

Income distribution
Percentage share of household income, by percentile group of households

Country	Year	Lowest 20%	Next-to-lowest 20%	Middle 20%	Next-to-highest 20%	Highest 20%	Highest 10%
Argentina	1970	4.4	9.7	14.1	21.5	50.3	35.2
Australia	1966 – 67	6.6	13.5	17.8	23.4	38.8	23.7
United States	1972	4.5	10.7	17.3	24.7	42.8	26.6

Yet Prebisch himself observes that his center/periphery theory is challenged by the Australian experience:

> Primary producing countries, on the periphery, have faced regularly deteriorating terms of trade . . . while the industralized economies at the centre of the capitalist world have retained the rewards of their productivity within their own borders, partly because their workers have been able to defend a level of wages which is, relative to wages elsewhere, high. Unfortunately Australia . . . falsifies this hypothesis; it is a country at the periphery, exporting raw materials, whose relatively high per capita income is no more skewed in its distribution than is the case in economies at the centre.[79]

That Australia, like Argentina, was a "dependent" country is stressed by the Australian economist N. G. Butlin:

More than any other growing new country of the time [the nineteenth century], Australia depended on the transfer of British resources,
particularly to supplement local savings. British funds dominated financing
of pastoral assets and were a major part of the finances required for communications development. This transfer, the disposal of the greater part of
exports to Britain and the purchase of most commodity imports in Britain,
all suggest a special dependent relationship of a relatively simple and rigid
sort.[80]

But the consequence was hardly exploitation:

Australian living standards appear to have been considerably above those in
Britain; the rate of growth in Australia was far higher than that in Britain;
the course of Australian economic activity was rather steadier than that of
Britain, despite quite violent economic fluctuations in the rest of the trading world; the rate of Australian growth was not intimately dependent on
export receipts; and the composition of output and the rate of growth appear to have been determined predominantly by local Australian
considerations.[81]

I conclude this chapter with the words of Argentine Guido di Tella,
spoken at the *Argentina y Australia* symposium:

It is sad, but evident enough, that countries exist which are superior to
others in certain periods of their history when it comes to setting and
achieving economic goals . . . Mediterranean culture does not appear to of-
fer a propitious base for the organization of a modern industrial society.
Until very recently, Spain did poorly. Italy did a little better, but not
much. We could then ask ourselves why a society based on colonial Spain,
that has received a massive flow of Spanish and Italian immigrants, located
in this corner of the world, should have done better.[82]

NOTES

1. Thomas F. McGann, *Argentina: The Divided Land*, p. 10.
2. V. S. Naipaul, *The Return of Eva Peron*, p. 166.
3. From a commencement address at Wesleyan University, June 1982.
4. Ezequiel Martínez Estrada, *Radiografía de la Pampa*, p. 10.
5. James R. Scobie, *Argentina: A City and a Nation*, p. 50.
6. *Ibid.*, p. 51.
7. McGann, *The Divided Land*, p. 23.
8. Figures from Scobie, *A City and a Nation*, p. 61.
9. The Spanish title is *Facundo: Civilización y Barbarie*. The book is a thinly disguised attack on Rosas. Sarmiento, as we shall see, played an important role in Argentina's political evolution.
10. McGann, *The Divided Land*, p. 26.
11. *Ibid.*, p. 27.
12. *Ibid.*
13. *Ibid.*, p. 30.
14. *Ibid.*, p. 33.

15. *Ibid.*, p. 31.
16. *Ibid.*, p. 32.
17. *Ibid.*, p. 33.
18. Carlos Rangel, *The Latin Americans: Their Love-Hate Relationship with the United States*, pp. 240 – 41.
19. McGann, *The Divided Land*, p. 40.
20. Gino Germani points out in his *Politica y Sociedad en Una Epoca de Transición* that 75 percent of Argentina's cultivable land was in the hands of 6 percent of the people in 1947 (p. 221).
21. Naipaul, *The Return of Eva Peron*, p. 119.
22. *Ibid.*, p. 179.
23. *Ibid.*, p. 171.
24. *The Boston Globe*, "Grumbling, gloom on rise in Argentina," October 3, 1981, p. 3.
25. For a more extensive discussion of dependency theory see Chapter 8.
26. Fernando Henrique Cardoso and Enzo Faletto, *Dependency and Development in Latin America*, p. 133.
27. *Ibid.*, pp. xv – xvi.
28. See, for example, Raul Prebisch, "Estructura socio-economica y crisis del sistema," pp. 167 – 264.
29. Cardoso and Faletto, *Dependency and Development*, p. xxii.
30. *Ibid.*, p. xxiv.
31. François Bourricaud, "The French Connection," p. 59.
32. Guillermo A. O'Donnell, *Modernization and Bureaucratic Authoritarianism: Studies in South American Politics*, p. 122.
33. u.n. Economic Commission for Latin America, *El desarrollo economico de la Argentina*, Mexico, 1959.
34. For an interesting treatment of this question see Michael Novak, "Why Latin America is Poor," pp. 66 – 75.
35. McGann, *The Divided Land*, p. 98.
36. *Ibid.*, pp. 110 – 113 passim.
37. *Ibid.*, p. 102.
38. *Ibid.*, p. 103. McGann believes that at the root of the Argentine institution of corruption was the highly centralized, rigid, but unenforceable Spanish colonial rule.
39. In *Leader and Vanguard in Mass Society: A Study of Peronist Argentina*, Jeane Kirkpatrick derives the following table from Almond and Verba's *The Civic Culture*:

	People will take advantage of you	No one much cares what happens to you	People generally help one another
Argentina	84%	69%	64%
U.S.	68	38	80
Britain	75	45	84
Germany	81	72	58
Italy	73	61	55
Mexico	94	78	82

40. McGann, *The Divided Land*, p. 108.
41. *Ibid.*, p. 100.
42. Naipaul, *The Return of Eva Peron*, pp. 107, 110 – 111, 119 – 120, 124, 149, 155, 159, 165.

43. Tomás Roberto Fillol, *Social Factors in Economic Development*, p. 3.
44. *Ibid.*, p. 13. Fillol's emphasis.
45. *Ibid.*, p. 14.
46. *Ibid.*, p. 22. Fillol's emphasis.
47. *Ibid.*, p. 21.
48. *Ibid.*
49. *Ibid.*, pp. 25, 26.
50. As with much of the literature of the period, mothers and daughters sometimes appear not to exist.
51. *Ibid.*, p. 33.
52. *Ibid.*, p. 47.
53. *Ibid.*, p. 55.
54. The principal source for the following historical review is Russel Ward, *Australia: A Short History*.
55. *Ibid.*, p. 29.
56. The quotation is from the 1823 report of a British commissioner, J. T. Bigge, cited in Ward, *Australia*, p. 41.
57. The 1827 words of a Scots surgeon, Peter Cunningham, cited in Ward, *Australia*, p. 4.
58. *Ibid.*, p. 43.
59. *Ibid.*, p. 44.
60. John Hirst in John Fogarty, Ezequiel Gallo, and Hector Dieguez, *Argentina y Australia*, p. 87.
61. Ward says that a proposal for a hereditary aristocracy was "laughed out of court" (p. 80).
62. Ward, *Australia*, p. 79. The Englishman was Sir Charles Dilke.
63. John Hirst, "La Sociedad Rural y la Política en Australia, 1850 – 1930," *Argentina y Australia*, pp. 77 – 96.
64. Ward, *Australia*, p. 107.
65. *Ibid.*, p. 112.
66. See, for example, Fogarty's views (p. 32) in *Argentina y Australia*.
67. Ward, *Australia*, p. 166.
68. *Ibid.*, p. 169.
69. Arthur Smithies, "Argentina and Australia."
70. Peter Cochrane, *Industrialization and Dependence*, pp. 3 – 4.
71. Theodore H. Moran, "The 'Development' of Argentina and Australia — The Radical Party of Argentina and the Labor Party of Australia in the Process of Economic and Political Development," p. 79.
72. *Ibid.*, p. 91.
73. *Ibid.*, p. 87.
74. Aldo Ferrer and E. L. Wheelwright, *Industrialization in Argentina and Australia: A Comparative Study* (preliminary draft), p. iii.
75. *Ibid.*, p. v.
76. D. W. McElwain and W. J. Campbell, "The Family," in A. F. Davies and S. Encel, *Australian Society*.
77. Income distribution in the United States, while not as badly skewed as Argentina's, is measurably less equitable than Australia's.
78. The income distribution difference is stressed by Alberto Petrecolla in *Argentina y Australia*. Petrecolla observes, ". . . there exists a notable difference in the distribution of income of the two societies, perhaps the most notable of the differences indicated in these sessions, with a much greater equality in the Australian case" (p. 230).
79. Quoted in Barrie Dyster, "Argentine and Australian Development Compared," p. 94.
80. N. C. Butlin, *Investment in Australian Economic Development 1861 – 1900*, p. 5.
81. *Ibid.*
82. Fogarty, Gallo, and Dieguez, *Argentina y Australia*, p. 183.

7

Spain and Spanish America

Here is a quiz for students of Hispanic-American history:

1. In what country during the period 1814 – 1876 were there seven constitutions, two civil wars, and thirty-five attempts by the military to overthrow the government (eleven of them successful)?
2. What was the first country which, in the face of political chaos and bloodshed, established a system under which liberals and conservatives would alternate in power?
3. In which country did one percent of the landowners own 42 percent of the land early in this century?
4. Which country experienced six peasant revolts and five urban uprisings between 1827 and 1917?
5. In which country in this century did civil strife in which foreign intervention played a key role lead to the installation of a military dictatorship that endured four decades?

The quiz is, of course, deceptive. The answer to each question is Spain. But in each case, the question evokes one or more Hispanic-American countries. Question one sounds like a number of countries in the hemisphere, Bolivia foremost among them. Question two brings Colombia to mind. Question three sounds like most Latin American countries. Question four suggests Mexico and perhaps Argentina. And question five evokes the Somoza dynasty in Nicaragua and (though of somewhat shorter duration) the Trujillo dictatorship in the Dominican Republic.

While the quiz itself strongly suggests the close parallels between recent Spanish history and Spanish-American history, a brief review of the former will be helpful. For this review I will be drawing principally on Pierre Vilar's *Spain — A Brief History*; E. Ramon Arango's *The Spanish Political System: Franco's Legacy*; and Eléna de la Souchère's *An Explanation of Spain*.

As we observed in the preceding chapter, one of the factors contributing to Argentina's and indeed all of Spanish America's independence was the Napoleonic Wars, whose Iberian extension is referred to as the Peninsular Wars. The French occupied Spain from 1808 to 1814, and Napoleon established his brother Joseph on the Spanish throne. Arango observes, "It is the opinion of many careful observers of Spanish history and politics that

132

perhaps only a crusade against foreign invasion — whether of ideas or troops — gives the Spanish people a sense of mission sufficiently strong to unify them."[1] This rare unity materialized during the French occupation, and widespread guerrilla warfare erupted.

In 1812, a legislative body at Cádiz produced a liberal constitution that drew not only from the rhetoric of the French revolution but also from a homebred Spanish liberalism that had evolved during the preceding century. When the British army under Wellington invaded Spain from Portugal, supported by Spanish guerrillas, the stage was set for the return of the Spanish Bourbon monarchy — now within a constitutional framework — in the person of Ferdinand VII. Ferdinand, however, rejected the Cádiz constitution and proceeded to rule (misrule is probably more apt) Spain as an absolute king for nineteen years. Vilar observes, "The masses of *España negra* (black — or reactionary — Spain) triumphed over the enlightened minority."[2]

Ferdinand's reign was chaotic and destructive. For the first six years, those committed to the Cádiz constitution plotted his overthrow. In 1820, a military force that was supposed to suppress independence movements in the American colonies turned on the king instead and forced him to restore the constitution. Three years later, Ferdinand was back in control, and the constitution was again junked. In 1824, following the disastrous Spanish defeat at Ayacucho in Peru, South America was effectively lost to the mother country.

Ferdinand died in 1833. His brother, Don Carlos, claimed the throne, as did Ferdinand's wife, Maria Cristina, in the name of their three-year-old daugher, Isabel. The first "Carlist" War was the result. Maria Cristina lasted as regent until 1839. She was forced to accept the Cádiz constitution in 1836, although it was replaced with a more conservative version in 1837. In that year, the lands of the Church were expropriated. But rather than being distributed to peasants, which could have changed the course of Spanish social and political history, they were sold, for the most part to the affluent.

Maria Cristina was ousted when progressive military elements led by General Baldomero Espartero succeeded in a *pronunciamiento* — a declaration by the military, the ultimate arbiter of power in Spain, as to how politics are to be ordered. In reflecting on what he describes as "The age of the *pronunciamiento*" (1832 – 75), Vilar says, "Caprice . . . is the natural regime of the Spanish people, who temper it at the top by the *pronunciamiento* and at the bottom by anarchy . . . it explains why even today the Spanish people look less to King or Parliament than to the Army or Revolution in the streets."[3]

Maria Cristina's daughter Isabel came of age in 1843 and was named Queen (Isabel II) following another *pronunciamiento* that removed Espartero. In 1844, General Ramon María Narváez gained control, and a constitution placing major power in his hands was decreed in the following year. The Carlist guerrillas again appeared but were suppressed by Narváez.

General Leopoldo O'Donnell arrived on the scene via another *pronunciamiento* in 1854. He and Narváez alternated in power until 1868. Seven *pronunciamientos* were attempted between 1864 and 1868, but only after both O'Donnell and Narváez died did power pass to new hands.

The period between 1868 and 1875 was marked by another try at constitutionality. The new charter called for a king, and Amadeo, son of the King of Italy, took the throne in 1870 after one of the provisional rulers, General Prim y Prats, sought unsuccessfully to arrange for a Hohenzollern to be monarch.[4] Prim y Prats was murdered the day Amadeo arrived, and continuing instability and violence, including the resumption of the Carlist war, led to Amadeo's abdication in 1873. The Bourbon line was restored the following year with the installation of Alfonso xii, son of Isabel ii.

Throughout the sixty-six-year period from the Peninsular Wars to the Restoration, the Spanish army continually intervened in politics. Its political orientation during those turbulent years was generally liberal, although not because of ideology: "The army was liberal only because it was against certain things dear to the hearts and minds of the conservatives"[5] (e.g. aristocratic prerogatives, the privileges of the Church). In the long run what was most significant about the military role was that ". . . it legitimized to the present day the tradition of military intervention in politics when such intrusion was deemed necessary to preserve national unity or to preserve the integrity of the armed forces."[6]

The eminent Spanish intellectual Salvador de Madariaga labeled the phenomenon of military involvement "praetorianism," bemoaning a condition in which ". . . a body of officers . . . controls the political life of the nation, giving but little thought to foreign affairs and intent on the preservation of power and on the administration and enjoyment of a disproportionate amount of the budget."[7] De Madariaga also observed that ". . . military education has disastrous effects on Spanish psychology. The Spanish character has an innate tendency to become overbearing. The military law of obedience from below and orders from above encourages such a tendency."[8]

A new constitution was enacted in 1876 that served as a backdrop to an arrangement between the Liberal and Conservative parties under which the parties alternated in power. The arrangement, which was managed principally by Conservative Antonio Cánovas del Castillo and Liberal Praxedes Sagasta, resulted in an unprecedented degree of political tranquillity. But the alternation scheme required predetermined election results, which were achieved by rigging, intimidation, and bribery in the electoral process, reminiscent, in several respects, of techniques employed by the Argentine conservatives for more than half a century. It was a charade that postponed once again the opportunity for the Spanish people to experience a working

democracy. Moreover, the tranquillity was that of stagnation, not progress.
The scheme

> froze the Spanish state in attitudes favorable to the elites, the liberal and
> conservative "consensus groups" that supported the alternating govern-
> ments. As in France, the values frozen were largely preindustrial, beneficial
> primarily to those socioeconomic elements seeking to delay industrializa-
> tion. . . . The lower classes, forced out of democratic politics and deprived
> of effective electoral expression, turned to direct action — strikes, violence,
> and assassinations — and to new sources of political inspiration, socialism
> and anarchism.[9]

Alfonso XII died at the age of twenty-eight in 1885. His queen, Maria
Cristina, took over as regent for her son, Alfonso XIII. During her regency,
Spain experienced the shattering humiliation of the Spanish-American War
of 1898, in which the only remaining Spanish colonies in the Western
Hemisphere and Asia (Cuba, Puerto Rico, and the Philippines) were lost
to the United States.

Alfonso XIII came of age in 1902. Sagasta was assassinated in 1903.
(Cánovas had died of natural causes in 1897.) The alternation scheme broke
down, and the Liberal and Conservative parties both experienced major
defections that led to a proliferation of new parties. Alfonso was not prone
to self-restraint, as were his mother and father, and he soon became an
active participant in politics. He succeeded in undermining government after
government (there were thirty-three of them between 1902 and 1923). Alfonso's rise to dominance was paralleled by increasing activism on the part
of the military, who had been humiliated and demoralized by the Spanish-
American War. In 1909, a call to active duty in Morocco of reserves from
Catalonia led to a bloody suppression of Catalan protesters. The first nationwide general strike, in 1917, was similarly put down. A year earlier,
the military had organized itself into "defense committees," the goal of which
was to assure that the military institution would not be subordinated to
civilian authority. "The army had once again become the arbiter of Spanish
politics, as it had been through most of the nineteenth century."[10]

The general strike had been prompted by the intensifying economic
problems of the masses, principally the consequence of inflation. Regional
separatist sentiment intensified, particularly in Catalonia. The Bolshevik
success in Russia reverberated through Spain, where the labor movement
was divided between socialists and anarchists. Assassinations and other
forms of political violence were daily occurrences. Unsuccessful military
operations in Morocco further aggravated a very volatile situation. Arango
observes:

> By the 1920's . . . the elites and the masses faced each other across barriers
> of fear and hatred while among the working classes themselves conflict was

growing deeper. The socialists and the anarchists loathed and mistrusted one another as only brothers can, and to this enduring animosity were added the Communists after 1917.[11]

Late in 1923, General Miguel Primo de Rivera, "a carouser, a voracious eater, a womanizer,"[12] orchestrated a *pronunciamiento* that signaled the end of the constitutional monarchy (although Alfonso XIII remained on the throne). Arango diagnoses the causes of the new dictatorship as "an upper class hermetically sealed in ignorance; a brutalized lower class maintained in a festering thraldom; a corrupt and unctuous clergy within a church bereft of decency or legitimacy; an army commanded by men not merely ignorant but stupid."[13]

Primo de Rivera conducted himself like any number of larger-than-life Hispanic-American *caudillos*. He initiated grandiose development projects. He spent enormous sums on an exposition in Seville (like Trujillo's 1955 – 56 International Fair in Santo Domingo). He instituted a rigid system of censorship. He pushed the state into a variety of new enterprises.

But he also attempted to reform the top-heavy army (the ratio of officers to enlisted men was the highest in Europe), and this was his undoing. The affected military officers took their grievances to the king who, unhappy in Primo de Rivera's shadow, sided with them. Primo de Rivera resigned early in 1930 and died soon thereafter in Paris, where, according to Arango, "he spent the last days of his life alternately whoring and confessing."[14]

The flimsy political fabric covering Alfonso soon unraveled as pressures for a new republic built rapidly toward a national consensus. With all his support gone, Alfonso abdicated on April 14, 1931, following overwhelming prorepublic votes in municipal elections.

The second republic and civil war

Arango draws a parallel between the German Weimar Republic and the Spanish Second Republic, born in 1931: they both "died simply because each was beyond the political capacity of its people."[15] He goes on to quote Harry Eckstein on Weimar:

This unalleviated democracy was superimposed upon a society pervaded by authoritarian relationships and obsessed with authoritarianism . . . German families were dominated more often than not by tyrannical husbands and fathers, German schools by tyrannical teachers, German firms by tyrannical bosses.[16]

Of the conditions in Spain at the time, Arango says:

The church was authoritarian (in Spain one is almost tempted to call it totalitarian); the army was despotic and infected with scandal . . . the school system was as authoritarian as the church itelf, and if run by the state was as corrupt and featherbedded as the state itself; the civil service was a spoils system ripened to the point of putrefaction; the family was ruled by a pater-familias who brooked no opposition.[17]

A liberal constitution was ratified in elections at the end of 1931 that brought to power a left-wing government. But the consensus for a republic did not extend to the way the republican concept was being implemented:

> The polity fractionalized into over twenty parties fanning from Left to Right, each desirous of a republic tailored to its own ideological nature and each unaware of or unconcerned with the procedural consensus that trans-forms political rhetoric into effective democracy.[18]

In a climate of what Arango terms "pentecostal politics,"[19] the "Red Biennium" was initiated. The Church was the principal target: the govern-ment abrogated the Concordat of 1851, abolished public financing of church personnel, closed all Catholic schools except seminaries, outlawed the Jes-uits, and abolished religious burials unless specifically willed by the deceased.

The government then turned its attention to the army, which was still top-heavy. Ignoring the grave costs Primo de Rivera had paid for a similar program, the government offered early retirement at full pay to most officers. Roughly half of them accepted, "and many of these then used their well-paid free time to plot against the Republican regime."[20]

Although the government had adopted a prodecentralization policy and granted autonomy to Catalonia, which actively supported the govern-ment, when the Basques sought similar treatment, they were turned down because of their conservative, pro-Church orientation. Thus another sworn enemy was created.

The government also failed to respond adequately to one of its own constituents: the land-hungry rural poor. An Agrarian Reform Institute was created (it was run by a journalist), but, after two years, the amount of land that had been distributed was minuscule.

It was not surprising, then, that the left was overwhelmed by the right in the elections of 1933. Aside from the voting blocs antagonized by the policies and failures of the Red Biennium, the left suffered from its own divisions: the anarchists refused to go to the polls "in the name of doctrinal purity."[21]

The rightist landslide initiated the "Black Biennium," essentially a period of reaction to the policies of the Red Biennium. The reactionary policies pursued by the government were within the bounds of the consti-tution, but when a rightist party (CEDA, the Spanish Confederation of Au-tonomous Rightist Parties) that was anathema to the left was brought into the governing coalition in 1934, Leftist leaders effectively renounced the constitution. "They did not content themselves with declaring their oppo-sition to the *program* of the Right, a stance within the concept of loyal democratic opposition; they declared themselves against the *existing institutions of the country* — institutions they themselves had created."[22]

When three CEDA members were named to cabinet jobs on October 1, 1934, the left responded with "the most intensive, destructive proletarian insurrection in the history of Western Europe to that date."[23] De Madariaga observes, "With the rebellion of 1934, the Left lost every shred of moral authority to condemn the rebellion of 1936."[24]

The uprising triggered violence throughout the country as clandestine militias representing groups across the political spectrum came out into the open. In virtually total chaos, elections were called for early 1936. The left was returned to power with a substantial majority. The moderate Indalecio Prieto and the increasingly radical Francisco Largo Caballero vied for control of the Socialist party. Prodded by Largo Caballero, whom Brian Crozier identifies as bearing more responsibility for the impending civil war than anyone else,[25] the government adopted increasingly radical policies. The war was triggered by the murder of rightist José Calvo Sotelo by the republican police force on July 12, 1936.

The Spanish Civil War, which lasted until April 1, 1939, was astonishingly costly. Approximately 600,000 Spaniards died, many of them in acts of almost insane violence and cruelty. Vilar says, "It would be absurd to underestimate the acts of violence on both sides which still dominate the memory of the average Spaniard today. . . . One must bear in mind that in certain aspects the events reflect a Spanish temperament. There were priests who blessed the worst of fusillades; mobs who hurled monks and nuns into their graves."[26]

More than half a billion dollars in gold reserves were wiped out. Two hundred and fifty thousand houses were destroyed, another 250,000 damaged. Fifty percent of railroad rolling stock was lost. A third of all livestock was wiped out. GNP dropped by 25 percent.

The Franco years

Generalisimo Francisco Franco, leader of the victorious Nationalists, thus inherited a nation in physical, institutional, and psychic shambles. As the quintessential *caudillo*, Franco ruled with an iron fist, especially during his first decade. Although his rhetoric was progressive and nationalistic, he "tried to freeze Spain into a sociopolitical mold similar to that discarded by England a century and a half ago."[27] The official statutes of Nationalist Spain state: ". . . the Chief assumes full and absolute authority. The Chief answers to God and to History."[28]

Franco had been backed by Nazi Germany and Fascist Italy, and his philosophy was clearly closer to them than to the Allies. He was an astute politican, however, and he equilibrated Spain's foreign policy to the ebb and flow of World War II. As the tide turned against Hitler, Franco became more neutral. As the Allies took the upper hand, they increasingly gained Spain's sympathies.

Active participation in World War II was out of the question. After suffering the near-mortal wounds of the Civil War, Spain needed time to recuperate and heal. During these first years, Franco pursued a policy of autarchy — self-sufficiency at a low level of consumption. The policy was in part dictated by realities imposed by World War II. But it was a policy that placed severe limits on the speed of Spain's recovery.

Spain's strategic position was enhanced by the shift in international dynamics toward the Cold War, and by the early 1950s it was possible to pursue a major base rights agreement with the United States. Spain was opened up to the rest of the world, Franco shifted his internal alliances from the traditional conservatives to the technocrats of *Opus Dei*, and the result was a sustained economic boom that has substantially transformed Spain economically, socially, and politically. A country that had been largely cut off from the rest of the world suddenly opened itself up to trade, investment, tourists, and above all ideas, particularly from Western Europe and the United States. The opening up brought about major changes in the way Spaniards saw the world.

Toward democracy

The boom particularly benefited the oligarchy, who had also done well during the period of autarchy. Franco tried to buy off labor with a progressive system of social benefits, but he continued to prohibit (1) the organization of labor unions independent of the government, and (2) strikes. Labor unrest intensified through the Franco years, and the labor movement came increasingly under far-left influence.

The effect of economic growth on the middle class was profound. "The increase in economic well-being was just enough to make the middle classes want even more, to make them want the remaining rights and privileges enjoyed by members of those classes in all the other Western countries, above all freedom of assembly and the right to organize into political parties and to form pressure groups."[29]

Franco's system was further strained by increasing student activism and by the dramatic shift in Church values and attitudes following the 1965 Vatican Council of Pope John XXIII, which brought the Church into the twentieth century with its focus on the human condition.

Spain was a very different country in 1975, when Franco died, than it was when he became *caudillo*, in 1936. Notwithstanding his goal of recreating a kind of nineteenth-century authoritarian state, Spain had taken many important strides toward the Western European model. But the divisions that had brought Spain so much political chaos and bloodshed still existed. In trying to build a modern democracy, King Juan Carlos had to confront a radicalized labor movement, intense separatist sentiment in the Basque country and Catalonia, and a military establishment some of whose members continued to see themselves as above the law. The intelligent and progressive policies of center-right Prime Minister Adolfo Suárez kept democracy alive through episodes of political, labor, and separatist violence from June 1976 to January 1981, when, in adverse economic conditions, Suárez resigned. Some military officers seized the opportunity of the transfer of leadership to Leopoldo Calvo Sotelo to attempt a coup, which was thwarted, largely by the skillful intervention of the king. In a major test of the democratic experiment, power was successfully transferred in 1982 from Suárez's center-right coalition to a center-left coalition under Socialist Felipe Gonzalez. Spain had joined NATO during the same year.

In circumstances in several respects similar to those of the Dominican Republic, Spain has clearly moved into the twentieth century. But its democratic roots need time to become firmly established, and the traditional centrifugal forces of Hispanic culture are still at work. Nonetheless, real progress has been made in constructing a pluralistic political system with which the majority of Spaniards can identify.

The economic picture

Spain is relatively well endowed with natural resources. It is second (after France) in total land area in Western Europe. It is the highest in land cultivated per person. Eléna de la Souchère asserts, "The soil in Spain is among the most productive in the world."[30] But it is true that many agricultural areas suffer from a shortage of rainfall, which brings de la Souchère to the conclusion that "at all times in Spanish history, irrigation should have been the prime national objective."[31]

Spain's mineral endowment is rich: it produces large quantities of iron, coal, copper, lead, mercury, tungsten, zinc, manganese, and sulfur. But, as was the case with irrigation, effective mining operations required complicated collective efforts. In de la Souchère's view,

> Coordination, foresight, method: these were the conditions indispensable to the achievement of prosperity. And it was precisely these conditions which the Iberian character found the most repugnant. At the very root of Spanish poverty, there is a divorce between man and the soil, between the individual energies of men and the collective discipline required for cultivation of the soil. Hence, Spanish mineral deposits, sometimes neglected and more often ceded to foreign development companies, have enriched only foreign stockholders and a few Spanish businessmen. . . . Still more grave is the way in which agricultural resources have been laid waste. Deforestation and greedy cultivation of the soil without care for the future, with no other thought than the immediate yield, have made way for the scourge of scourges: erosion.[32]

Except in some northern provinces, particularly Catalonia and the Basque country, the industrial revolution largely passed Spain by until the middle of the twentieth century. And agricultural production increased very slowly, partly because Spain was slow to apply technological advances, partly because of an archaic pattern of land distribution that, among other inefficiencies, kept large tracts of good land in the hunting preserves of the oligarchy. We are again reminded of Latin America when de la Souchère observes that demographic expansion

> was not accompanied by those compensating phenomena which occurred everywhere else in Europe: an increase in the global volume of consumer goods and their redistribution through salary raises, progressive taxes, and, most importantly, by a form of land distribution or at least by shares in agrarian revenue. . . . The capital fact isolating Spain from these other nations . . . is the failure of each attempt to parcel out the great landholdings in the southern part of the Peninsula.[33]

While de la Souchère speaks of "collusion between Spanish oligarchical forces and foreign capital [which] guaranteed to the latter a de facto monopoly over the major activities of the Peninsula,"[34] it is clear that she attributes Spain's underdevelopment principally to cultural factors. These same factors have much to do with the large foreign presence in the Spanish economy.

The boom that started in the early 1950s, when Franco dropped his autarchy policy in favor of economic internationalism, is confirmed by a number of indicators:

- per-capita GNP increased by 4.5 percent annually during the 1951– 58 period
- total real GNP increased two and one-half times from 1953 to 1969
- electricity consumption increased from 416 kilowatt hours per capita in 1955 to 764 kilowatt hours in 1963
- 47 percent of homes had refrigerators in 1960; 85 percent of homes had refrigerators in 1969
- 1 percent of homes had television sets in 1960; 74 percent of homes had them in 1969.

Nonetheless, after Turkey and Greece, Spain is the poorest country in Western Europe, although it is usually counted as a developed country. Per-capita GNP in 1980 was $5,400, compared with $7,920 for the United Kingdom, $11,730 for France, and $13,590 for West Germany. Life expectancy and adult literacy are now comparable to Western European standards. Major inroads have been made against illiteracy in this century. According to Arango, 44 percent of adult Spaniards were illiterate in 1920, 30 percent in 1931, and 23 percent in 1940.[35] The World Bank records 13 percent illiteracy in 1960.

Spanish culture

Much has been written about Spanish national character. In his book *The Modernization of Puerto Rico — A Political Study of Changing Values and Institutions*, Henry Wells develops a profile of Hispanic character from this extensive literature. He believes the profile is apt for both Spain and Spanish America.

In Wells's opinion, at the foundation of the Hispanic world view are four fundamental value premises:

1. *Fatalism* ("life is shaped by forces beyond human control")[36]
2. *Hierarchy* (society is naturally hierarchical; one's position depends on one's birth)
3. *Dignity* ("the person has intrinsic worth or integrity,"[37] but this has nothing to do with rights, initiative, enterprise, or equality of opportunity)
4. *Male superiority* (from which flow authoritarianism, paternalism, and machismo)

Wells perceives links among the values of hierarchy, dignity, and male superiority that explain an "addiction to strong leaders and acceptance of authoritarian rule."[38] He goes on to say, "Hispanic peoples have never found democracy particularly attractive precisely because they attach little value to widely shared power."[39]

José Ortega y Gasset singled out what he calls "particularism" as "the most widespread and dangerous characteristic of modern Spanish life."[40] He defines particularism as

> that state of mind in which we believe that we need pay no attention to others. . . . Taking others into account implies at least an understanding of the state of mutual dependence and cooperation in which we live. . . .
> Among normal nations, a class that desires something for itself tries to get it by agreement with the other classes. . . . But a class attacked by particularism feels humiliated when it realizes that in order to achieve its desires it must resort to these organs of the common will.[41]

Wells examines Hispanic individualism, with its high content of pride, and relates it to the rarity of collective action and organization in Hispanic societies, with obvious costs for development. Ortega y Gasset notes one of these costs: "Incapable of perceiving the excellence of his neighbor, the proud man impedes the perfecting of the individual and the refining of his class."[42] He goes on to link this individualism to another phenomenon that gets in the way of progress:

> The perfect Spaniard needs nothing; more than that, he needs nobody.
> This is why our race are such haters of novelty and innovation. To accept

anything new from the outside world humiliates us. . . . To the true Spaniard, all innovation seems frankly a personal offense.[43]

In its most extreme form, Spanish individualism approaches misan-
thropy. Arango introduces Part 3 of *The Spanish Political System* with an
anonymous epigram: "For the Spaniard it is not enough to have heaven
guaranteed for himself; he must also have hell guaranteed for his neighbor."[44]
One particularly important consequence, in my view, of the set of
values and attitudes flowing from Spanish individualism is the failure of the
Spanish — and Latin American — elite to develop a sense of noblesse oblige.[45]
The histories of Barbados and Australia make clear, I think, that the noblesse
oblige of the British aristocracy, doubtlessly related to the concept of fair
play, had much to do with the progressive evolution of those two societies.
We recall, for example, that, in 1710, Christopher Codrington, an affluent
Barbadian planter, left his estate to an organization that educated slaves.
We remember that the British Parliament played a key role in defending
the interests of the Barbadian masses against the efforts of the plantocracy
to preserve its power and privileges in the nineteenth century. Parliament
played a similarly constructive role as Australia moved toward greater social
equality and national independence. And the Australian upper classes have
traditionally demonstrated concern for the society as a whole. Early achievement of virtually complete adult literacy by these two countries reflects, I
believe, at least in part, a well-developed sense of noblesse oblige with roots
in British culture.
In *Englishmen, Frenchmen, Spaniards*, de Madariaga takes note of "the
tendency towards social, political, and moral disorder which has often been
observed in societies of the Spanish race . . . [they are] instinctively hostile
to association, rebellious to discipline and to technique, and used to inverting
the scale of social services in favour of such groups as are most closely related
to the individual . . ."[46] He subsequently observes, ". . . the family is . . .
the strongest of the group units in Spanish life"[47] and "the family in Spain
is often a self-sustained unit . . . more extended than [the] English or French."[48]
In both Spain and Spanish America the family is enlarged by the institution
of *compadrazgo* — godparents, who are often chosen from a higher social
level, much as a rich and powerful "patron" is often sought by a poor "client"
in these same societies. The relationship between godparents and godchil-
dren often approaches the intensity of the relationship between natural
parents and children.
We have noted repeatedly in the chapters treating Spanish American
countries that the radius of identification and trust rarely extends beyond
the family. This phenomenon is applicable to Spain as well. It is an important facet of Hispanic culture that impedes the kind of broader association
that facilitates political compromise and economic activity.
The brief recounting earlier in this chapter of Spanish history since
1808 strongly suggests the brittle nature of politics in Hispanic societies.

Positions are rigid, and individuals and groups often seem to be uncomfortable in the middle ground.

An anecdote comes to mind. When Alfonso Robelo resigned from Nicaragua's Junta of National Reconstruction in April 1980 and criticized the increasingly authoritarian nature of the Sandinista government, I tried to explain to one of the commanders of the revolution and a cabinet minister why the Sandinista labeling of Robelo as "a traitor" was not going to go down well in the United States. This required that I explain our concept of dissent. I failed completely with the commander, a highly intelligent Marxist-Leninist who knew little of the United States and Canada. And I didn't do much better with the minister (who, by the way, has since defected), who had studied for a number of years in the United States. After my lengthy explanation, during most of which he seemed uncomprehending, he suddenly smiled broadly and said, "Now I understand. You're talking about civil disobedience."

That evening I explained my frustration to a Nicaraguan who has a Ph.D. from a prestigious u.s. university and knows the United States very well. He confirmed that there is no adequate word in Spanish for "dissent" and then went on to explain, "You must remember that most of us have grown up in church schools where we learned that dissent was heresy."

Before turning to some further comparisons between Spain and the Hispanic American countries, I want to return to two aspects of the Hispanic profile developed by Henry Wells: (1) attitudes about work, and (2) child-rearing.

With respect to the former, Wells's words echo observations that appear throughout this book. He speaks of "disdain for physical labor, money-making, technological skills, and nonhumanistic learning" in the upper class subculture.[49] Although those Spaniards and particularly those Spanish-Americans (who are far more numerous) who have to fight for survival perforce live lives of unrelieved toil and drudgery, the attitudes toward work of the classes above them are influenced by the attitudes of the elite. For those who have escaped from subsistence, little pleasure or satisfaction derives from work:

> All occupations in which we engage out of necessity are painful to us.
> They weigh down our life, hurt it, tear it to pieces. . . . The man who
> works does so in the hope . . . that work will lead to his liberation, that
> some day he will stop working and start really living.[50]

Not unrelated is the "mañana" attitude of the stereotypical Latin American. Interestingly, writing about Spain in 1908, Havelock Ellis had this to say: "Let us . . . consider a characteristic which is today very familiar both to natives and to visitors — the tendency to delay everything to a remote tomorrow. To every demand the Spaniard responds with a cheerful Mañana."[51]

With respect to child-rearing, Wells stresses its authoritarian nature in Puerto Rico and the heavy emphasis on respect. He quotes Elena Padilla: "The child has no voice in family matters, not even in matters which pertain to him directly and exclusively. He has to be unfailingly obedient, for obedience is the hallmark of respect."[52] The emphasis on masculinity dominates the upbringing of boys. Wells quotes Sidney Mintz: "Beginning about the time when they start to toddle, boys are taught that aggressiveness is male and that they should be aggressive."[53] Wells goes on to observe, "Boys tend to be treated more indulgently than girls, but neither sons nor daughters are allowed to develop feelings of independence."[54] He cites the findings of David Landy, who studied a peasant village in Puerto Rico and concluded that the way boys are reared results in "dependent and insecure adults."[55]

To be sure, Wells is talking about Puerto Rico, not Spain. There is, however, a strong presumption of parallelism between Spanish and Puerto Rican child-rearing, in part because Puerto Rico was a Spanish colony until 1898. Child-rearing practices generate a particularly persistent inertia: the way a person is treated as a child importantly determines the way that person will behave as a father or mother. Moreover, while I have been unable to find any extensive treatment of child-rearing in Spain, its authoritarian nature has been mentioned by the anthropologist Michael Kenny ("Part of the child's training is directed to accepting the father's word as law and to viewing the mother as the source of all virtue")[56] and Carmelo Lison-Tolosana (the children "possess little initiative of their own. In the plots they carry out the work as the father orders; in the house the mother rules everything").[57]

Spain's impact on Spanish America

There is compelling evidence of the profound, even decisive, influence of Spanish culture on Spanish America. In his book *Culture and Conquest: America's Spanish Heritage*, George Foster examines the patterns in which Spanish culture has substantially supplanted indigenous culture across much of the spectrum of human activity — from farming and fishing to the organization of towns and techniques of midwifery. To be sure, Indian cultures have survived and continue to influence national culture in such countries as Mexico, Guatemala, Ecuador, Peru, and Bolivia.

> But overriding the Indian-based characteristics are the generic Spanish similarities, stemming from the time of the Conquest and giving Hispanic America a cultural unity which has led anthropologists, historians, and philosophers to think in terms of a common Contemporary Hispanic American culture. . . . Although following separation from Spain, a series of independent nations emerged, each with peculiar geographical, economic, and social characteristics and with local traditions and histories, the supranational resemblances even today, a century and a half later, are so pronounced that, in anthropological concept, all countries together constitute a single culture area.[58]

Several others have drawn similar conclusions from different perspectives. Octavio Paz observes that "New Spain did not seek or invent: it applied and adapted. All its creations, including its own self, were reflections of Spain."[59] Claudio Véliz says, "To understand the personality of Don Quixote is to take the first step toward understanding of the Latin American intellectual . . ."[60] Charles Wagley says, "The ideal patterns which are common throughout Latin America and which seem to profoundly influence the behavior of most Latin Americans are mainly patterns of behavior and institutional forms that derive from the Iberian Peninsula of the sixteenth and seventeenth centuries. . . ."[61] And Carlos Rangel says, "The Spanish American New World was the Spanish Old World, with a few serious additional problems."[62]

These and other observers have analyzed aspects of Latin America's "national" character and have focused on several characteristics that are prominent in the analyses of Spanish national character earlier in this chapter:

Individualism. Charles Gibson distinguishes the North American's concept of the individual from the Hispanic American concept. He believes that the North American view is a political, social, and economic way of looking at the individual that leads toward equality of opportunity and social consciousness, while the Hispanic American view, by focusing on dignity, honor, and the soul, discourages democracy and "allows the individual, or a small group of individuals, to take advantage of others and to exploit rather than change the society."[63] Rangel refers to "This inability to become part of the whole, to feel involved in the collective destiny . . ."[64] De Madariaga, in projecting this individualism to the level of the whole society, speaks of "the brittle quality of its collective self which . . . we find exemplified in the Disunited States of Spanish America (the fruit of dictatorship and separation) as opposed to the United States of Anglo-Saxon America."[65] And Paz adds, "The [Mexican] Revolution has not succeeded in changing our country into a community, or even in offering any hope of doing so."[66]

Caudillismo/Machismo. Foster generalizes: "Although authority may be flouted, power is respected and desired, power as exercised by the political *caudillo*, the strong man, or the ruthless yet successful military general or business man."[67] Gibson says, "One need not look far in the colonial period to find expressions of authority, political and of other kinds. The general atmosphere of dictatorship — its preoccupation with personal power and with self-assertion, its neglect of the 'rights' of individuals — existed from the beginning."[68] Paz says, "It is impossible not to notice the resemblance between the figure of the *macho* and that of the Spanish conquistador. This is the model — more mythical than real — that determines the images the Mexican people form of men in power: *caciques*, feudal lords, hacienda owners, politicians, generals, captains of industry."[69] And finally de Madariaga (speaking of Spain, but with reference to Latin America): ". . . dictatorship [is] observable not only in the public man, statesman, general, cardinal, or king at the head of state, but in every one of the men at the head (or on the

way thereto) of every village, city, region, business firm, or even family . . ."⁷⁰

Law vs. Personalismo. The common irrelevance of law to reality in Latin
America has been frequently commented upon. Foster observes, "In spite
of, or perhaps because of, a long authoritarian tradition in Church and State,
laws and regulations often are considered things to be avoided, and satisfaction is taken in an individualism and a freedom of spirit and action which
sometimes approach anarchy. . . . *Personalismo* — an effective personal
working relationship with the right people — rather than impersonal principle is more often than not the basis on which government, and business
as well, functions."⁷¹ Gibson says, "Law leads a life of its own . . . it is an
academic subject, separated from reality by the continuing assumption that
its significance and application are in doubt. Routine business is conducted
around the law, in fees and bribes, in personal loyalties, in codes of honor,
in tax evasion, and in embezzlement. Such activities continue to be regarded
as natural and expectable, as in the colonial period."⁷² And Paz adds, "In
Spanish America, liberal democratic constitutions merely served as modern
trappings for the survival of the colonial system. This liberal, democratic
ideology, far from expressing our concrete historical situation, disguised it,
and the political lie established itself almost constitutionally. The moral
damage it has caused is incalculable. . . ."⁷³

Social Rigidity. Of the colonial period, Gibson observes that "Neither
the revolutions nor anything else subverted the existing social order. Lower
classes remained subordinate, and significant change occurred only between
creoles and peninsulars at the uppermost level of social rank."⁷⁴ Rangel adds,
". . . the social structure set up in the sixteenth century continues to weigh
down Latin American society in the twentieth."⁷⁵ Kalman Silvert notes that
"Iberian society has grown much more specialized in economic matters since
the beginning of this century, but the attempt is invariably made to see that
the changes do not disrupt the social pecking order, the conditions of im-
mobility, and the distribution of economic, social, and political power which
characterized the traditional order."⁷⁶

Attitudes about Work. The view of several observers is summarized in
the words of Foster: "Unlike the traditional attitude of predominately Protestant societies, work is not thought to be a positive value; it is regarded as
a necessary evil, something people must do to live, but something to be
avoided. . . ."⁷⁷

In sum

While it is well ahead of the countries of Hispanic America in most
key indicators of human progress, Spain is well behind the democracies of
Western Europe and North America, Australia, and Japan. What has stood
in Spain's way? What we have seen in this chapter strongly suggests that
its failure to build a viable and stable political system with which most

Spaniards could identify has been a decisive factor. That failure has been accompanied by chronic political upheaval or the oppressive stability of dictatorship. The former has been highly discouraging to entrepreneurial activity; growth has occurred in the latter, but it has resulted in benefits markedly skewed toward the upper strata of Spanish society.

A combination of (1) the high degree of authoritarianism that Spaniards experience all their lives, and (2) the low value that attaches to work and practical achievement has probably suppressed the entrepreneurial instinct and performance of Spaniards, thereby also contributing importantly to reduced rates of economic growth.

I do not want to leave the impression that I believe Spanish culture is static, that it is destined to relive perpetually the political instability, slow growth, and social injustice that have characterized it in the past. On the contrary, there is much evidence that Spanish culture is changing, particularly as a consequence of the internationalist policies initiated in the early 1950s that have permitted far greater access to the more progressive cultures of Western Europe and the United States. It may well be that many Spaniards now see the world in substantially the same way as Western Europeans. If that is true, or if it will be true before long, then democracy, economic progress, and increased social justice may well be Spain's destiny.

I believe Spanish America's failure to keep pace with North America is also principally explained by the same cultural factors, which have led to alternating political instability and rigid dictatorship, and to suppression of the entrepreneurial instinct and entrepreneurial performance. I want now to turn to some aspects of the North – South relationship in the Western Hemisphere.

NOTES

1. Arango, *The Spanish Political System*, p. 17.
2. Vilar, *Spain — A Brief History*, p. 57.
3. *Ibid.*, p. 64.
4. Prim y Prats's interest in a Hohenzollern contributed to the outbreak of the Franco-Prussian war of 1870.
5. Arango, *The Spanish Political System*, p. 22.
6. *Ibid.*
7. Quoted in Arango, pp. 21, 22.
8. *Ibid.*, p. 22.
9. *Ibid.*, pp. 32 – 33.
10. *Ibid.*, p. 35.
11. *Ibid.*, p. 47.
12. *Ibid.*, p. 49.
13. *Ibid.*
14. *Ibid.*, p. 53.
15. *Ibid.*, p. 59.
16. *Ibid.*, p. 80.
17. *Ibid.*, p. 81.

18. *Ibid.*, p. 60.
19. *Ibid.* The destructive consequences for Spanish democracy of the uncompromising poli-
    cies and actions of the Spanish left during the "Red Biennium" are not unlike the con-
    sequences of the Allende government's similar actions and policies in Chile forty years
    later. See Chapter 8, page 159.
20. *Ibid.*, p. 66.
21. *Ibid.*, p. 68.
22. *Ibid.*, pp. 70 – 71.
23. Stanley Payne, quoted in Arango, *The Spanish Political System*, p. 72.
24. Quoted by Arango, p. 72.
25. Quoted in Arango, p. 76.
26. Vilar, *Spain — A Brief History*, p. 113. Sarmiento, writing in 1851, made a relevant
    observation in *Facundo* (p. 103): "Terror is a sickness of the spirit which infects people,
    like cholera, small pox or scarlet fever. And after you have worked for 10 years to
    inoculate against it, the vaccine fails to work. Don't laugh, people of Hispanic Amer-
    ica, when you see such degradation! Remember that you are Spanish, and that is how
    the Inquisition educated Spain! This sickness we carry in our blood. Be careful, then!"
27. Arango, *The Spanish Political System*, p. 119.
28. Quoted in Arango, p. 103.
29. Arango, p. 268.
30. De la Souchère, *An Explanation of Spain*, p. 16
31. *Ibid.*, p. 17.
32. *Ibid.*, p. 18.
33. *Ibid.*, p. 98 – 99.
34. *Ibid.*, p. 121.
35. Arango, *The Spanish Political System*, p. 65.
36. Wells, *The Modernization of Puerto Rico*, p. 23.
37. *Ibid.*, p. 24. The Spanish *dignidad* is a stronger word than "dignity"; loss of *dignidad*
    implies shattering consequences for a member of an Hispanic society.
38. *Ibid.*, p. 28.
39. *Ibid.*, p. 29.
40. José Ortega y Gasset, *Invertebrate Spain*.
41. *Ibid.*, pp. 49 – 50.
42. *Ibid.*, p. 156.
43. *Ibid.*, pp. 152 – 53.
44. Arango, *The Spanish Political System*, p. 109.
45. James Michener comments on the absence of noblesse oblige in *Iberia*, p. 356.
46. Salvador de Madariaga, *Englishmen, Frenchmen, Spaniards*, p. 50.
47. *Ibid.*, p. 140.
48. *Ibid.*, p. 141.
49. Wells, *The Modernization of Puerto Rico*, p. 32.
50. Ortega y Gasset, quoted in Carlos Rangel, *The Latin Americans, Their Love-Hate Rela-
    tionship With the United States*, p. 192.
51. Havelock Ellis, *The Soul of Spain*, pp. 391 – 92; Ellis goes on to mention that in the
    seventeenth century, Sir Francis Bacon speaks of "notorious delays" in negotiating with
    Spaniards.
52. Wells, *The Modernization of Puerto Rico*, p. 44.
53. *Ibid.*, pp. 44 – 45.
54. *Ibid.*, p. 45.
55. *Ibid.*
56. Michael Kenny, *A Spanish Tapestry: Town and Country in Castile*, p. 62.
57. Carmelo Lison-Tolosana, *Belmonte de los Caballeros*.
58. Foster, *Culture and Conquest*, pp. 2 – 3.
59. Octavio Paz, *The Labyrinth of Solitude: Life and Thought in Mexico*, p. 104.

60. Claudio Véliz, *The Centralist Traditions of Latin America*, p. 148.
61. Charles Wagley, *The Latin American Tradition*, p. 3.
62. Rangel, *The Latin Americans*, p. 182. Rangel had in mind particularly slavery in its various forms in the New World in mentioning "additional problems."
63. Charles Gibson, *Spain in America*, pp. 213 – 14.
64. Rangel, *The Latin Americans*, p. 208.
65. In Hugh M. Hamill, ed., *Dictatorship in Latin America*, p. 33. One is reminded of Latin America's disappointing experiments with economic integration during the last three decades (e.g., the Latin American Free Trade Association, the Andean Group, the Central American Common Market) and the implications for these experiments of Hispanic individualism.
66. Paz, *The Labyrinth of Solitude*, p. 175.
67. Foster, *Culture and Conquest*, p. 4.
68. Gibson, *Spain in America*, p. 211.
69. Paz, *The Labyrinth of Solitude*, p. 82.
70. Hamill, ed., *Dictatorship in Spanish America*, p. 33.
71. Foster, *Culture and Conquest*, p. 4.
72. Gibson, *Spain in America*, p. 212.
73. Paz, *The Labyrinth of Solitude*, p. 122. Earlier (p. 40) Paz speaks of lying as institutionalized in Mexico: "Lying plays a decisive role in our daily lives, our politics, our love-affairs and our friendships. . . ." We are reminded of Mendieta's diagnosis of Central America's ills.
74. Gibson, *Spain in America*, p. 207.
75. Rangel, *The Latin Americans*, p. 185.
76. Kalman H. Silvert, *Essays in Understanding Latin America*, p. 24.
77. Foster, *Culture and Conquest*, p. 4.

8

Spanish America and the United States

A conventional wisdom has evolved in the Latin American and North American intellectual communities that blames the United States for Latin America's ills. It goes under the name of "dependency theory." The theory, as espoused by André Gunder Frank[1] and others, goes something like this: Latin America is poor because we are rich. Many of its people do not eat enough because we eat too well. International capitalism, largely guided by Wall Street, has depressed the prices of what Latin America produces while charging Latin America exorbitant prices for what it imports from the United States and other developed countries. U.S. corporations that invest in Latin America are both bleeding it dry and conspiring to install or shore up right-wing dictatorships. The United States government supports rightist dictators and opposes truly popular movements to perpetuate its privileged imperialistic position.

A variant, evolved by ECLA's Fernando Henrique Cardoso and Enzo Faletto,[2] argues that the Latin American elites have betrayed their national loyalties by serving as lackeys for the interests of U.S. (and in the nineteenth century, British) imperialism.

While dependency theory highlights some truths — e.g., the consequences, particularly for small countries, of world price fluctuations for undiversified economies; the "export" of recession from the rich countries to the poor countries — it is, in my view, both fundamentally flawed and a major impediment to progress in Latin America.

The U.S. economy is substantially self-sufficient: according to World Bank figures, exports and imports represented about 18 percent of GNP in 1980, quite possibly the highest in the nation's entire history and importantly reflecting the higher costs of imported energy. (In 1960, the figure was slightly more than 10 percent.) The 1980 ratio for West Germany was 47 percent, the United Kingdom 45 percent, France 38 percent, and Japan 26 percent. The 18 percent figure for the United States is a prima facie argument that the bulk of its economic growth is attributable to domestic production and its internal market. As an example, the city of Springfield, Massachusetts, is about as important a market as all five Central American countries together.[3] Moreover, about 55 percent of U.S. trade is with developed countries; about 15 percent is with Latin America. (It was about 30 percent in

1950.) Thus, trade with Latin America currently represents something less than 3 percent of GNP.

Although Argentina, Brazil, and Mexico are all now about as self-sufficient as the U.S., many Latin American economies are far more dependent on trade. Some may thus argue — not very convincingly, I think — that trade has made Latin America poor. Fidel Castro may have so argued at one time, although it is clear that now he would welcome the reopening of trade with the U.S. But it is patently unreasonable to argue that trade has made the United States rich. Trade — particularly trade with Latin America — is just not that important to the U.S. in comparison to other countries. And Latin America's trade with the United States is declining: in 1950 it represented almost 50 percent of Latin America's world trade total; in 1980 it accounted for about 32 percent.[4]

On the other hand, for those Latin American economies, particularly the smaller ones, whose foreign trade is a much higher percentage of GNP, "dependency" has more substance. But what are the options? The dependency theorists, many of whom are Marxists, call for an end to dependency by disengagement from the international capitalist system. But as Cuba clearly demonstrates, this really means substituting one dependency for another. Moreover, policies aimed at self-sufficiency for small countries are patently infeasible and antieconomical.

The relationship between the quantities of food eaten in the U.S. and the quantities eaten in Latin America is limited. Reduced food consumption in the United States would *not* result in higher food consumption in Latin America. In fact, the reverse is more likely true: lower food consumption in the U.S. will mean lower demand for Latin America's exports, which means lower incomes — and lower food consumption — in Latin America. The nutrition problem in Latin America is principally a consequence of low incomes and inequitable income distribution.

Nobody has yet produced a convincing, documented argument that long-term movements in the terms of trade — the relationship between the prices of what is exported and what is imported — have operated against Latin America's interests as essentially a producer of primary products, particularly in relationship to the terms of trade for the United States. The only clear exception is the price of oil, which has also adversely affected the United States and most of the developed countries of the West. And, of course, Mexico, Venezuela, Ecuador, and Peru have benefited from the oil price rise.

As the world's largest exporter of primary products (about 30 percent of its total exports), the United States itself has a stake in what happens to the prices of primary products. And we must remember that the United States, Canada, and Australia all grew rapidly in the nineteenth century as exporters of primary products (and, we should note, the three encouraged foreign investment, principally from Britain). It is also worth noting that Latin America is increasingly an exporter of manufactured goods. For example, in 1960, such goods accounted for 3 percent of Brazil's exports. In 1979, they accounted for 39 percent.

Table 5 surely provides little support for dependency theory[5]:

Table 5. Terms of trade (relationship of export prices to import prices [indexed])

	1960	1970	1975	1980
Latin America (all)	—	100	114	123
Latin America (oil exporters)	—	100	181	243
Latin America (nonoil exporters)	—	100	86	76
United States	115	—	100	82

In his book *The Spirit of Democratic Capitalism*,[6] Michael Novak examines the economic impact of u.s. multinational corporations in Latin America. He concludes that the economic significance of the multinationals is vastly exaggerated, as is the extent of their profits. To start with, u.s. investment overseas is 5 percent of its total investment (underscoring again its economic self-sufficiency). More than 70 percent of its overseas investment is in Western Europe, Canada, Australia, and Japan. Its investments in Latin America account for less than 20 percent of its worldwide total, which means less than 1 percent of its total investment. And they also represent a very small proportion (perhaps 1 – 2 percent) of total domestic and foreign investment in Latin America.

Novak cites research done by an International Labor Organization economist, Joseph Ramos, which demonstrates that "The average rate of return on u.s. investments in Latin America has not been particularly high, either before 1950 or during the years 1950 to 1977. This return has been higher than in Canada but about the same as Europe, Australia, Asia, and Africa."[7]

The multinationals have undeniably involved themselves in Latin American politics, often unwisely and sometimes irresponsibly. But it must be kept in mind that they operate in circumstances where due process and continuity of policy are the exception; where it is common for multinationals to become targets of nationalistic politicians, to say nothing of the far left; and where an uncompensated expropriation may be the bottom line. In any event, the multinationals have learned many lessons during the past twenty years, perhaps foremost among them the importance of being "good corporate citizens."

I have observed multinational corporations in the five Latin American countries in which I have worked. I have had innumerable conversations with North Americans and Latin Americans about the costs and benefits of the multinationals. I always ask, "On balance, would the country be better off if they had never come?" Very few answer, "Yes." In most cases, at least until recently, there would have been a lapse of many years or even decades before national entrepreneurs or governments initiated comparable enterprises. Even where contracts were inordinately favorable to foreign capital, which was not uncommon in the early part of this century but is very rare today, jobs, foreign exchange earnings, and government revenues were created that otherwise would not have existed.

Interestingly, some researchers have found, to their "shock," that there is a correlation between the degree of dependency, as measured by trade and capital data, on the one hand, and income inequality and political participation, on the other. But the correlations "go strongly and significantly in the *opposite* direction from that predicted by dependency theory. By most of the measures we have devised, more dependent economies grow faster, rather than more slowly; they have more rather than less equal land tenure structures; and, according to our measures of capital dependency, they have more constitutional stability and less militarism."[8]

With respect to the allegation that the United States supports (some on the left in Latin America and in the U.S. would say "creates") right-wing dictatorships, I believe that an objective reading of U.S. policy toward Latin America during the past two decades will demonstrate that above all the U.S. has tried to nurture the democratic center, which has not always been easy to find. (As we have already noted, Yankee evangelism was a factor in the Nicaraguan, Haitian, and Dominican interventions early in this century.) For reasons that are central to the thesis of this book, Latin America has tended to produce the same kinds of authoritarian governments since independence that it knew during three hundred years of colonial status, and one of the thorniest dilemmas U.S. policymakers have faced is how to deal with these dictatorships. They have clearly gotten too cozy with some, particularly in Republican administrations. But the costs of a hostile policy toward them can also be high. Jimmy Carter alienated the Argentine military over human rights issues only to see U.S. influence in Argentina, including influence over human rights, vanish. The Carter administration also contributed to the demise of Anastasio Somoza in Nicaragua, only to see a new authoritarianism replace the old. But the basic point remains valid: U.S. policies have consistently shown a preference for the democratic center.

There are other reasons to conclude that dependency theory is in large measure mythical. Both Latin America and North America are richly endowed with resources. The U.S. started the nineteenth century in roughly the same economic shape as Latin America. U.S. economic involvement in Latin America for most of the nineteenth century was extremely limited. (To be sure, British involvement, particularly in Argentina, was substantial.) By the end of the century, the U.S. had become a world power — more importantly as a result of foreign (European) investment, by the way — while most Latin American countries were essentially the same stagnant, exploitative, inequitable societies they had been since the sixteenth century as Iberian colonies.

Does dependency theory explain the currents of militarism, authoritarianism, and political instability common to most Latin American countries in the nineteenth and twentieth centuries? Does it explain the substantial illiteracy and serious public health problems that exist in many of these countries to this day? Included in that group of countries are some — e.g., Bolivia, Paraguay — in which u.s. involvement has been negligible, at least until the last few decades. Indeed, in a number of these countries, there is evidence that the United States has been more concerned about education and health — to say nothing of human rights — than the national governments.

The view of Carlos Rangel

Carlos Rangel's view of the hemisphere is diametrically opposed to that of Frank, Cardoso, Faletto, and Prebisch. He believes Latin American history has been determined principally by Hispanic culture and that that history "is a story of failure."[9] He documents this assertion with the following:

> (1) the disproportionate success of the United States in the same "New World" during a parallel period of history; (2) Latin America's inability to evolve harmonious and cohesive nations, capable of redeeming, or at least reasonably improving, the lot of vast marginal social and economic groups; (3) Latin America's impotence in its external relations — military, economic, political, cultural, et cetera — and hence its vulnerability to outside . . . influences in each of these areas; (4) the notable lack of stability of the Latin-American forms of government, other than those founded on dictatorships and repression; (5) the absence of noteworthy Latin-American contributions in the sciences or the arts (the exceptions I could quote merely prove the rule); (6) [Latin America's] population growth rate, the highest in the world; (7) Latin America's feeling that it is of little if any use to the world at large.[10]

In reviewing New World history, Rangel observes, "As late as 1700, the Spanish American empire still gave the impression of being incomparably richer (which it was!), much more powerful, and more likely to succeed than the British colonies of North America."[11] He goes on to emphasize the debility of the North American confederation born in 1776, surrounded by enemies and facing major obstacles to the formation of a federal state.

It was not long thereafter (1783 – 84) that Francisco de Miranda, a Spanish military officer born in Venezuela, toured the newly formed United States from South Carolina to New England. Miranda kept a diary from which Rangel quotes liberally:

> At his first American barbecue, Miranda observed that "the very first magistrates and people of note ate and drank with the common folk, passing the plate around, and drinking out of the same glass. A more purely demo-

cratic assembly could not be imagined. America incarnates all that our
poets and historians imagined about the mores of the free peoples of ancient Greece.

In Charleston, South Carolina, he attended a court session, which
was open to the public, according to the English custom, and commented:
"I cannot express the satisfaction I felt watching the workings of the admirable system of the British Constitution. God forgive me: but what a contrast to the system now current in Spain!" The government of the State of
South Carolina also met with his admiration because it was "altogether
democratic, as are all the States," with separate and distinct executive, legislative, and judiciary branches.

He was surprised to disembark in Philadelphia "without ceremony or
registration formalities." Pondering on the North Americans' ability to
make and build things, he reminisced about Benjamin Franklin, inventor of
a "new stove, which produces more heat with one third the coal or wood
normally required . . ." He admired the absolute freedom of religion for
which Philadelphia had been famous ever since its founding by William
Penn. In general, he declared Philadelphia to be "one of the most pleasant
and best-governed cities in the world."

Miranda was only displaying common sense when he attributed the
virtues and the prosperity he observed in North American society, not to
any abuse of power over other nations (impossible at any rate for the fledgling government), but simply to "the advantages of a free government over
any form of despotism" — something that "very few Frenchmen or Spaniards familiar with the United States are able to discern, not having been
penetrated by the wonderful secrets of the British Constitution."

On his way from Philadelphia to New York, he stopped to admire
the landscape and the prosperity of New Jersey, "the pleasant appearance
and the strength of its inhabitants . . . the degree of development and the
activity of the farming community. It would be hard to find a corner or
plot on which no house stands . . . and I can say that I have never met a
man who seemed ill-dressed, hungry, sick, or unemployed. . . . The land,
as we see it, is divided . . . into small plots called *farms*. As a result the
land is far better cultivated and the density of houses — houses of simple
appearance, it is true — is far greater than in other countries." And yet, "it
must be said the soil is extremely poor and sandy; but it is watered and
tended by hard-working farmers. This fact, and the fact that the people are
governed by an independent government, has led them to riches even in
the face of harsh nature."

From New York Miranda went on to New England. He recorded
one of his most meaningful observations in Providence, Rhode Island. He
had been taken to see a mine equipped with a kind of pump, a "machine to
evacuate water by evaporation, invented and built by a Mr. Joseph Brown.
The cylinder must measure some two feet by ten; it is of iron and had
been cast by Mr. Brown himself. With the use of this machine, water from
three hundred feet below the surface can be pumped out at a rate of a
hundred gallons a minute. What a difference in the character of these two
nations! In Mexico, or in any of our colonies in Spanish America, there is
no such machine, there is nothing to compare to it. Thus our richest gold

and silver mines are readily lost to us. Here such a machine is invented to draw water from a mine producing only iron. . . ."

In Boston, Miranda marveled at this society that viewed as permissible all that was not expressly forbidden by law, a society that trusted the truth of all statements unless proven false. His luggage arrived, and he remarked that the customs officials let him through without even opening his trunks, "on my simple assurance that they did not contain any commercial goods."

Near Salem, Massachusetts, he made observations similar to those he recorded in New Jersey: "The soil seems poor and is poor. Farming consists mostly of pasture grazing, corn, and rye. But such is the industrious spirit with which freedom fills these people that a small plot of land allows them to feed their large families, pay heavy taxes, and live well and pleasantly, a thousand times happier than the slave-owning landlords of rich mines and fertile lands in Mexico, Peru, Buenos Aires, Caracas, and all the Spanish American world."

These homely truths, describing the reasons for the United States' prosperity and subsequent power, and antedating the onset of that country's relations with Latin America, are ignored nowadays in favor of complicated explanations based on a causal connection between the wealth of the one half of the hemisphere and the poverty of the other. Such explanations attribute the poverty of Latin America to Yankee exploitation — which is said to be the main cause, perhaps the *only* cause, of their progress and our want. Anyone who still wishes to read Miranda's words today must do so in utmost privacy, for no one refers to his writing publicly any longer. The fact is that an age that thrives on myths would be bewildered by an explanation as clear, as simple, as obviously true as Miranda's — an explanation given by one of Spanish America's great men, one of its great heroes.[12]

Miranda's impressions contrast sharply with Simon Bolívar's final judgment on Latin America, pronounced in 1830, the year of his death:

> I was in command for twenty years, and during that time came to only a few definite conclusions: (1) I consider that, for us, [Latin] America is ungovernable; (2) whosoever works for a revolution is plowing the sea; (3) the most sensible action to take in [Latin] America is to emigrate; (4) this country [Great Colombia, later to be divided into Colombia, Venezuela, and Ecuador] will ineluctably fall into the hands of a mob gone wild, later again to fall under the domination of obscure small tyrants of every color and race; (5) though decimated by every kind of crime and exhausted by our cruel excesses, we shall still not be tempting to Europeans for a reconquest; (6) if any part of the world were to return to a primeval chaos, such would be the last avatar of [Latin] America.[13]

Rangel notes that most Europeans expected Mexico to defeat the United States in the war fought from 1846 to 1848. He also observes that, in 1879, the Chilean navy was stronger than the United States navy and that up to that time, ". . . the United States was mainly a producer of agricultural and mineral raw materials. It participated in world commerce mainly by trading these raw materials for manufactured goods and by encouraging foreign investment, the very same situation that today is alleged to be sufficient cause for Latin America's underdevelopment."[14]

Yet nineteen years later, the United States navy destroyed the Spanish navy. The United States succeeded where the French had failed in building the Panama Canal (it was started in 1904 and completed in 1914). And by World War I, the United States had become a first-rank world power.

Of the U.S. interventions in the Caribbean basin in this century, Rangel says, ". . . the United States strictly adhered to its policy of not tolerating any situation in the Caribbean that might threaten its control of the seaways leading to the canal. This is the *main* reason for North American intervention in the Caribbean, a fact generally ignored in Latin America, where it is agreed that the main (if not the only) object of Marine landings was the protection of (supposedly) vital North American economic interests. Ignoring the primary cause of United States intervention allows critics of that country to take the next step and pin on these interventions the bulk of responsibility for the developmental lag of the countries involved. No one stops to remember the conditions in the Dominican Republic, Nicaragua, etc. *before* these interventions."[15]

Rangel goes on to say:

> The United States has rightly been blamed for having tolerated or openly supported such dictators as Trujillo and Somoza. But it would be wrong to infer that this style of leadership appealed to Woodrow Wilson or Franklin Roosevelt, whose governments supported it. No less misleading is the extrapolation that there must be a deep affinity between the North American political or economic system and the coercive regimes of the client states. When national security is at stake, nations, whatever their form of government, are not particularly scrupulous in choosing their means of protecting it; the American democracy, in fact, may perhaps show greater concern than other countries because of the nature of its institutions.[16]

Rangel is not a raving Americanophile. He is a highly respected Venezuelan journalist who, with his wife Sofía, hosts a popular news program on Venezuelan television. In addition to U.S. links with Trujillo and Somoza, he is critical of the "sordid"[17] U.S. role in converting Panama from a Colombian province to an independent country and of the failure of the United States to share canal revenues fairly with Panama. He quotes Talleyrand in labeling the U.S. intervention in the Dominican Republic in 1965 "worse than a crime; it was a mistake."[18] He is also fully aware of "the darker aspects of North American society, such as racial discrimination, the excesses of consumerism, the disquieting power of the 'military-industrial complex' . . ."[19]

But he flatly rejects dependency theory, which he describes as "an almost general belief in Latin America today."[20] He expresses the fear that "by echoing this line of thought, we Latin Americans are starting on a new cycle in our self-delusion over the causes of our frustration. We are once again refusing to admit that the reasons for North American success and Latin American failure are to be found in the qualities of North Americans and in the defects of Latin Americans."[21] The concluding sentence of Gibson's *Spain in America* comes to mind:

> But what the colonial and modern history of Spain in America so steadfastly informs us is that Spanish America is less concerned with progress than we are.[22]

Rangel goes on to say what is for many Latin Americans unthinkable:

> A sincere, rational, scientific examination of North American influence on Latin America's destiny would have to dispense with prejudging the issue . . . keeping open the possibility that the United States' overall contribution may have been positive.[23]

The high costs of the dependency theory myth

There is a clear link between the Vietnam tragedy and the blossoming of dependency theory in the United States. Those who saw u.s. intervention in Vietnam as a blatant act of American imperialism, ordered by an immoral government elected by a corrupted society, were able to persuade many others — mostly young people — that u.s. policies and actions in Latin America were similarly imperialistic and immoral. The demise of Salvador Allende in Chile in 1973, "engineered," according to the prophets of dependency theory, by the u.s. government, strengthened their arguments about the destructive, exploitative role of the United States in Latin America. (The dependency theorists downplay the internal factors — the military, the middle class, Allende's tampering with Chile's traditional democratic institutions, and his unsound economic policies — which in my view and the view of others[24] vastly overshadowed the u.s. role, some elements of which were clearly unsavory.)

Dependency theorists often point to u.s. interventionism — in Nicaragua, Haiti, and the Dominican Republic early in this century and in recent years in Guatemala, the Dominican Republic, Chile, and now Central America — as evidence of u.s. exploitation of Latin America. In all these cases, as Rangel points out, the principal motivation for the intervention has been a security concern, not u.s. economic interests. The early interventions were mounted principally to prevent European powers from obtaining strategically important bases near the Panama Canal at the time of World War I; the later interventions all related to what was viewed —rightly or wrongly — as a communist threat that would inevitably involve u.s. security. In none of these cases was there a truly significant u.s. economic interest. The only one that was close was Allende's Chile. But there, u.s. copper interests had already been substantially nationalized by the predecessor Frei administration.

The United States *does* have economic interests in Latin America, and those interests are not inconsequential, e.g., Venezuela and Mexico are important sources of oil; bauxite deposits around the Caribbean basin are also important; and the Latin American market, particularly with its promise in the long term, cannot be ignored. Clearly, these interests have to be taken into account in national policymaking, and indeed they have been historically. Moreover, u.s. companies operating in Latin America have influenced u.s. policies, as indeed have the AFL-CIO, church groups, and intellectuals. But in all the cases of intervention, the dominant consideration has been national security.

The interventions understandably make many people uncomfortable and appear to buttress the case of the dependency theorists, particularly in the wake of Vietnam. In any event, for the past ten or more years, high school and college students in the u.s. have heard a great deal of dependency theory from their teachers. Peer pressure operates: few students have the courage to challenge a conventional wisdom that recent history appears to confirm and that can be emotionally satisfying to people who are guilt-ridden because Americans are so much better off than Latin Americans. The students don what Mark Falcoff has labeled "our Latin American hair-shirt."[25] Many professors have been enjoying it for some time.

Dependency theorists stress that u.s. society itself is sick, greedy, materialistic, inequitable, and exploitative — the stark contrasts with Latin America notwithstanding. The u.s. government is the ultimate expression of what is bad in the society, most particularly in its policies toward Latin America. The policies and rhetoric of the Reagan administration appear to reinforce this view. The basic message to the student is, "You cannot ever trust your government to do the decent or right thing." Another legacy of Vietnam.

The students graduate and go out into the world. Some end up in professions where their views on Latin America count:

> · Some become reporters for influential newspapers. They give the benefit of the doubt to Latin American "liberation" movements and give no benefit of any doubt to the u.s. government. The article of Pulitzer Prize winner Shirley Christian of the *Miami Herald*, "Covering the Sandinistas," in the March 1982 *Washington Journalism Review*, makes a convincing case that *The New York Times*, *The Washington Post*, and CBS all gave too much benefit of the doubt to Nicaragua's Sandinistas.

· Some end up in editorial departments of influential newspapers. One such person, with whom I had dealings recently, was carrying around the idea that the United States was exploiting Latin America in the *eighteenth* century.

· Some end up as congressmen. One visited Nicaragua in 1981, while I was there. He came to Managua convinced that the Sandinistas were really well-intentioned democratic reformers and that U.S. embassy personnel in Nicaragua weren't sufficiently enlightened or sensitive to appreciate that. He left Nicaragua with essentially the same viewpoint, in part because he chose not to spend much time with embassy personnel.

· Some students become professors. They attend the annual meetings of the Latin American Studies Association (LASA). In the LASA meeting in Bloomington, Indiana, in October 1980, they gave a standing ovation to Sergio Ramírez and Miguel D'Escoto, two high officials of a Nicaraguan government that is pushing its people back into authoritarianism, albeit of a new variety, and, in the process, abusing human rights in many of the same ways Somoza did. The LASA audience then proceeded to heckle and jeer James Cheek, one of the Foreign Service's most distinguished and enlightened Latin Americanists, who had played a key role in disengaging the U.S. from Somoza.

And there are many others who do not end up in positions where they influence U.S. policy toward Latin America but in whom linger the precepts — the self-doubt, the mistrust of U.S. society and government —on which dependency theory rests. I am not now talking of that healthy suspicion of power and human nature that guided those who shaped the United States constitution. I am talking about a mistrust, a hostility, a cynicism that strain the fabric of society. Those who have managed the affairs of the U.S. government who have succumbed to the arrogance of power have helped to nurture these feelings of doubt and mistrust, to be sure. But the dependency theorists magnify and distort their errors and give no credit where it is due. And, as I reflect on what the U.S. government has done in Latin America during my twenty years in AID, I conclude there is much to be proud of: e.g., the Alliance for Progress, its genesis as a reaction to the Cuban revolution and its incomplete achievements notwithstanding; efforts to move away from paternalism and build "a mature partnership" in the early 1970s; the ratification of a new Panama Canal treaty, a bipartisan achievement that returned sovereignty over the Canal to Panama; a strong message to the Dominican military in 1978 that preserved that country's promising democratic experiment; and a sincere and forthcoming effort to build a new relationship with Nicaragua after the Sandinistas came to power.

Dependency theory erodes Americans' belief in themselves and in their society. But it may have even more pernicious consequences for Latin America. As Jean-Francois Revel has observed,[26] self-criticism is a rare commodity in Latin America. Most Latin American intellectuals are inclined to blame the United States for Latin America's shortcomings. This is true of the writers — Gabriel García Márquez, Miguel Asturias, Pablo Neruda, for example — and of the economists, Raul Prebisch and the ECLA school foremost among them.

In contrast, self-criticism is *over*developed in U.S. intellectual circles, with the result that U.S. intellectuals are telling Latin American intellectuals just what they want to hear: that Latin America would be a wonderful place if only it could break out of the clutches of the Yankee devil. The two tendencies reinforce each other, erode the quality of scholarship both in the U.S. and in Latin America, and lead those Latin American intellectuals and politicians who want to do something about Latin America's condition down a dead-end street.

Dependency theory implies that Latin America is impotent, the course of its history determined by outside forces.[27] Dependency theory both patronizes and paralyzes Latin America. Yet Latin America *can* determine its own destiny. Venezuela's architect's role in OPEC, Brazil's industrialization, and Peru's development of its fishmeal industry are cases in point.

Above all, Latin America needs to see itself objectively. Dependency theory may be comforting, but it is a debilitating nostrum that diverts Latin America's attention from that indispensable coming to grips with itself.

NOTES

1. Andre Gunder Frank, *Capitalism and Underdevelopment in Latin America*.
2. Their book, *Dependency and Development in Latin America*, is discussed in Chapter 6.
3. Central America's population is about 20 million. The discrepancy in per-capita income between Central America and the United States reduces this to about one million people. Further adjustments for income distribution, consumption of Central American products, and consumption of European, Japanese, and other Latin American products, may well reduce this to something like 200,000 people — the population of Springfield — in terms of effective demand for U.S. products.
4. The source of the Latin America-U.S. trade figures is Sergio Bitar, "Latin America and the United States: Changes in Economic Relations During the 70's."
5. The source of the figures for Latin America is an ECLA document, cited in Bitar's article: the source for the United States is the World Bank's *World Development Report 1982*.
6. Excerpts from the book appeared in the March 1982 *Atlantic Monthly* article, "Why Latin America is Poor."
7. *Ibid.*
8. R. R. Kaufman, Daniel S. Giller, and Harry I. Chernotsky, "Preliminary Test of the Theory of Dependency," p. 304.
9. Rangel, *The Latin Americans*, p. 6.
10. *Ibid.*, p. 67.
11. *Ibid.*, p. 21.

12. *Ibid.*, pp. 25 – 29.
13. *Ibid.*, p. 6.
14. *Ibid.*, p. 22.
15. *Ibid.*, p. 37.
16. *Ibid.*, pp. 37 – 38.
17. *Ibid.*, p. 33.
18. *Ibid.*, p. 37.
19. *Ibid.*, p. 45; Rangel goes on to inquire, "What could Latin America's criticism draw on if not on the North American's criticism of themselves?"
20. *Ibid.*, p. 44.
21. *Ibid.*
22. Gibson, *Spain in America*, p. 216.
23. Rangel, *The Latin Americans*, p. 44. As an example, Rangel observes (p. 193), "Only the influence of other Western countries, particularly of the United States, has been able to make a dent in the Latin American's contempt for work."
24. See, for example, Paul E. Sigmund, *The Overthrow of Allende and the Politics of Chile, 1964 – 76.*
25. Mark Falcoff, "Our Latin American Hairshirt," pp. 58 – 65. In the same vein, Rangel says (p. 15), ". . . the West today is afflicted with an absurd feeling of guilt, convinced that its civilization has corrupted the other peoples of the world, grouped as the 'Third World,' who, had they not been exposed to Western culture, would have remained happy as Adam and flawless as diamonds."
26. Jean-Francois Revel, "The Trouble with Latin America," pp. 47 – 50.
27. Sergio Bitar says in his article "Latin America and the United States: Changes in Economic Relations in the 70's," p. 2, "The initial emergence of dependency theories had provided significant stimulus to quantitative analysis. But in time, given their scarce capacity to engender policy formulations, these concepts lost some of their initial impact."

9

What it all means

Is culture the principal determinant of the course and pace of development in the cases we have considered?

Costa Rica *is* different from Nicaragua, indeed from most Hispanic countries. Some may say that Costa Rica's remoteness or the small number of Indians, or the unique topography of its rich Central Plateau, or the temperate climate of that plateau, or the relatively late date of Costa Rica's settlement, or its racial homogeneity are the real explanations of the difference. And, indeed, all these factors may be relevant. But *how* have they made Costa Rica different? By influencing how Costa Ricans see the world. There is still a perceptible Spanish influence in that world view. But it is more attenuated than in most other Hispanic American countries. Costa Rica is different from Nicaragua *because Costa Ricans are different from Nicaraguans*.

Nicaragua and the Dominican Republic have not strayed as far as Costa Rica from the mainstream of Hispanic-American culture. Their histories bear strong resemblance to one another, and to Spain's. Their current levels of development, as measured by the indicators of Table 2 (page 10), are very close to one another. Both are well behind Costa Rica. The Dominican Republic is involved in a promising experiment with democracy; Nicaragua continues to suffer under authoritarianism, albeit of a new variety.

The Dominican Republic is far ahead of Haiti, with which it shares an island, in all indicators of development. Yet, in economic production, Haiti, as the French slave colony Saint Domingue, was far ahead of Spanish Santo Domingo — and the rest of the New World — just two hundred years ago. Today, Haiti is by far the poorest country in Latin America. Its standard of living is much more akin to that of sub-Saharan Africa, where are found the roots of the Haitian people.

The roots of the Barbadian people are in the same African soil, and the Barbadians, too, were slaves in the New World. But their masters were English. The slaves were beneficiaries of significant acts of English noblesse oblige starting early in the eighteenth century, and English colonial rule grew increasingly enlightened in pace with the steady march of Britain itself toward a modern democracy. That colonial rule continued until 1966, albeit with substantial autonomy in this century. Barbados, which is far ahead not only of Haiti but also of the Dominican Republic and, by a narrower

164

margin, Costa Rica, is much more English than African, black skin pigmentation notwithstanding.

Haiti is much more African than French. Ninety percent of Haitians cannot communicate in French. French influence was exercised largely through a brutal slavery system until Dessalines effectively ended that influence by defeating Napoleon's expeditionary force and slaughtering the Frenchmen (and women and children) who remained in Haiti. While the French-speaking, mostly mulatto elite has looked to France for its literary and artistic inspiration, French political theory and practice, at least as they have evolved in the past two centuries, have had little impact. The French slave system, on the other hand, appears to have had an enduring, demoralizing influence on how Haitians see the world.

Argentina, so much bigger and richer than Nicaragua and the Dominican Republic, is nonetheless unmistakably in the same Hispanic-American cultural mainstream. The history of each country since independence bears strong resemblances to Spanish history during the same period. If resource endowment can make economic progress and democracy happen in any country, that country should have been Argentina. Indeed, economic progress did occur, particularly during the period 1880 – 1930. But Argentina has failed to build a viable political system that could command the allegiance of its people, and political polarization, chronic instability, and authoritarian government have taken a heavy toll on economic progress. And there is evidence that authoritarianism and negative attitudes about work at all levels of society have taken a heavy toll on entrepreneurship, on creativity.

Australia, like Argentina, is blessed with natural resources. Its level of economic development was comparable to Argentina's until 1930. But in the last half century, it has left Argentina far behind and kept pace with the industrialized democracies of the West. Today, Australia is among the most successful countries in the world, its per-capita income about $10,000, its democratic institutions assuring its citizens not only of increasing prosperity but also of increasing social justice. The political and economic evolution of Australia is so similar to that of Canada and the United States that it is difficult not to conclude that British culture has played a decisive role in all three, the differences in their colonial histories notwithstanding. And indeed, while there are some important differences between Australia and Barbados, there are also some striking similarities.

In each of the cases I have discussed, the world view of the society has expressed itself in ways that have affected the society's cohesion, its proneness to justice and progress, and the extent to which it taps human creative potential. And, I believe, those are factors that importantly explain why some societies are more successful than others.

In the case of Latin America, we see a cultural pattern, derivative of traditional Hispanic culture, that is anti-democratic, anti-social, anti-progress, anti-entrepreneurial, and, at least among the elite, anti-work.

Racism?

The basic message of this book — that culture is the principal determinant of development — is, I recognize, a highly controversial one. Some people with whom I have discussed the thesis have labeled it racist, which it most assuredly is not. Racism implies genetic superiority/inferiority, a concept that is unproven, that I reject, and that is repugnant to me. Some reflection on the book — e.g., on the differences between Haiti and Barbados and how they have come about, and on the fact that Hispanic culture is the dominant culture for some full-blooded Indians and blacks as well as most mestizos and whites in Hispanic-American societies — will demonstrate that race as a physiologically differentiated concept is irrelevant to the thesis.

Thomas Sowell (see Chapter 5) has been accused of racism, which is a little ironic, since he is black. In a recent *Harper's* article, James Traub observed, "Separated from the libertarian economic policy that they suggest, Sowell's various inferences seem less menacing and unacceptable. It is, for example, simply *a matter of received wisdom* that some values are economically more useful than others . . ."[1] (My italics.) And that is precisely the point. There is nothing intrinsic or immutable about culture. It is transmitted and received. And it changes, while genes do not, at least not in time frames that are relevant to this discussion.

That culture changes is self-evident. Something happened in Costa Rica that makes Costa Rican descendants of Spanish colonizers different from the descendants of Spaniards who settled elsewhere. The slaves in Haiti and the slaves in Barbados came essentially from the same African culture; their two cultures are now dramatically different. Swedes, Irishmen, Japanese, Italians, and Jews whose ancestors migrated to the United States may still label themselves by their ethnic extraction, but even though the old ethnicity persists in some forms, it has usually receded before the dominant American culture, and they are first and foremost Americans. And even Spain, notwithstanding a cultural momentum that has endured some five hundred years without significant deviation, a momentum so powerful that its influence is still dominant in much of the Western Hemisphere, even Spain may be experiencing a process of cultural change that is bringing it, at last, into twentieth-century Europe.

It may well be that Franco's decision in the early 1950s to open up the Spanish economy to the world initiated that process. If so, a major transformation may be occurring in a matter of a few decades. Of more limited scope, but nonetheless impressive because of the rapidity with which supposedly intractable attitudes have changed, is what has happened to the views of white Americans on race questions in the past twenty years. A 1978 *Scientific American* article presents data that document an increase in liberal, prointegration racial attitudes on the part of American whites from about 40 percent of the white population in 1963 to about 60 percent in 1976.[2]

As Jacob Bronowski demonstrated so effectively in the BBC television series *The Ascent of Man*, the basic direction of human cultural change has clearly been toward progress. While that basic direction is upward, some societies have obviously progressed more rapidly than others, and some have not progressed at all. Moreover, cultural change in a given society at a given time can be regressive. Its movement is not supported by a ratchet: countries can slip back, and that includes developed countries. Britain's disappointing economic performance since World War II may reflect both an attenuation of entrepreneurship and a weakening of the national consensus by class divisions. The Vietnam war and Watergate have had traumatic consequences for the way many Americans see themselves, their society, and their government; trust and cohesiveness have eroded. And both countries, as well as a number of other advanced countries, may be experiencing significant changes in values and attitudes as a result of unprecedented affluence, changes whose negative consequences could, in the long run, outweigh the positive ones.

Culture, to recapitulate, is transmitted and received, and it changes. Racist theories imply that culture is inborn and static. Those theories are totally inconsistent with the thesis of this book.

Yankee boosterism?

I also recognize that there will be readers who will criticize this book as an expression of cultural arrogance or chauvinism, particularly at a moment in history when its message runs counter to strong currents of criticism of, even disenchantment with, the United States, both at home and abroad.

To begin with, although some may interpret the book as Yankee boosterism, that is principally because of its Western Hemisphere focus. I am advocating the liberal, democratic capitalist model of the West, not necessarily the American version of it. I believe the Western model, extending from the Swedish variant with a heavier social content to the American variant with a lighter social content, offers the best way of organizing a society that humankind has yet been able to devise. People who live in such societies are likely to live happier, more creative, more fulfilling lives than people in authoritarian systems of the left or right. And the economies of liberal, democratic capitalist societies are likely to work better.

I also believe the Western model is relevant to the needs and aspirations of poor countries, and that sustained practice of it can be an important means of bringing about constructive cultural change.

I have an abiding faith in the American system *for Americans*. I am proud of the achievements of U.S. society, and am particularly impressed by its ability to change, to adapt, and to progress. It may be true that Spain is the most difficult country in the world to govern because every man is a king, as someone — I forget who — has observed. But surely the United States, with its staggering ethnic and racial diversity and its great size, is among the world's most difficult countries to govern.[3] Its great success is eloquent testimony to the virtues of its system.

That does not mean I advocate that other countries adopt the American variant of the Western model. Nor does it mean I am not troubled by the flaws in the u.s., e.g. an income distribution pattern skewed toward the more inequitable end of the developed country range (see the table on page 128); the insufficient priority assigned to public education, symbolized by the low prestige and salary levels of the teaching profession; and the degree of political apathy suggested by the fact that roughly 40 percent of eligible American voters do not vote in presidential elections.

I also appreciate that the book may be viewed as an unbalanced assault on Hispanic — and Hispanic-American — culture that perceives no redeeming features. The book's focus on those aspects of culture that are most relevant to development omits the artistic dimension of culture, particularly literature, painting, and, to a lesser degree, music, a dimension in which Spain's and Spanish America's contribution is impressive. Moreover, in the social dimension of culture, there are aspects of Hispanic-American culture from which North Americans can learn, e.g., the way the elderly are treated.

But I stand on the basic message of the book: human development is frustrated in most Hispanic-American countries — and most Third World countries — by a way of seeing the world that impedes the achievement of political pluralism, social equity, and dynamic economic progress. And that way of seeing the world has been driven, without significant deviation, by the momentum of centuries.

This is not to say that Hispanic-American culture has been wholly static. Some change has occurred, particularly in this century, and above all as a consequence of Latin America's exposure to North American culture through motion pictures, television, radio, newspapers, and magazines; through the large number of Latin Americans who study in the United States; through the enormous flow of Latin-American immigrants — hundreds of thousands each year — to the United States; and through the substantial u.s. presence in Latin America (e.g., the Peace Corps). North American cultural "penetration" of Latin America has had positive *and* negative consequences, just as has Latin American cultural "penetration" of the United States, principally through immigration. But it is obvious from the thrust of this book that I believe that, on balance, Latin America has benefited from this exposure. I want to repeat the words of Rangel that appear in Chapter 8:

A sincere, rational, scientific examination of North American influence on Latin America's destiny would have to dispense with prejudging the issue . . . keeping open the possibility that the United States' overall contribution may have been positive.[4]

North American, and Western European and Japanese, influence on Hispanic America notwithstanding, deviation from traditional Hispanic culture has been modest, and indeed Spain itself may be deviating more sharply from that traditional culture than is Hispanic America.

What can be done about it

This brings us to the final issue of this book: what can societies do both to assure that their values and attitudes change in ways that enhance progress, and to accelerate the process?

In posing that question we cross the frontier of scientific knowledge. While many social scientists have observed and analyzed cultural change, very few have addressed the question of how one consciously guides and accelerates it, and most of those few have treated the question speculatively and intuitively. My own prescriptions, which follow, are admittedly speculative and intuitive. One of my principal hopes for this book is that it will stimulate interest by a number of disciplines, e.g., anthropology, sociology, political science, economics, psychology, and psychiatry, in the question of what measures societies can take to influence their cultural evolution.

The starting point has to be a recognition that the thesis of this book has validity. That recognition is going to be very difficult to achieve, above all in Latin America, where dependency theory has deep emotional roots and is widely subscribed to. I can only hope that the argument of the book is sufficiently compelling to cause some Latin American (and North American and European) intellectuals to reflect objectively on it.

To design and orchestrate a coherent program of cultural change that stands a chance of working, it is necessary to identify those values and attitudes that get in the way and those that need to be introduced or strengthened. This means a process of candid national introspection that produces an agenda of goals for cultural change.

The next question is what means to employ. Seven such means occur to me (there are doubtless many others): leadership, religious reform, education and training, the media, development projects, management practices, and child-rearing practices.

Leadership

History records a number of government leaders who have significantly changed the values and attitudes of their societies: Lenin, Kemal Ataturk, Lincoln and Franklin Roosevelt, Gandhi and Nehru, Mao, and in Latin America, Castro and Romulo Betancourt. The changes may not always have been for the good in all or even most respects, but it is clear that each leader changed the course of his country's history importantly by influencing the values and attitudes of his society.

If leaders are convinced that cultural factors are major obstacles to progress, they will make cultural change an explicit and high-priority part of their program of government. Among the tools they can use are speeches, anticorruption campaigns, and legislative programs that force social change. They can also, by their example, contribute to changed popular expectations by living simply, by dealing civilly with their opposition, and by pursuing policies that encourage participation and a sense of belonging.

In Chapter 2 we saw how Nehru addressed himself to some cultural obstacles to Indian development. Here I would like to use some examples from the recent history of the Dominican Republic. I have already alluded to one example: the decision of former President Antonio Guzmán (1979 – 1982) not to seek reelection. *Caudillismo* implies *continuismo*, and Guzmán struck an important blow for democratic leadership with his decision.

More recently, Guzmán's successor, Salvador Jorge Blanco, effectively attacked *caudillo* mythology when he said, in his February 27, 1983, State of the Nation address:

> I try to express through my conduct that the President of the Republic is a human being, like any other, and not a messianic personage, an instrument of destiny, an indispensable and unsubstitutable being without whose presence everything would collapse, threatening even the survival of the Nation.
>
> I try to express daily that the President is the first servant of the Nation and not somebody who makes himself absolute owner of its destiny by virtue of magical individual qualities, or by force, or by intrigue.
>
> Our Presidency has been a simple and accessible presidency, human and of the people, without diminution of the respect due this office for reasons of state and because of the nature of the exercise of power.

Among other efforts to change Dominican values and attitudes, President Jorge Blanco is undertaking a campaign against tax evaders, including prosecution and imprisonment, a practice very rare in Latin America.

Religious reform

As is explicit in the earlier chapters of this book, religion is a powerful determinant of culture. One can disagree with some of Weber's analysis and ideas, but it seems to me apparent that Protestantism in general and Calvinism in particular *have* played a role in the success of many industrialized nations as well as some high-middle-income ones (e.g., Trinidad and Tobago, Barbados). It also seems apparent to me that traditional religions, while they may help people endure lives near the margin of survival, often *do* stand in the way of a progress their adherents earnestly desire. The role of Vodun in Haiti is a case in point.

Catholicism since Pope John XXIII has carried a much stronger "this world," social equality, and ethical message. The traditional tension between capitalism and Catholicism, however, coupled with the powerful momentum of traditional Catholic authoritarianism, has guided a part of the recently stimulated social concern toward "liberation theology," in which ecclesiastical authoritarianism may be replaced by Marxist authoritarianism.[5]

Religious reform can be a potent agent of positive cultural change when it: (1) stresses the future and the concept of progress, (2) encourages an ethical code that helps to extend the radius of trust in a society, (3) discourages authoritarianism, and (4) encourages the belief that human beings *can* control their destinies.

I appreciate that there are numerous obstacles to religious reform, among them the fundamental interpretation of the relationship between a deity or deities and humans, the long-standing traditions of a church, and the fact that the policies of most churches are usually determined by older people. On the other hand, culture can change without the involvement of religion — for example, attitudes about family size — and failure of religion to stay abreast or ahead of such changes may jeopardize its influence.

Education and training

The efficacy of education as an agent of cultural change has been mentioned by a number of scholars: e.g., Myrdal, McClelland, Banfield, and Inkeles and Smith.[6] Whereas all of them see education as an ingredient in cultural change, there is little consensus on what should be done with education to maximize its impact.

I believe education can rigidify culture as well as make it more progressive. Education in Hispanic America does both. It imparts tools to the neglected masses that are indispensable to social and economic mobility. But it often also reinforces the traditional world view for both the masses *and* the elite at all levels in the education system by the use of authoritarian pedagogical techniques, including dictation-cum-rote-memorization, and the suppression of dissent.

My sense is that a shift to participatory pedagogy, including techniques that encourage more initiative and cooperation at lower levels of the system and emphasize seminars and case-method at the upper levels, may be even more important than curriculum changes that, for example, stress less theory and more practical application (which may well be desirable, too).

One country — Venezuela — became sufficiently concerned five years ago about *how* its children learn that it set up a Ministry for the Development of Human Intelligence. The minister, Luis Alberto Machado, saw his responsibility as teaching Venezuelans to think:

> Consider this, the mathematics they teach in Harvard and Moscow are the same as they teach in Caracas and Bogotá, and the potential of all the students is absolutely equal. Why are the results so different? Why do the

Nobel Prize winners come from their universities instead of ours?
. . . in some manner, many students have been taught to think.[7]

The u.s. children's television program "Sesame Street" has been adapted
for Latin American audiences in ways clearly designed to change fundamental values and attitudes. Among other issues, "Plaza Sésamo" takes on
sex roles:

> . . . women should have careers as top professionals . . . it is acceptable
> for a man to pursue less "macho" fields such as music, and . . . couples
> might share household responsibilities.
>   In a region where male dominance of society remains overwhelming,
> the idea is just short of revolutionary.[8]

In 1969, David McClelland collaborated with David G. Winter in the
book *Motivating Economic Achievement*, which was based on experiments in
motivation training of males in India. The goal of the training program was
to develop "a disposition to accept new ideas and try new methods; a read-
iness to express opinions; a time sense that makes men more interested in
the present and future than in the past; a better sense of punctuality; a
greater concern for planning, organization and efficiency; a tendency to see
the world as calculable; a faith in science and technology; and, finally, a
belief in distributive justice."[9]

The results of the training program were not conclusive, although the
authors were encouraged. Unfortunately, expected funding for continuation
of the experiment did not materialize, and, to my knowledge, little has been
done with the idea since. I believe it would be worth resurrecting.

The media

During the past thirty years, people's world views have been increasingly influenced by radio, television, motion pictures, and, with growing
literacy, newspapers and magazines. The media today are highly important
shapers of popular values and attitudes. They can contribute to the building
of a national consensus about cultural change, and they can play a key role
in bringing about that change.

To return to the example of the Dominican Republic, that country is
blessed with unusually high quality newspapers, particularly *Listín Diario*
and *El Caribe*, the two papers that circulate most widely. Rafael Herrera,
editor of *Listín Diario*, has for two decades been communicating to his wide
readership a vision of a modern, progressive democracy, principally through
his highly readable editorials. His has been a telling voice for national
reconciliation and cohesion, for moderation, tolerance, and social justice. It
is not surprising that his editorial following President Jorge Blanco's 1983
State of the Nation address singled out those portions quoted above.[10]

Development projects

People who are designing development projects may be in a position both to increase the effectiveness of such projects and to further the process of cultural change by considering carefully the cultural implications of what they are doing. Development projects often fail, or fall far short of their goals, because the values and attitudes of the intended beneficiaries are ignored. Consequently, in the last ten years or so, anthropologists have increasingly been active participants in project design and evaluation.

In addition to increasing the effectiveness of development projects in general by considering cultural factors, project designers can emphasize projects that are likely to accelerate the process of cultural change. I have already referred to two possible examples, pedagogical reform and entrepreneurship training. Some others, none of which are particularly novel but that may not have been approached heretofore principally for their cultural change potential, include:

- programs to expand the numbers of well-trained social scientists
- programs of value and attitudinal research
- promotion of agricultural cooperatives, community development organizations, and other associations based on mutual interest in which the participant learns both the value and the tools of association
- projects that encourage dialogue among business, labor, and intellectual groups, and among political parties
- projects that identify and train leaders
- education and training programs that expose people to more progressive cultures
- efforts to decentralize governmental power and decision-making

An excellent example of a development project (actually it has so many facets that "program" would be more apt) that has significantly modernized people's attitudes and values is the complex of activities that has bloomed around a successful milk cooperative in India's Gujarat state. The program is often referred to as "the Anand Pattern"; Anand is the small city where the cooperative dairy plant and the National Dairy Development Board, which is responsible for replicating the Anand Pattern throughout India, are located.

Starting in the late 1940s with a handful of milk producers who banded together to protect themselves from gouging middlemen, the cooperative structure has grown to embrace hundreds of thousands of milk producers, the majority of whom own no more than one or two buffaloes. The milk producers, or often their wives or children, bring milk to convenient collection points twice a day. The amount of milk, its purity, and its butterfat content, are measured by modern instruments, and the producers are paid each day. Producers are provided with scientifically formulated feed for their animals at reasonable prices. They also receive technical assistance from qualified veterinarians. The cooperative maintains a pool of high-quality breeder stock, and artificial insemination is used widely by the producers.

Cooperative members have experienced substantial increases in their incomes. But there may have been even more dramatic changes in the way they see the world. Each day there is a lesson in modern technology and fair play. Each day there is a reward for hard and intelligent work. Participation in the village-level cooperatives is practical training in democracy. Attitudes about health, nutrition, and family size have changed. Age-old social patterns have broken down: ten years ago untouchables stood in separate lines; today, segregated lines do not exist.

The Anand Pattern has emphasized — and achieved — profitability. Most of the profits have been plowed back into its burgeoning complex of activities. The cooperative has diversified into a variety of products, including baby formula, high-protein food for children, and chocolate. Anand has spawned a promising oilseed cooperative, a primary health-care program, a graduate school of rural management. It has converted money-losing, government-owned dairies in New Delhi and Bombay into highly efficient, modern, money-making operations.

What has happened at Anand in the past twenty-five years demonstrates compellingly that cultural change can result from development activities that involve their participants in progressive ways of organizing human enterprise.

Management practices

Several authors, perhaps foremost among them Inkeles and Smith, have stressed the modernizing role of industrialization. Work in the factory, Inkeles and Smith point out, encourages openness to new experience, the acquisition of information, the development of judgment and opinion, future orientation, optimism, trust, cooperative effort, and planning.[11] Thus, industrialization, a national goal in most poor countries, can itself be a powerful instrument of cultural change.

Tomás Roberto Fillol believes that modern democratic management practices can be an important engine of cultural change in Argentina. The manager who explains rather than commands, who encourages communication in his organization, who encourages and rewards initiative, can create an environment in which "workers feel they are recognized by their superiors; responsibilities and a certain degree of autonomy are *truly* delegated by all levels of management; all levels of personnel identify with their jobs, the enterprise, and its goals; workers willingly cooperate with each other and with all levels of management in the pursuit of personal, but common material advantages; individuals are free to discuss problems arising from their jobs with superiors and workmates and willingly take advantage of such opportunities."[12]

Fillol does not expect significant changes in the basic values and attitudes of people of Hispanic culture who are exposed to modern democratic management for the first time. "But their anxiety, their rancor, their rage and forced suppression of it during working hours may have considerably declined. . . . Above all, people will not need to discharge their anxiety, rage, and aggression on their subordinates and especially their children . . ."[13] The real payoff in cultural change will thus appear in subsequent generations, in Fillol's view.

I believe Fillol has captured an important truth that has applicability for organizations in general, private *and* public. I think he may even underestimate the capacity for change of people first exposed to enlightened management. In any event, a part of that important truth is his focus on child-rearing, a focus shared by so many people discussed in earlier chapters.

Child-rearing practices

Concern about child-rearing practices is a thread that runs throughout this book, connecting such people as David McClelland, Edward Banfield, Salvador Mendieta, Malcolm Walker, Robert Rotberg, and Tomás Roberto Fillol. Part of that concern relates to the values and attitudes parents communicate to children orally and by example. Whatever changes in the values and attitudes of parents that are brought about by leaders, churches, schools, the media, etc., should be substantially transmitted to their children in this way. But the parent socializes the child in another way that may be both far more important for cultural change and far less susceptible to modification: the way in which the parent relates to the child.

In the opinion of many psychologists and other social scientists, the *way* the parent communicates with the child may be more important than *what* the parent communicates. The way the mother and father treat the child may be the principal determinant of the child's self-image and self-confidence, emotional stability, judgment, degree of optimism, capacity and motivation for achievement, and sense of trust. Needless to say, those characteristics are transcendentally important both for individuals and for societies.

A powerful inertia sustains parenting techniques from one generation to the next. What the child experiences, both consciously and subconsciously, as it is raised is its principal preparation for the parental role it will later assume. There may be a quite different world view between one generation and the next (e.g., between immigrant parents and their native-born children), but the character of the parents and the children may be very similar, no doubt in part for genetic reasons but also importantly because of the inertia implicit in approaches to child-rearing. And character, in such facets as creativity, social adaptability, and judgment, can have much to do with the way a society really works. It is not at all improbable for someone who believes in democratic interpersonal relationships to be authoritarian because of the emotional and psychic damage done by authoritarian parents.

We — all of us, in poor, middle-income, and rich countries — need to know much more about what makes for successful parenting. Psychologists and psychiatrists have done a great deal of work on this subject in recent decades. Part of the problem resides in disagreements among professionals, and further research is needed both to resolve issues about which there is debate and to explore as yet unstudied aspects of the parent–child relationship. But much is already known, and perhaps the biggest problem is in communicating this knowledge effectively to prospective parents. One way this can be done is through parenting courses in the last year of primary studies in countries where many students terminate formal education at the primary level, and at the secondary and university level in all countries.

In any event, there is so much evidence that child-rearing practices importantly influence culture that no country concerned with human progress can afford to ignore the question.

Obviously, the mere listing and brief discussion of seven ways that occur to me to accelerate cultural change do not constitute a reliable and efficacious program. My hope is that the need for cultural change will be taken seriously by political and intellectual leaders and that these and/or other approaches will be studied and adapted or reinforced as conditions in a given country dictate.

In concluding this book I want to repeat my awareness that numerous noncultural factors affect development. I also want to repeat my appreciation of the monumental difficulties in accelerating constructive cultural change. But if underdevelopment *is*, importantly, a state of mind, there is no choice but to try.

NOTES

1. James Traub, "You Can Get It If You Really Want It," p. 31.
2. D. Garth Taylor, Paul B. Sheatsley, and Andrew M. Greeley, "Attitudes toward Racial Integration," pp. 42 – 49.
3. For the same reasons, the u.s.s.r. also belongs among the most difficult countries to govern.
4. Carlos Rangel, *The Latin Americans: Their Love-Hate Relationship With the United States*, p. 44. Rangel is referring not just to the cultural aspects but to the full array of relationships, including the military interventions by the u.s.
5. The point is treated in depth in Michael Novak's *The Spirit of Democratic Capitalism*. I might also mention in passing that there is an increasingly noticeable tension between capitalism and Protestantism, and perhaps Judaism as well. Both are experiencing heightened concerns with questions of equity.
6. Alex H. Inkeles and David H. Smith, *Becoming Modern: Individual Change in Six Developing Countries*.

7. "Brain Power," *The New York Times*, March 4, 1984, p. 41.
8. ". . . In Mexico, Latin Values Stressed," *The New York Times*, September 29, 1983, p. c17.
9. David C. McClelland and David G. Winter, *Motivating Economic Achievement*, p. 9. The words quote a summary of Inkeles's views formulated by Myron Weiner.
10. "Mensaje Optimista" ("Optimistic Message"), *Listín Diario*, 28 February 1983, p. 6.
11. Inkeles and Smith, *Becoming Modern*, p. 19.
12. Tomás Roberto Fillol, *Social Factors in Economic Development*, p. 97.
13. *Ibid.*, pp. 98 – 99.

Bibliography

Almond, Gabriel A., and Verba, Sidney. *The Civic Culture*. Boston and Toronto: Little Brown and Company, 1963.

Arango, E. Ramon. *The Spanish Political System: Franco's Legacy*. Boulder, Colorado: Westview Press, 1978.

Banfield, Edward C. *The Moral Basis of a Backward Society*. Glencoe, Illinois: The Free Press, 1958. Published through the Research Center in Economic Development and Cultural Change, University of Chicago.

Biesanz, Karen, Mavis, and Richard. *Los Costarricenses*. San Jose: Editorial Universidad Estatal a Distancia, 1979.

Bosch, Juan. *Composición Social Dominicana*. Santo Domingo: Colección Pensamiento y Cultura, 1970.

Bourricaud, Francois. "The French Connection." *Caribbean Review*, Spring 1982.

Busey, James. "Foundations of Political Contrast: Costa Rica and Nicaragua." *Western Political Quarterly*, September 1958.

Butlin, N. C. *Investment in Australian Economic Development 1861 – 1900*. Cambridge, England: At the University Press, 1964.

Cardoso, Fernando Henrique, and Faletto, Enzo. *Dependency and Development in Latin America*. Berkeley and Los Angeles: University of California Press, 1979.

Corten, André and Andrée. *Cambio Social en Santo Domingo*. Rio Piedras, Puerto Rico: Instituto de Estudios del Caribe, University of Puerto Rico, 1968.

Christman, Henry M., ed. *The American Journalism of Marx and Engels*. New York: New American Library, 1966.

Cochrane, Peter. *Industrialization and Dependence*. St. Lucia, Queensland, Australia: University of Queensland Press, 1980.

Crassweller, Robert D. *Trujillo: The Life and Times of a Caribbean Dictator*. New York: Macmillan, 1966.

de la Souchère, Eléna. *An Explanation of Spain*. New York: Random House, 1964.

de Las Casas, Bartólome. *A Very Brief Account of the Destruction of the Indies*, 1544.

Delpar, Helen, ed. *The Encyclopedia of Latin America*. New York: McGraw-Hill, 1974.

de Madariaga, Salvador. *Englishmen, Frenchmen, Spaniards*. London: Oxford University Press, 1931.

Dyster, Barrie. "Argentine and Australian Development Compared." *Past and Present* 84, August 1979.

Ellis, Havelock. *The Soul of Spain*. Reprint. Westport, Connecticut: Greenwood Press, 1975.

Estrada, Ezequiel Martínez. *Radiografia de la Pampa*. Buenos Aires: Editorial Losada, 1942.

Falcoff, Mark. "Our Latin American Hairshirt." *Commentary*, October 1976.

179

————. "Somoza, Sandino, and the United States: What the Past Teaches — and Doesn't." *This World*, Fall 1983.

Ferrer, Aldo, and Wheelwright, E. L. *Industrialization in Argentina and Australia: A Comparative Study*. Preliminary draft. Buenos Aires, Instituto Torcuato di Tella, 1966.

Fillol, Tomás Roberto. *Social Factors in Economic Development*. Cambridge, Massachusetts: MIT Press, 1961.

Foster, George. *Culture and Conquest: America's Spanish Heritage*. Chicago: Quadrangle Books, 1960.

Frank, Andre Gunder. *Capitalism and Underdevelopment in Latin America*. New York: Monthly Review Press, 1967.

Galbraith, John Kenneth. *The Nature of Mass Poverty*. Cambridge and London: Harvard University Press, 1979.

Gámez, José Dolores. *Historia de Nicaragua*. 1899. Reprint. Banco de America, 1975.

Germani, Gino. *Politica y Sociedad en Una Epoca de Transición*. Buenos Aires: Editorial Paidos, 1962.

Gibson, Charles. *Spain in America*. New York: Harper Colophon Books, 1966.

Gold, Herbert. "Caribbean Caudillo: Magloire of Haiti." *Nation*, February 5, 1955.

Hagen, Everett E. *On the Theory of Social Change: How Economic Growth Begins*. Homewood, Illinois: The Dorsey Press, 1962.

Hamill, Hugh M., ed. *Dictatorship in Latin America*. New York: Alfred A. Knopf, 1965.

Hanke, Lewis. *The Spanish Struggle for Justice in the Conquest of America*. Boston and Toronto: Little, Brown and Company, 1965.

Harrison, Lawrence E. "Costa Rica Shows a Better Way." *Boston Globe*, April 27, 1982.

————. "Some Hidden Costs of the Public Investment Fixation." *International Development Review* 12, 1970/2.

————. "Waking from the Pan American Dream." *Foreign Policy*, Winter 1971 – 72.

Hazard, Samuel. *Santo Domingo Past and Present with a Glance at Hayti*. 1873. Reprint. Santo Domingo: Editoria de Santo Domingo, 1974.

Herskovitz, Melville J. *Life in a Haitian Valley*. New York: Octagon Books, 1964.

Hertz, J. H., ed. *The Pentateuch and Haftorahs*. London: Soncino Press, 1961.

Hippler, Arthur E. "The Yolngu and Cultural Relativism: A Response to Reser." *American Anthropologist*, 1981.

Hirst, John. "La Sociedad Rural y la Política en Australia, 1850 – 1930." In *Argentina y Australia*, edited by John Fogarty, Ezequiel Gallo, and Hector Dieguez. Buenos Aires: Instituto Torcuato di Tella, 1979.

Hodges, Wallace. "Poverty Linked to Voodoo Spirits." *Baltimore Sun*, November 15, 1981.

Hoyos, F. A. *Barbados: A History from the Amerindians to Independence*. Macmillan Caribbean, London and Basingstoke, 1978.

Hunte, George. *Barbados*. New York: Hastings House, 1974.

Huntington, Samuel P. *Political Order in Changing Societies*. New York and London: Yale University Press, 1968.

". . . In Mexico, Latin Values Stressed." *The New York Times*, September 29, 1983.

Inkeles, Alex H., and Smith, David H. *Becoming Modern: Individual Change in Six Developing Countries*. Cambridge, Massachusetts: Harvard University Press, 1974.

James, Preston E. *Latin America*. 3rd ed. New York: Odyssey Press, 1959.

Kaufman, R. R.; Giller, Daniel S.; and Chernotsky, Harry I. "Preliminary Test of the Theory of Dependency." *Comparative Politics* 7, April 1975.

Kenny, Michael. *A Spanish Tapestry: Town and Country in Castile*. London: Cohen and West, 1961.

Kinzer, Stephen. "Grumbling, Gloom on Rise in Argentina." *Boston Globe*, October 3, 1981.

Kirkpatrick, Jeane. *Leader and Vanguard in Mass Society: A Study of Peronist Argentina*. Cambridge, Massachusetts and London, MIT Press, 1971.

"Latin America and the United States: Changes in Economic Relationships During the 70's." Mimeographed. Washington, D.C.: Woodrow Wilson International Center for Scholars, The Smithsonian Institution.

Lewis, Arthur W. *The Theory of Economic Growth*. Homewood, Illinois: Richard D. Irwin, Inc., 1955.

Leyburn, James G. *The Haitian People*. New Haven and London: Yale University Press, 1966.

Lison-Tolosana, Carmelo. *Belmonte de los Caballeros*. Oxford: Clarendon Press, 1966.

Logan, Rayford W. *Haiti and the Dominican Republic*. London, New York, Toronto: Oxford University Press, 1968.

López, José Ramón. *La Paz en la República Dominicana*. 1915. Reprint, Santiago: Universidad Católica Madre y Maestra, 1975.

McClelland, David C. *The Achieving Society*. Princeton: D. Van Nostrand Company, Inc., 1961.

————, and Winter, David G. *Motivating Economic Achievement*. New York: The Free Press, 1969.

McElwain, D. W., and Campbell, W. J. "The Family." In *Australian Society*, edited by A. F. Davies and S. Encel. New York: Atherton Press, 1965.

McGann, Thomas F. *Argentina: The Divided Land*. Princeton: Van Nostrand Co., 1966.

MacLeod, Murdo J. *Spanish Central America — A Socioeconomic History 1520 – 1720*. Berkeley: University of California Press, 1973.

Martin, John Bartlow. *Overtaken by Events*. Garden City, New York: Doubleday & Company, 1966.

Melendez, Carlos. *Historia de Costa Rica*. San José: Editorial Universidad Estatal a Distancia, 1981.

Mendieta, Salvador. *La Enfermedad de Centro-América*. 3 vols. 1912. Reprint. Barcelona: Tipografía Maucci, 1936.

"Mensaje Optimista." *Listín Diario*, February 28, 1983.

Michener, James. *Iberia*. New York: Fawcett Crest, 1968.

Millett, Richard. *Guardians of the Dynasty*. Maryknoll, New York: Orbis Books, 1977.

Moran, Theodore H. "The 'Development' of Argentina and Australia — The Radical Party of Argentina and the Labor Party of Australia in the Process of Economic and Political Development." *Comparative Politics* 3, October 1970.

Moya Pons, Frank. *Historia Colonial de Santo Domingo*. Santiago, Dominican Republic: Universidad Católica Madre y Maestra, 1974.

Murray, Gerald S. *La Loma: Paternalism in a Caribbean Community*. Honors thesis, Harvard College, 1968.

Myrdal, Gunnar. *Asian Drama: An Inquiry into the Poverty of Nations*. New York: Pantheon, 1968.

Naipaul, V. S. *The Return of Eva Peron*. New York: Vintage Books, 1981.

Novak, Michael. *The Spirit of Democratic Capitalism*. New York: American Enterprise Institute/Simon and Schuster, 1982.

————. "Why Latin America is Poor." *Atlantic Monthly*, March 1982.

O'Donnell, Guillermo A. *Modernization and Bureaucratic Authoritarianism: Studies in South American Politics*. Berkeley: Institute of International Studies, University of California, 1973.

Ortega y Gasset, José. *Invertebrate Spain*. New York: W. W. Norton Co., 1937.

Paz, Octavio. *The Labyrinth of Solitude: Life and Thought in Mexico*. New York: Grove Press, 1961.

Prebisch, Raul. "Estructura socioeconómica y crisis del sistema." ECLA *Review*, second semester, 1978.

Rangel, Carlos. *The Latin Americans: Their Love – Hate Relationship with the United States*. New York and London: Harcourt Brace Jovanovich, 1977.

Revel, Jean-Francois. "The Trouble with Latin America." *Commentary*, February 1979.

Rotberg, Robert. *Haiti: The Politics of Squalor*. Boston: Houghton Mifflin Co., 1971.

Samuel, Wilfred S. *The Jewish Colonists in Barbados in the Year 1680*. London: Purnell and Sons, Ltd., 1936.

Sarmiento, Domingo. *Facundo: Civilización y Barbarie*. Buenos Aires: Espasa-Calpe Argentina, S.A., 1951.

Schoenrich, Otto. *Santo Domingo: a Country with a Future*. New York: Macmillan, 1918.

Schumpeter, Joseph A. *Capitalism, Socialism and Democracy*. 3rd ed. New York: Harper Bros., 1950.

————. *The Theory of Economic Development*. Cambridge, Massachusetts: Harvard University Press, 1951.

Scobie, James R. *Argentina: A City and a Nation*. New York: Oxford University Press, 1964.

Seligson, Mitchell A. "Trust, Efficacy and Modes of Political Participation: A Study of Costa Rican Peasants." *British Journal of Political Science 10*, 1980.

Sharpe, Kenneth Evan. *Peasant Politics: Struggle in a Dominican Village*. Baltimore and London: Johns Hopkins University Press, 1977.

Sigmund, Paul E. *The Overthrow of Allende and the Politics of Chile, 1964 – 76*. Pittsburgh: Pittsburgh University Press, 1977.

Silvert, Kalman H. *Essays in Understanding Latin America*. Philadelphia: Institute for the Study of Human Issues, 1977.

Smith, Adam. *Wealth of Nations*. New York: Random House, 1937.

Smithies, Arthur. "Argentina and Australia." *American Economic Review 55*, May 1965.

Sowell, Thomas. "Three Black Histories." *Wilson Quarterly*, Winter 1979.

Stephens, John L. *Incidents of Travel in Central America, Chiapas and Yucatan*. 2 vols. 1841. Reprint. New York: Dover Publications, 1969.

Stone, Samuel. *La Dinastía de los Conquistadores*. San José, Costa Rica: Editorial Universitaria Centroamerica, 1975.

Taylor, D. Garth; Sheatsley, Paul B.; and Greeley, Andrew M. "Attitudes toward Racial Integration." *Scientific American 238*, June 1978.

Thiel, Bernardo Augusto. *Monografía de la Población de la República de Costa Rica*. 1900.

Traub, James. "You Can Get It if You Really Want It." *Harper's*, June 1982.
Trejos, Gonzalo Chacon. *Costa Rica es Distinta en Hispano América*. San José: Imprenta Trejos Hermanus, 1969.
United Nations Economic Commission for Latin America. *El desarrollo económico de la Argentina*, 1959.
Vega, Eugenio Rodríguez. *Apuntes para una Sociología Costarricense*. San José: Editorial Universidad Estatal a Distancia, 1979.
Véliz, Claudio. *The Centralist Traditions of Latin America*. Princeton: Princeton University Press, 1980.
Verba, Sidney, and Pye, Lucian, eds. *Political Culture and Political Development*. Princeton: Princeton University Press, 1965.
Vilar, Pierre. *Spain — A Brief History*. Oxford et al.: Pergamon Press, 1967.
Wagley, Charles. *The Latin American Tradition*. New York and London: Columbia University Press, 1908.
Walker, Malcolm T. *Politics and the Power Structure: A Rural Community in the Dominican Republic*. New York and London: Teachers College Press, Columbia University, 1972.
Ward, Russel. *Australia: A Short History*. Sydney: Ure Smith, 1979.
Weber, Max. *The Protestant Ethic and the Spirit of Capitalism*. New York: Charles Scribner's Sons, 1950.
———. *The Religion of China*. New York: Macmillan, 1951.
———. *The Religion of India*. Glencoe, Illinois: The Free Press, 1958.
Welles, Sumner. *Naboth's Vineyard: The Dominican Republic 1844 – 1924*. Mamaroneck, New York: Paul P. Appel, 1966.
Wells, Henry. *The Modernization of Puerto Rico: A Political Study of Changing Values and Institutions*. Cambridge, Massachusetts: Harvard University Press, 1969.
Wheelock Román, Jaime. *Imperialismo y Dictadura*. Mexico City: Siglo Veintiuno Editores, S.A., 1975.
Wiarda, Howard J. *Dictatorship, Development and Disintegration*. Ann Arbor, Michigan: Xerox University Microfilms, 1975.
World Bank. *World Development Report 1980*.
———. *World Development Report 1981*.
———. *World Development Report 1982*.

Index